Society without God

Phil Zuckerman

Society without God

*What the Least Religious Nations
Can Tell Us about Contentment*

New York University Press • *New York and London*

NEW YORK UNIVERSITY PRESS
New York and London
www.nyupress.org

First published in paperback in 2010.

Library of Congress Cataloging-in-Publication Data

Zuckerman, Phil.
Society without God / Phil Zuckerman.
p. cm.
Includes bibliographical references and index.
ISBN-13: 978–0–8147–9723–5 (pb : alk. paper)
ISBN-10: 0–8147–9723–7 (pb : alk. paper)
ISBN-13: 978–0–8147–9714–3 (cl : alk. paper)
ISBN-10: 0–8147–9714–8 (cl : alk. paper)
1. Religion—Controversial literature. 2. Religion and sociology. I. Title.
BL2775.3.Z83   2008
306.6094—dc22   2008018213

New York University Press books are printed on acid-free paper,
and their binding materials are chosen for strength and durability.
We strive to use environmentally responsible suppliers and materials
to the greatest extent possible in publishing our books.

Manufactured in the United States of America

For Stacy, Ruby, Flora, and August

Contents

Acknowledgments

The research for this book was financially supported in part by Pitzer College and the European Union Center of California, as well as two generous grants: the Jack Shand Research Award from the Society for the Scientific Study of Religion, and the Joseph Fichter Research Award from the Association for the Sociology of Religion. My great appreciation goes out to these institutions and organizations.

I would also like to recognize and sincerely thank the following people for their significant help and support: Azadeh Afsar, Lars Ahlin, Steve Bruce, Andrew Buckser, Theo Calderara, Michelle Cadeau, Alice Elbek, Jørgen Elbek, Lonni Fogsgaard, Göran Gustafsson, Richard Halladay, Sandy Hamilton, Sonja Bossow Jakobsen, Hans Jørgen Lundager Jensen, Karen-Lise Johansen, Jesper Jühne, Lindsay Kennedy, Iben Krogsdal, Lene Kühle, Kjell Lejon, Christel Manning, Kirsten Foss Marstal, Amatzya Mezahav, Maja Müller, Elof Nelson, Nilla Norberg, Jens Peter Schjødt, Madeleine Svensson, Carina Tannenberg, Cecilia Thurman, Tage Vester, Lars Villemoes, and the many individuals who agreed to participate in an interview with me.

I would like to further express my deepest gratitude to Stacy Elliott, Jennifer Hammer, Neils Tage Hansen, Hans Raun Iversen, Benton Johnson, Edna Kovanda Klein, and Marvin Zuckerman for their invaluable input, work, and encouragement.

Introduction

THE WORLD SEEMS more religious than ever these days.

Across the Middle East, fervent forms of Islam are growing more popular and more politically active. Muslim nations that were somewhat secularized 40 years ago—such as Lebanon and Iran—are now teeming with fundamentalism. In Turkey and Egypt, increasing numbers of women are turning to the veil as an overt manifestation of reinvigorated religious commitment. But it isn't just in the Muslim world that religion is thriving. From Brazil to El Salvador, Protestant Evangelicalism is spreading with great success, instilling a spirited, holy zeal throughout Latin America. Pentecostalism is proliferating, too—vigorously—and not only throughout Latin America, but in Africa and even China. In the Philippines, tens of thousands of people are committing themselves to new religious movements such as El Shaddai, with its powerful theology of prosperity. And many nations of the former Soviet Union, which had atheism imposed upon them for decades, have emerged from the communist era with their faith not only intact, but strong and vibrant. Even in Canada, a nation hardly known for its religious vitality, there is evidence of a spiritual and religious renaissance. To quote a leading sociologist of religion, Peter Berger, "most of the world is bubbling with religious passions."[1]

Here in the United States, religion is definitely alive and well. In fact, religion in the United States—in terms of church attendance and belief in God, Jesus, and the Bible—is stronger and more robust than in most other developed democracies. Simply driving around Southern California, where I live, it seems like every third bumper sticker is an ad for Jesus, God, or the Bible. But America's religious fervor isn't just to be found on bumper stickers. I was recently in Tucson, Arizona, and was struck by the many prominent billboards all around the city, advocating prayer and worship of the Lord. In addition to the proliferation of religious bumper stickers and billboards, Christianity in America today is being steadily broadcast from radio stations and television channels with unprecedented dynamism. As for the nation's politicians, both Republicans and Democrats seem to be more

1

publicly religious than ever, going out of their way to emphasize their faith. And Americans seem to like it that way. After all, nobody seemed to care when, back in 2004, George W. Bush said that his invasion of Iraq was inspired by the result of his prayerful consultations with God. If anything, that admission gained him more credibility among Americans, not less.

In sum, from Nebraska to Nepal, from Georgia to Guatemala, and from Utah to Uganda, humans all over the globe are vigorously praising various deities; regularly attending services at churches, temples, and mosques; persistently studying sacred texts; dutifully performing holy rites; energetically carrying out spiritual rituals; soberly defending the world from sin; piously fasting; and enthusiastically praying and then praying some more, singing, praising, and loving this or that savior, prophet, or god.

But this is not occurring everywhere. In fact, there actually are some notable pockets of irreligion out there.

They may be few and far between, but there are indeed some significant corners of the world today, however atypical, where worship of God and church attendance are minimal. These unusual, exceptional societies—rather than being more religious than ever—are actually *less* religious than ever. In fact, they aren't very religious at all. I am referring to two nations in particular, Denmark and Sweden, which are probably the least religious countries in the world, and possibly in the history of the world. Amidst all this vibrant global piety—atop the vast swelling sea of sacredness—Denmark and Sweden float along like small, content, durable dinghies of secular life, where most people are nonreligious and don't worship Jesus or Vishnu, don't revere sacred texts, don't pray, and don't give much credence to the essential dogmas of the world's great faiths.

In clean and green Scandinavia, few people speak of God, few people spend much time thinking about theological matters, and although their media in recent years has done an unusually large amount of reporting on religion, even this is offered as some sort of attempt to grapple with and make sense of this strange foreign phenomenon out there in the wider world that refuses to disappear, a phenomenon that takes on such dire significance for everyone—except, well, for Danes and Swedes. If there is an earthly heaven for secular folk, contemporary Denmark and Sweden may very well be it: quaint towns, inviting cities, beautiful forests, lonely beaches, healthy democracies, among the lowest violent crime rates in the world, the lowest levels of corruption in the world, excellent educational systems, innovative architecture, strong economies, well-supported arts, successful entrepreneurship, clean hospitals, delicious beer, free health care, maverick filmmaking, egalitarian social policies, sleek design, comfortable bike paths—and not much faith in God.

I lived in Scandinavia for 14 months, from May 2005 through July 2006.[2] I was accompanied by my wife and two daughters, and we had a baby while there. We lived in Aarhus, Denmark's second largest city. Over the course of our stay, I observed as much of Danish society as I could, studied and read as much of Scandinavian history and culture as I could, traveled around Denmark as much as I could, and also interviewed as many people as possible, asking them about life in such a nonreligious society, as well as about their own religious belief—or rather, as was often the case—its absence. I talked to whomever I could in whatever social situations I found myself, be it waiting in line at a cafeteria or chewing on chips at a neighbor's dinner party. But in addition to countless informal conversations such as these, I conducted nearly 150 formal, structured, in-depth interviews.[3] With my tape recorder in hand, along with a notepad and pen, I sat down and spoke with Danes and Swedes of all ages and various educational backgrounds, from folks who had Ph.D.s to many whose formal education never went beyond the seventh or eighth grade. The people I interviewed were from tiny rural villages, medium-sized towns, as well as large cities. And they represented a vast array of different occupations, including cooks, nurses, computer technicians, professors, artists, lawyers, slaughterhouse workers, preschool teachers, heart surgeons, farmers, police officers, journalists, high school teachers, submarine officers, psychiatrists, social workers, graphic designers, stay-at-home moms, grocery store clerks, engineers, shop stewards, small business owners, physical therapists, tax consultants, casting directors, secretaries, postal workers, students, janitors, the unemployed, and even one bass player. It was through these in-depth conversations with so many people from both Denmark and neighboring Sweden that I was able to get a deep sense of life among relatively nonreligious folks, and had the opportunity to reflect upon and analyze the nature of life in a society where belief in God is muted, minimal, and marginal. This book is thus a personal reflection and sociological analysis of what I found, experienced, and learned while living in one of the least religious societies on earth.

But it is much more than that. Along with focusing a sociological lens on the nonreligious, irreligious, or religiously indifferent men and women who make up the majority of people living in Scandinavia today—relatively secular people who are part of an important and largely understudied segment of humanity—this book also addresses additional important matters.

First of all, I argue that society without God is not only possible, but can be quite civil and pleasant. This admittedly polemical aspect of my book is aimed primarily at countering the claims of certain outspoken, conservative Christians who regularly argue that a society without God would be hell on earth: rampant with immorality, full of evil, and teeming with depravity. Well, it isn't. Denmark and Sweden are remarkably strong, safe, healthy, moral, and prosperous societies. In fact, a good case could be made that they are among the "best" countries in the world, at least according to standard sociological measures. In an age of growing religious fundamentalism and strengthening ties between religion and politics—in the United States as well in as many other countries—this is important information. It is crucial for people to know that it is actually quite possible for a society to lose its religious beliefs and still be well-functioning, successful, and fully capable of constructing and obeying sound laws and establishing and following rational systems of morality and ethics. Worship of God can wane, prayer can be given up, and the Bible can go unstudied, yet people can treat one another decently, schools and hospitals can still run smoothly, crime can remain minimal, babies and old people can receive all the care and attention they need, economies can flourish, pollution can be kept at a minimum, speeding tickets can be paid, and children can be loved in warm, secure homes—all without God being a central component of everyday life.

A second goal of this book is to consider and analyze the unique contours of the worldviews of secular men and women who live their lives without a strong religious orientation.

For example, how do they think about and cope with death? It is widely accepted that religion exists because humans need some way to deal with the impending fact of their own demise. That is, everyone is more or less afraid to die (or so the theory goes), and so people turn to religion for comfort and some sort of psychological balm in the face of death. This may certainly be the case for many people—but not everyone, and certainly not for millions of Danes and Swedes. Many Scandinavians are able to live their lives perfectly well without any great fear of, or worry about, the Grim Reaper. I interviewed so many people over the course of my stay who did not fear death—didn't even give it much thought—and were able to live their lives contentedly, being more or less comfortable with the fact that at some point in the near or distant future they will cease to exist. Along these lines, one of the most interesting individuals that I interviewed was Anne, a 43-year-old hospice nurse from Aarhus. I was completely surprised when she told me that in her many years of experience working with the dying, she found that it was generally the *atheists* who had an easier time calmly accepting their impending fate, while the Christians often had the hardest time facing death, often being wracked with worry and anxiety. Such a finding raises serious challenges to the commonly held notion that fear of death is simply part of the human condition, and that humans subsequently "need" religion to quell this "universal" fear.

Or consider the meaning of life. Along with the fear of death, many people argue that religion exists because it provides existential answers to the great, burdening questions of why we are here and what it is all about. Sure, millions of humans may desire answers to these questions, and thus may turn to religion for answers. But not most Danes and Swedes. I interviewed many people who flatly proclaimed to me that they believe that there is ultimately *no* meaning to life. And yet these very same people continued to live moral, loving, satisfying, and prosperous lives, despite the taken-for-granted meaninglessness of it all. Again, the existence of millions of such men and women living secular lives in largely secular societies adds new dimensions—and perhaps raises significant challenges—to certain taken-for-granted theories and explanations of religion as a necessary or inevitably integral part of the human condition.

A final goal of this book is to explore and attempt to explain how and why certain societies are nonreligious in today's otherwise extremely religious world. Whereas Denmark and Sweden are certainly at the head of the pack, several other nations, such as Great Britain and the Netherlands, are also characterized by remarkably low levels of religion. Why is it that a handful of such countries—most abundantly concentrated in Western Europe—are not all that concerned with God or Jesus or life after death? What is it about these societies that has resulted in religion being relatively insignificant and marginal? I will try to address these questions by using and expanding upon several prominent sociological theories and by drawing heavily upon my own extensive research while living in Denmark.

As for that year of living in Denmark, let me now offer some initial observations.

• • •

The first thing that I noticed upon our arrival in Scandinavia was this: no cops.

We had been in Aarhus for only a few days when I suddenly became aware of the absence of a police presence of any kind: no police cars to be seen, no motorcycle officers, and no policemen or policewomen on foot patrol. I expressed my curiosity to my wife one sunny day as we were riding our bikes to the beach: "Where are all the police?" She shrugged her shoulders, offered a few speculative theories, and then kept on pedaling.

We rode past the university district, through downtown, past the old cathedral, through numerous intersections, past shopping centers and malls, alongside the train station, down by the waterfront, past the harbor, and straight on to the beach full of sunbathers. And at no time during that 20-minute bike ride did we see any police. Now mind you, Aarhus is not some tiny village tucked away in a remote bog somewhere out in the Nordic hinterlands. It is a thriving municipality full of industry and culture, with a population of a quarter of a million. And as I walked through the bustling downtown with my kids a few days later, meandering through the crowds, strolling along the canal, passing many busy cafes and restaurants, I noticed it yet again: no cops. It was a strange feeling. After all, back home in Claremont, California—a rather small town by American standards, with a population of about 33,000—I see police nearly every single day.[4] But I wasn't seeing any in Aarhus. Not even one. So I started to keep a daily tab. The result: a grand total of 31 days passed before I finally saw any police presence. And what is even more remarkable is that despite the significant lack of a police presence in Aarhus, the violent crime rate there is among the lowest in the world for a city of that size. For example, in 2004, the total number of murders in the city of Aarhus was one. Clearly, something is keeping Danes from murdering one another, and it isn't heavy policing.

Nor is it fear of the Lord.

I mention this because many people assume that religion is what keeps people moral.[5] For example, Dr. Laura Schlessinger—the famous radio host, television personality, and best-selling author—has declared that it is simply impossible for people to be moral without religion or God.[6] For many people, including Dr. Laura, it is the belief in and fear of God that keeps murder rates down. But that doesn't seem to be the case for Scandinavians. Although they may have relatively high rates of petty crime and burglary, and although these crime rates have been on the rise in recent decades,[7] their overall rates of violent crime—such as murder, aggravated assault, and rape—are among the lowest on earth. Yet the majority of Danes and Swedes do not believe that God is "up there," keeping diligent tabs on their behavior, slating the good for heaven and the wicked for hell. Most Danes and Swedes don't believe that sin permeates the world, and that only Jesus, the Son of God, who died for their sins, can serve as a remedy. In fact, most Danes and Swedes don't even believe in the very notion of "sin." Almost nobody in Denmark and Sweden believes that the Bible is divine in origin. And the rate of weekly church attendance in these Nordic nations is the lowest on earth. In addition, even though a sizeable proportion of Danes and Swedes definitely do believe in God, the God they claim to believe in is generally some vague, distant notion of their own interpretation—not the literal, punishing, vengeful, merciful, or forgiving God of the Bible. And the significance that they place on their belief in this vague, distant God is quite minimal and, well, rather underwhelming. As Danish sociologist Ole Riis notes, "It is only a minority of the Scandinavians who ascribe great importance to God in their lives. The typical attitude is lukewarm and a bit skeptical."[8]

To be sure, there are some committed fundamentalists here and there, and you can even find a well-attended Pentecostal church if you look for it. But True Believers in Denmark and Sweden are fewer and farther between than in most other countries, existing only as a miniscule minority at the fringes of society. As Denmark expert Andrew Buckser has observed, "Few avow a firm belief in a well-defined God, and most look to science rather than religion to make sense of their world."[9] According to Swedish scholar Eva Hamberg, less than 20 percent of Swedes claim to believe in the existence of a personal God, and "for many of those Swedes who still believe in God, this belief is more or less unimportant."[10]

So the typical Dane or Swede doesn't believe all that much in God.[11] And simultaneously, they don't commit much murder. But aren't they a dour, depressed lot, all the same? Some Americans might suspect that Scandinavians' marked detachment from the Lord would breed widespread despair. As they forgo prayer, let their Bibles gather dust, fail to praise Jesus on a regular basis, and remain more or less indifferent to the Lord Almighty, don't these religiously tone-deaf Nordics find themselves feeling empty deep down in their souls? Aren't they unhappy? Not according to Dr. Ruut Veenhoven of Erasmus University. Dr. Veenhoven is a leading authority on worldwide levels of happiness from country to country. He recently ranked 91 nations on an international happiness scale, basing his research on cumulative scores from numerous worldwide surveys. According to his calculations, the country that leads the globe—ranking number one in terms of its residents' overall level of happiness—is little, peaceful, and relatively godless Denmark.[12]

As an American living there, I found the low levels of religiosity in Scandinavia fascinating, and even, I'll admit, a relief at times. For a nonbeliever/agnostic such as myself, life in the strongly religious United States can be somewhat exasperating. Although I can definitely recognize and appreciate the enormous good that religion can generate in terms of providing community, instilling hope, strengthening family bonds, emphasizing love and forgiveness, and embellishing life with important rituals and rites of passage, it still isn't always so easy for me to live in a country as religious as the United States, where praying is as ubiquitous as dieting, where police chiefs of major cities can explain a rise in crime within their jurisdiction as being caused by Satan,[13] where governors can entreat the public to use prayer as a primary method with which to confront natural disasters,[14] and where school board members consistently challenge the teaching of human evolution in high school biology classes. In all honesty, for me personally, living in Denmark was like a year-long breath of secular fresh air.

Of course, I must acknowledge that religion hasn't disappeared from Danish or Swedish culture altogether. One of the reasons I have titled this book *Society without God* as opposed to *Society without Religion* is because many elements of the Lutheran religion definitely continue to permeate Danish and Swedish culture. For example, the majority of Danes and Swedes are still tax-paying members of their respective national churches, most Danes and Swedes prefer to get married in church, and a large majority of Danes and Swedes still choose to baptize their children under the auspices of a pastor (who, by the way, is usually a woman these days). Additionally, most Danes will see their sons and daughters go on to be confirmed in the church in early adolescence. But even these overt vestiges of Lutheran religiosity are seldom performed out of a sense of faith or spiritual conviction. Rather, Danes and Swedes overwhelmingly engage in these Christian rituals out of a sense of cultural tradition. For example, nearly all of the people that I talked to said they paid about 1 percent of their annual income in taxes to support their national church simply because "that's just what one does." It almost never had anything to do with God, Jesus, religious conviction, or faith. And nearly everyone I interviewed who got married in church did so solely for the "tradition" or "romance" of it, preferring the aesthetics of a church ceremony over a bland ceremony in city hall. One of my closest friends while living in Denmark was Mikkel, a 39-year-old pastor[15] within the national Danish Lutheran Church. He has been the leader of a small congregation in a quiet village about 15 miles outside of Aarhus for several years. He has performed over 200 weddings. He always meets with the couples and talks with them before marrying them. He asks them why they want to get married in the church as opposed to city hall. He summarized the responses:

You would expect that quite a lot of them would say, well, "That's to have the blessing of God." Now I think that out of these 200, it would be like 10 who have mentioned God. Maybe 2 or 3 of them would say it's to have the blessing of God. But like 10—which is about 5 percent—would mention God. The rest of them would look at me like, "Why do you ask this question? Obviously it's because of tradition, Mikkel"—they think that it's a joke that I even ask. "This is tradition. It has to be a real wedding, you know, with the white dress in this old church."

As for the widespread practice of baptizing babies, this is also generally done for the sake of tradition rather than for the sake of the babies' souls. Most people I interviewed said that they had their children baptized to please Granny, not God. For an example of a thoroughly secular Scandinavian who would still baptize her child despite her lack of belief in God, consider Lise, a 24-year-old Dane who works as a computer technician in Aarhus. Lise is from a small town in central Jutland, and was raised by parents who did not believe in God and did not go to church. None of Lise's friends growing up believed in God—indeed, God was simply something that was never talked about in her social world. Like her family and friends, Lise does not believe in God, nor does she believe in Jesus, nor in the devil or heaven or hell—although like many Danes, she has no problem off-handedly admitting that "there is more between heaven and earth." Lise is currently engaged, and I wondered, if she were to have kids, would she raise them to be religious?

No.

Will you have them confirmed?

Yeah, and baptized.

Because. . .?

It's the norm. It's what we do.

And that was that. When I pushed her on why she would baptize her baby even though she doesn't believe in the central tenets of Christianity, she just shrugged her shoulders and again explained that it is simply what Danes do. Another Danish woman that I interviewed was Gitte, who is 40 years old and works as a preschool teacher in Aarhus. Gitte is a third-generation nonbeliever, that is, her grandparents as well as her parents did not believe in God. And she doesn't either. And yet she had her two children baptized. I asked her how she could sit in a church and listen to a pastor say all those religious words about God and Jesus while performing the sacred ritual of baptism over her children if she didn't even believe in Jesus or God or anything like that. She said that the words had no meaning for her at all, but that the ritual itself was a nice experience, and that she ultimately understood the entire ceremony as "just a piece of cultural performing."

As for confirmation—again, most people I talked to said they went through the process simply because that is just "what everybody does," and the party, gifts, and money that come along with it are something most 14-year-olds have a difficult time refusing. Thus, even though most Scandinavians engage in a variety of nominally religious rituals and Christian life-cycle ceremonies, they rarely do so for theological reasons. From baptism to paying church taxes, from confirmation to church weddings, the popular Lutheran components of most Scandinavians' lives are best understood as simply secular traditions with religious trappings.

Most Danes and Swedes are characterized by a strong belief in reason and rationality. In fact, 82 percent of Danes accept the evidence for Darwin's theory of human evolution, among the highest proportion of evolution-believers in the Western world.[16] And yet, most Danes and Swedes do simultaneously identify themselves as Christian. How is that possible? How can one reject the holiness of the Bible, not believe in Jesus, not believe in sin, salvation, or resurrection—not even believe in God—but still call oneself Christian? I pursued that very question repeatedly throughout my year of research. For the vast majority of Danes and Swedes that I spoke with, when they said they were Christian, they simply meant it in terms of cultural heritage and history, and when I asked them what the designation "Christian" meant to them, they almost invariably all stressed the same things: being kind to others, taking care of the poor and sick, and being a good and moral person. They almost never mentioned God, Jesus, or the Bible in their explanation of Christian identity. When I specifically asked these Nordic Christians if they believed that Jesus was the Son of God or the Messiah, they nearly always said no—usually without hesitation. Did they believe that Jesus was born of a virgin or that he rose from the grave? Such queries were usually met with genuine laughter—as though the mere asking was rather silly.

Take the example of Anders, who is from Aarhus, is in his mid-forties, and owns a small corner market. Anders does not necessarily know if he believes in God or not, he doesn't believe in the divinity of Jesus, he doesn't believe in heaven or hell, and is sure that the Bible is merely a work of human creation. But he still considers himself a Christian. As he explains:

I'm believing in good things in human beings, which are the real things of Christianity. You can't kill other people. You have to help old people, and so on and so on. I think those are some good rules to live by. That's why I am a Christian man.

Consider Elsa, a 56-year-old Swedish human resources consultant from southern Sweden. No belief in God, Jesus, heaven, or hell, or the Bible, yet she calls herself a Christian. I asked her what that meant, and she replied:

To be a decent human being and respect other people and, yeah, to be a good person.

Not your typical American understanding of being Christian, that's for sure. While one can certainly find such sentiments among liberal, mainline American Christians,[17] Anders and Elsa offered fairly straightforward articulations of what could most easily be characterized as secular humanism.

The differences between Scandinavia and the United States—at least when it comes to religion—are thus quite remarkable and rather numerous. I spent my sojourn in Denmark in a relative state of awe, constantly noting how different things were in Aarhus when compared to, say, Anaheim. Whereas in the United States one cannot flip through radio stations or television channels without coming across preachers weighing in against sin and the need for salvation, and a football or basketball game can seldom begin without a prayer to Jesus, and 75 percent of Americans claim to believe in the existence of hell,[18] in Denmark and Sweden, people are far more interested in their families, their homes, their bikes, local politics, their careers, the weather, and even their favorite British or Brazilian soccer players than anything remotely theological. And as for belief in hell—only 10 percent of Danes and Swedes believe in the existence of such a place—the lowest national rates of belief in hell in the world.[19] While lovely, old churches dot the landscape of Denmark and Sweden, and while children are taught about Christianity as part of the elementary school curriculum, religion is distinctly muted in Scandinavia in a way that most Americans would find hard to fathom. Let me offer two examples to further illustrate this point: politics and the playground.

First, politics and religion, a topic I broached earlier on. In the United States, it is generally the rule that if a politician wants to be successful, he or she must not only be a regular churchgoer and a "person of faith," but must express that publicly and frequently. Most Americans these days prefer that their governors, senators, and presidents believe in God, praise God, and even base their decisions on prayer and consultation with God.

Consequently, an atheist in America has about as much chance of being elected president as a member of Al-Queda. But it's just the opposite in Denmark and Sweden. In these countries, politicians are expected to keep whatever religious beliefs they may have to themselves, and if they have no religious beliefs, well, that's even better. If a politician were to discuss his or her faith publicly, or were to base any decision-making on prayer, or were even to refer to God now and then in public addresses, that individual would quickly be out of a job. Or rather, would never even have gotten the job to begin with.

Consider the results from a recent international survey that asked people from different countries if they agreed or disagreed with the following proposition: "Politicians who don't believe in God are unfit for public office." Sixty-four percent of Americans agreed, but only 8 percent of Danes and 15 percent of Swedes did so.[20] A second question in the same survey asked people how they felt about the following statement: "It would be better for our country if more people with strong religious beliefs held public office." A full 75 percent of Americans agreed with that proposition, but only 12 percent of Danes and 30 percent of Swedes agreed, placing Denmark in the number one slot worldwide among countries whose citizens do not want religious people holding public office. In the words of Anders Fogh Rasmussen, Denmark's current prime minister: "Religion is and has to be a personal matter . . . it is dangerous when personal beliefs are over-ruled by religious laws, where an individual's beliefs must comply with 1,000-year-old commandments and scriptures, and where society has to conform to religious commands. In Denmark, we differentiate between religion and politics."[21]

For a second example of just how different the United States and Scandinavia are when it comes to religion and its place in society, let's consider the playground. In most elementary schools across America, if a child admits to not believing in God or Jesus, that child can expect a certain degree of trouble. It is quite possible that he or she will be shunned at school, or worse. When my own daughter was six years old, she was swinging on one of the swings on the school playground during recess. When her friend asked her if she believed in God, my daughter replied "no." Her friend immediately stopped swinging, damned my daughter to hell, and walked away—never to swing with her again.

And yet, in Scandinavia it is virtually just the opposite situation: to publicly profess a belief in God or Jesus marks you the strange one, the deviant one, the oddball. As Sarah, a 20-year-old grocery clerk from a tiny village in Jutland, explained to me:

Young people think that religion is kind of taboo. As a young person, you don't say, "I'm a Christian and I'm proud of it." If you do that, you often get picked on.

It is thus the rare believing Christian child on the Scandinavian playground who may face shunning, ridicule, or worse. Torben was just such a child. Beginning in the fifth grade, when his strong belief in God and Jesus became known, ridicule and harassment became routine. He changed schools a number of times, and finally found refuge in a private Christian school. "I still have scars," he lamented tearfully during the course of our interview. He is now 25 years old, married, and pursuing a degree in theology. He told me that he quit the national Danish Lutheran Church a few years ago because of its tolerant attitudes toward homosexuality. He now worships at a "free" church. He believes that the Bible is the literal word of God, that Adam and Eve actually existed, that Jesus died for our sins, that the devil is real, and that all non-Christians will go to hell. I asked him if he thought that all Jews would go to hell.

That's what I believe. I don't like it, but that's what my Bible tells me.

And all Buddhists and Hindus?

Yes.

Whereas many Americans would consider Torben of sound mind, most Scandinavians would find his religious beliefs disquieting, bizarre, and possibly the result of mental instability. That is, whereas Torben's religious beliefs are fairly common in the United States, in Scandinavia, he is an extreme rarity. I asked Andreas, a 33-year-old public high school teacher in the city of Odense, how many of his students share the beliefs of Torben. "Two or five percent," he replied.

One could go on and on detailing the many differences between the overt religiosity of the United States and the widespread secularism of Denmark and Sweden. For unlike in the United States, in Scandinavia there is no national anti–gay rights movement, there are no mega churches with "ATMs for Jesus" installed on-site where people can donate money to the church using a credit card, there are no popular, successful preachers haranguing "sodomites" or sinners on the radio airwaves, there are no political candidates who say that they decided to run for public office because "God told them to," there are no "Jesus fish" imprinted on advertisements in the yellow pages, there are no school boards or school administrators who publicly doubt the evidence for human evolution (and seek to limit its teaching), there are no judges who make rulings based on what the Bible says, there are no religiously inspired "abstinence only" sex education curricula, there is no viable anti-abortion movement, there are no parental groups lobbying schools and city councils to remove Harry Potter books from school and public libraries, there are no "natural history museums" that erect installations depicting Adam and Eve,[22] there are no restaurants that include Bible verses on their menus and placemats, there are no "Faith Nights" at national sporting events, where popular athletes praise God and preach Christianity to stadiums full of sports fans—all of which can be found within America's thriving religious landscape.

What is life like in such countries, so unlike the United States, where religious faith is almost invisible and God is relegated to the deeply private margins of society? And what about the individual men and women who live in Denmark and Sweden today? What is their (nonreligious) outlook on life? Of course, there are always nonbelievers in every society, even the most fundamentalist. And yet only in Scandinavia is nonbelief considered normal, regular, mainstream, common. Thus, to be a nonbeliever is one thing, but to be a nonbeliever in a society that thinks nothing of nonbelief and considers it typical and normative—that is something sociologically significant.

Lars was one such individual.

It is hard to say whether or not Lars is a "typical" Scandinavian. But he surely comes close. I'd like to end this introduction with a brief portrait of him, because of all the people I met and interviewed over the course of my year in Denmark, Lars made one of the more positive impressions on me. It was an impression of contentment and sanity, as well as a strong love of life. I was happy to have met Lars, and happy to have been able to sit with him for about an hour and a half on a snowy, cold, dark night in the middle of February, in a cozy house by the Kattegat sea, and ask him about his life and his beliefs.

Lars is 77 years old. He is in great shape and his face flushed with energy as we talked. He was raised in Copenhagen, but currently lives on the island of Fyn. He is retired now, but he spent many years as the headmaster of a small high school. Politically, he is right of center. He has two daughters and has been married to the same woman for over 50 years. His father was a strongly devout Christian, and was one of the leaders of his congregation. Lars's mother, however, was an atheist, as was her father, and Lars recalled that her father was deemed ineligible for promotions as a result of his atheism, which—back in the 1800s—was considered quite a problem when made public.

As Lars explained, his mother and father did not get along:

My father was the head of the biggest—a big group of Christians. . . . He was not the priest, but he was a teacher. He was head of it . . . the congregation. And my mother was an atheist. And they divorced when I was four years old.

Lars and his two brothers were thus raised mostly by their mother, although they did see their father from time to time, and even went with him to his congregation on occasion. Lars considers himself an atheist, and says that he always was an atheist—and he pointed out that he even refused to go through the confirmation process, which was quite an unusual move 65 years ago. However, he was married in the church. I asked him why, and he replied with a laugh:

That's because the mother-in-law has great power, you see.

Lars's mother passed away in 2003, and I was curious about the durability of her atheism as she aged. In her last days, did she ever turn to God?

No . . . she had three months left; then she would have been 108 years.

She lived that long?

You can look on her tombstone—it's in our town—1895 to 2003.

She just passed away . . .

Yes.

But she always stayed an atheist?

Always.

We talked a bit more about her death—how she was cremated without a Christian funeral, as was her wish. I looked at Lars—who is coming up on 80—and asked him about his own impending death.

What do you think happens after we die?

Oh . . . my old teacher in biology always said the chemicals you are made of have a value of about 4 Danish crowns and you have to pay back as soon as possible, so it goes down right to the crematorium. And I think the same . . . But . . . no, no.

You don't believe in life after . . . ?

No . . . I don't know, I don't know. I know—for me—when it's finished, it's finished.

But if you think "when it's finished, it's finished," then what is the point of it all? What is the meaning of life?

The meaning of life? I have my time on the earth and it's my duty to do it as well as it's possible for me. I try to be a good father . . . I have wonderful years.

How do you cope in your life when things are bad or you have something sad in your life? What do you do?

What should I say? . . . I have no sad moments. You know what I mean. I've been a very happy man. Everything I want, every job I ask for—I got my wife, two highly educated daughters, four grandchildren with brains running.

So you're happy?

Yes. Of course, I've had moments when I was . . . unsatisfied and angry and then that's your own fault, I think. Yes, but I have never been in a situation where I felt that I needed something to support me.

We talked of many more things: his recollections of the German occupation of Denmark during World War II, the recent influx of Muslim immigrants into Denmark, the night he was honored at a dinner at the high school where he used to be headmaster, and how 500 people stood up and toasted him, which he described as "the golden moment" of his life. But what most struck me about Lars throughout the course of the interview was his general warmth and what seemed to me to be an honest and totally unfeigned happiness and satisfaction with life. He seemed to have had it all: a strong, long marriage, loving daughters and granddaughters, a satisfying career, a lovely home on Denmark's greenest island, good health—and all without belief in God.

It is my deep desire to recognize and understand people like Lars—and to fathom and describe the culture that produces so many individuals like him—which comprises the underlying motivation of this book.

As stated at the beginning of this chapter, we currently live in a world bubbling with religious passions. But that makes the recognition of people like Lars—people who are not caught up in this bubbling passion—all the more provocative and interesting. And it renders an analysis of relatively "godless societies" such as Denmark and Sweden all the more pressing.

1

Society without God

In Holland . . . the whole nation, at its core, seemed so ungodly. Here one
could (and many did) contest the very existence of God at every turn. People
openly disbelieved every aspect of religion . . . almost everything was secular
here. God was mocked everywhere . . . and yet nobody was struck by a thun-
derbolt. Society worked without reference to God, and it seemed to function
perfectly. This man-made system of government was so much more stable,
peaceful, prosperous, and happy than the supposedly God-devised systems I
had been taught to respect.   —Ayaan Hirsi Ali[1]

WHAT ARE SOCIETIES like when faith in God is minimal, church attendance is drastically low, and religion is a distinctly muted and marginal
aspect of everyday life? If people don't do much in the way of praying, they
aren't too concerned about their soul's salvation, and they don't instill in
their children a strong belief in Jesus, what might be the overall condition of
such a relatively secular society? Having recently lived in just such a society,
I can confidently declare that the answer is not chaos, selfishness, criminal-
ity, or societal decay. As I stated in the Introduction, despite their relative
secularity, Denmark and Sweden are not bastions of depravity and anarchy.
In fact, they are just the opposite: impressive models of societal health.

The connection between religion—or the lack thereof—and societal
health is admittedly complex. It is difficult to definitively establish that secularism is always good for society and religion always bad. However, the opposite claim is equally difficult to substantiate: that secularism is always bad
for a society and religion always good. To be sure, in some instances, religion can be a strong and positive ingredient in establishing societal health,
prosperity, and well-being. And when considering what factors contribute
to the making of a good society, admittedly religion can be a positive force.
Here in the United States, for example, religious ideals often serve as a ben-
eficial counterbalance against the cutthroat brand of individualism that is so
rampant and dominating. Religious congregations in America serve as community centers, counseling providers, and day-care cites. And a significant

amount of research has shown that moderately religious Americans report greater subjective well-being and life satisfaction, greater marital satisfaction, better family cohesion, and fewer symptoms of depression than the nonreligious.[2] Historically, a proliferation of religious devotion, faith in God, and reliance on the Bible has sometimes been a determining factor in establishing schools for children, creating universities, building hospitals for the sick and homes for the homeless, taking care of orphans and the elderly, resisting oppression, establishing law and order, and developing democracy. However, in other instances, religion may not have such positive societal effects. It can often be one of the main sources of tension, violence, poverty, oppression, inequality, and disorder in a given society. A quick perusal of the state of the world will reveal that widespread faith in God or strong religious sentiment in a given country does not necessarily ensure societal health.[3] After all, many of the most religious and faithful nations on earth are simultaneously among the most dangerous and destitute. Conversely, a widespread lack of faith in God or very low levels of religiosity in a given country does not necessarily spell societal ruin. The fact is, the majority of the most irreligious democracies are among the most prosperous and successful nations on earth.

It is that last point that I want to focus on and establish in this chapter: that some of the least religious nations in the world, particularly those in Scandinavia, are simultaneously among the most prosperous and successful societies out there. Just to be perfectly clear here: I am not arguing that the admirably high level of societal health in Scandinavia is directly *caused* by the low levels of religiosity. Although one could certainly make just such a case—arguing that a minimal focus on God/the afterlife and a stronger focus on solving problems of daily life in a rational, secular manner have led to positive, successful societal outcomes in Scandinavia— that is not the argument I wish to develop here. Rather, I simply wish to soberly counter the widely touted assertion that without religion, society is doomed.

If you can smell my axe starting to grind here, your nostrils are in good working order. I will admit that I do feel the personal need to challenge and explicitly counter the claim that without religion, society is doomed. This claim deserves to be challenged because, aside from being poor social science, it is a highly political claim that is regularly promulgated by some of America's most popular and most influential Christian conservatives. These individuals do not represent or speak for the majority of believers in America, but together they do comprise a formidable and uniquely zealous chorus that reaches the hearts and minds of millions of people on a regular basis. I am referring to people like Pat Robertson, the successful televangelist and founder of the Christian Coalition, who regularly condemns secularism. Robertson has publicly stated that the existence of secular Americans can potentially destroy the foundations of society, and that when school boards push for secular science curricula over religious beliefs, God's punishment will ensue. Robertson has argued that when a society is without religion, "the result will be tyranny."[4] Furthermore, according to Robertson, any nation that accepts and tolerates homosexuality "can expect the judgment of God and the full weight of God's wrath against them."[5] And then there is the recently deceased Jerry Falwell, another successful televangelist and founder of the Moral Majority. Falwell publicly declared that the terrorist attacks of September 11, 2001, were caused by Americans who angered God by pushing secularism. "God will not be mocked," Falwell declared on Robertson's widely syndicated television show *The 700 Club*. "I really believe that the pagans, and the abortionists, and the feminists, and the gays and lesbians . . . all of them who have tried to secularize America—I point the finger in their face and say, you helped this happen."

"Well," replied Pat Robertson, "I totally concur."

More recently, Christian conservative media pundit, Ann Coulter, has written in one of her best-selling books that societies which fail to grasp God's significance are headed toward slavery, genocide, and bestiality[6] and that when Darwinian/evolutionary theory is widely accepted in a given society, all morality is abandoned.[7] Best-selling author and enormously successful conservative Christian journalist and television personality Bill O'Reilly has similarly declared that a society that is not full of religion and spirituality and fails to live "under God" will be a society of anarchy and crime,[8] where lawbreakers are allowed to run wild.[9] O'Reilly further argues that secular societies are necessarily "weak" and "chaotic" and that in secular cultures, the only creed people believe in is "personal gratification."[10] Super successful conservative radio and television commentator Rush Limbaugh has argued that if a society exists in which the majority of people do not believe that they ultimately must answer to God for their behavior, the result will be "national disaster."[11] Conservative pundit William Bennett has argued that "the only reliable answer" for combating societal ills is widespread religious faith, and that without religion, a society is without "the best and most reliable means to reinforce the good" in social life and human relations.[12] For Bennett, religion is "fundamental" to a "vital society."[13] Paul Weyrich, founder of the right-wing, conservative think tank Heritage Foundation, has argued that secular humanists threaten the "very survival" of society.[14]

But conservative Christian Americans aren't the only ones that broadcast this perspective. Oxford-trained philosopher Keith Ward has recently argued that societies that lack strong religious beliefs are essentially immoral, un-free, and irrational.[15] He claims that any nonreligious society without a strong belief in God is a society "beyond morality . . . and freedom" and ultimately predicated upon "the denial of human dignity."[16] Contemporary philosophy professor John D. Caputo has declared that people who are without religion and who do not love God are nothing more than selfish louts, thereby implying that a society with a preponderance of irreligious people would be a fairly loveless, miserable place.[17]

The assertions of Robertson, Falwell, Coulter, O'Reilly, and others quoted above, will be countered in my discussion below, as I shall make it very clear that a relative lack of religion in a given society does not necessarily lead to societal chaos, but is actually strongly correlated with impressively high levels of societal health, social well-being, and an admirably moral social order. For as I traversed the bike paths of Aarhus, as I walked my children to and from their schools, as I strolled the streets of Copenhagen, Stockholm, Odense, Gothenburg, and Silkeborg, and as I hiked along the coastline of Denmark and in the woods of Sweden, as I frequented the banks, bars, bakeries, and bookstores of Jutland, and as I traveled around wider Scandinavia, I could not avoid the striking sociological fact that here were societies in which religion is markedly weak, and yet at the same time, they are extremely healthy, well-functioning, and manifestly sensible.

•   •   •

"But what about China? North Korea? The former Soviet Union? Or the very first officially declared 'atheist' nation on earth, Albania? Surely these irreligious societies can hardly be characterized as exemplars of societal health."

That assertion is often leveled at me when I broach the matter of irreligion being correlated with healthy, prosperous societies. It is a seemingly logical assertion, and therefore one that merits a careful response.

I'll start with Albania.

In the late 1960s, the communist dictator of Albania, Enver Hoxha, outlawed religion and declared Albania to be the first atheist nation in the world. He forbade Albanians from giving religious names to their children, he razed churches and mosques, and he outlawed possession of Qu'rans, Bibles, and religious icons. Anyone caught with these items faced imprisonment. Like most fascist leaders, Hoxha was insanely paranoid. His political and economic policies were disastrous, and he single-handedly ruined his nation by oppressing, starving, and demoralizing Albanians for decades. Although Hoxha died in 1985 and Albania is no longer under his wicked boot, the nation today is extremely poor, its infrastructure is a mess, and its level of societal health is relatively low. Not a pretty picture when it comes to society without God.

And North Korea isn't any prettier. It is one of the most un-free, destitute societies on earth today. Similar to what happened in Albania, in North Korea, religion is severely repressed, with the only truly acceptable and legal "religion" being worship of its brutal dictator, Kim Jong Il. In China, another communist dictatorship, religion is also kept on a very tight leash. Indeed, even the most benign forms of religious worship can land you in prison. And simultaneously, indicators of societal health in China are distinctly unimpressive. What about the former Soviet Union? Yet another example of a communist dictatorship that was hostile to religion and sought to promote atheism over faith among its citizens. And like all communist dictatorships the world has ever known, the former Soviet Union was a gruesome exercise in repression, paranoia, and injustice, resulting in frightfully dismal levels of societal health.

Based on these examples of ostensibly anti-religious or nonreligious countries—Albania, North Korea, China, the former Soviet Union— one could quite easily make a very strong case that whenever religion is stomped out and replaced by atheism or state secularism, the resulting situation for such a society is horrid: corruption, inequality, poverty, suicide, injustice, and a whole slew of other societal, economic, and political maladies ensue. In sum, it may very well be that when nations turn away from God, they suffer the consequences.

Not so fast.

There is something else—something very significant—that all of these supposedly "godless" nations have in common. In each case, religion wasn't abandoned by the people themselves in a natural process over several generations. Rather, the "abandonment" of religion was decreed by vicious dictators who imposed their faithlessness on an unwilling, decidedly un-free citizenry. Just because Enver Hoxha of Albania banned religious faith in favor of atheism, that does not mean that he succeeded in changing what was in Albanians' hearts and minds. In fact, despite decades of "official" atheism in Albania, belief in God was never abandoned by the Albanians themselves; recent surveys indicate that today over 90 percent of Albanians believe in God.[18] They may have hidden their holy books while Hoxha was in power, and pretended to be atheists to avoid arrest, but their belief in God clearly held fast. The same can be said for much of the former Soviet Union; though the citizens of these former communist nations came under Soviet occupation and were subjected to forced secularization for decades, we now see that belief in God wasn't successfully stamped out, and is even rather robust in many former Soviet states.[19] For instance, 96 percent of Romanians and Moldovans currently claim to believe in God, as well as 93 percent of Georgians and 87 percent of Lithuanians.[20]

As for North Korea, unfortunately, we cannot even attempt to know what is in people's hearts and minds there because the dictatorial regime in power is so brutally totalitarian that it won't allow social scientists to carry out unfettered research. Social science on religion has also been hindered in China, for decades. However, in recent years more has been accomplished, and nearly all scholars of religion in China are in agreement that governmental estimates of religion are severe undercounts.[21] Some scholars have even argued recently that rather than being among the least religious nations in the world, China may in fact be one of the *most* religious nations in the world today.[22] But again, with the absence of democracy and the freedom it brings to social inquiry, we just can't be sure.

This discussion thus leads to a crucially important matter when looking at any country in terms of its religiosity: is it a dictatorship or a democracy? When religion is repressed by a dictator—that is, when a nonelected cabal or individual fascist takes over a country and attempts to forcibly abolish belief in God—such a country cannot be assumed to be truly void of religion. When we are dealing with a situation of governmentally forced atheism, what we might call "coercive" or "imposed" atheism, we cannot assume the people themselves have actually lost their faith in God.

In order to find societies where religion is truly, genuinely, and *verifiably* weak—where it can be observed that the majority of people honestly don't believe much in God, don't go to church much, and don't concern themselves much with religious or theological matters—we must look at free, open, democratic nations where atheism has not been enforced upon an unwilling population by a threatening, powerful regime. In such societies, if people lose faith in God, forget about their Bibles, stop going to

church, and stop praying to Jesus, we can safely assume that such secularization is an organic process. That is, the majority of people have stopped
being religious of their own volition. Such nations can be more accurately
described as societies where religion is truly weak. And it is to such societies that we must look in establishing the fact that relatively irreligious
societies are not bastions of depravity, but quite the opposite.

• • •

The best tool we have for assessing levels of religiosity among large populations or at the national level is the survey—an admittedly weak, problematic tool. Surveys of religiosity are riddled with methodological flaws,
including: (1) nonrandom samples, (2) low response rates, (3) adverse
political or cultural climates, (4) problematic cross-cultural terminology,
and (5) surface answers. First, if the sample of people participating in a
given survey was not selected randomly, then the responses they offer are
nongeneralizable to the wider population or country of which they are
members. Second, concerning low response rates: most people do not respond to surveys. They hang up the phone, toss the soliciting mail into the
trashcan, shut the door on the inquisitor, or simply walk away from the
sociologist on the street corner with clipboard in hand. Surveys with low
response rates may provide interesting information concerning the minority of self-selecting people responding, but they cannot be generalized to
the wider society or nation. A third methodological problem involves the
political or cultural climate of a given country. In a totalitarian country
where atheism is governmentally enforced by dictators and risks are present for citizens viewed as disloyal (e.g., China or North Korea), individuals will be reluctant to admit that they do believe in God. Conversely, in
a society where religion is heavily enforced by the government and risks
are present for citizens viewed as nonbelievers (e.g., Saudi Arabia or Iran),
individuals will be reluctant to admit that they don't believe in Allah. A
fourth methodological shortcoming relates to problematic cross-cultural
terminology. Meanings and definitions of specific words or categories seldom translate well from country to country. Signifiers such as "religious,"
"secular," "believe in," or "God" have dramatically different meanings and
connotations in different cultures. They are laden with historical, political,
social, and theological implications that are unique to every given country and its subcultures. Thus, making cross-national comparisons of religious beliefs between markedly different societies is tenuous, at best. A
final methodological weakness of surveys is the distinctly "surface" nature

of the responses that they generate. This is an especially acute weakness when it comes to trying to discern people's religiosity. For example, if a survey question asks someone "Do you believe in God?"—what does a response of "yes" actually mean? It could mean so many different things to so many different people. Indeed, as I found in my research, what a Dane or Swede means when responding "yes" to the question of God-belief is often qualitatively different than what an American usually means when responding "yes." In short, belief in God is such a vast, nuanced, personal, open-ended, culture-bound matter that a mere "yes" or "no" response to the question doesn't really tell us much. It just barely scratches the surface. Such is the case with most survey questions on religion. However, while admitting to all of the methodological problems outlined above, I would still argue that surveys aren't completely useless. They do offer some valuable information, even if that information is partial, limited, or sketchy. I am thus in full agreement with Robert Putnam, who argues that "we must make do with the imperfect evidence that we can find, not merely lament its deficiencies."[23]

That said, let's consider some recent survey data illustrating the relatively low levels of religiosity in Denmark and Sweden. Although Denmark (population 5.4 million) and Sweden (population 9 million) are separate nations with their own distinct landscapes and cultural idiosyncrasies, they are still about as similar as any two modern nations can be: their languages are mutually intelligible; their geographies and histories have been closely interwoven over the centuries; their economic, legal, and political systems are remarkably similar; and it is thus possible to speak of them as constituting if not exactly the same society, at least societies that are extremely close in nature.[24] And that is certainly true with regard to their comparable lack of devoutness.

I'll start with *belief in God*. While over 90 percent of Americans claim to believe in God, one study reports that only 51 percent of Danes and 26 percent of Swedes claim to believe in a God.[25] Another study found even lower rates, reporting that only 24 percent of Danes and 16 percent of Swedes claim to believe in a "personal God."[26] When asked "How important is God in your life?" (with 10 meaning "very important" and 1 meaning "not at all"), only 23 percent of Swedes and 21 percent of Danes chose 7–10—among the lowest such levels in the world.[27] And *belief in life after death* may be as low as 30 percent and 33 percent among Danes and Swedes respectively—compared to 81 percent of Americans.[28] Only 18 percent of Danes and 31 percent of Swedes believe in *heaven*—compared to 88 percent of Americans.[29] And only 10 percent of Danes and Swedes believe in *hell*—the lowest rates of hell-belief in the world.[30] As for belief in the existence of *sin*, Danes and Swedes are again at the very bottom of international rankings, with only 21 percent of Danes and 26 percent of Swedes believing in its existence.[31] Concerning *the nature of the Bible*, only 7 percent of Danes and 3 percent of Swedes believe that the Bible is the actual/literal word of God[32]—compared to 33 percent of Americans.[33] When it comes to *religious service attendance* (excluding weddings, funerals, and christenings), only 12 percent of Danes and 9 percent of Swedes attend church services at least once a month,[34] and only 3 percent of Danes and 7 percent of Swedes go at least once a week.[35] As for *prayer*, only 21 percent of Danes and 20 percent of Swedes claim to pray several times in a given month.[36] And only 15 percent of Danes and 12 percent of Swedes claim to have ever had a "religious experience."[37] When a sample of 18–29-year-olds from various countries were asked if religion gives them comfort and strength, only 24 percent of Danes and 20 percent of Swedes said "yes."[38] Finally, one recent study asked Danes what they thought were the most important goals when it came to fostering certain qualities in their children: 87 percent chose "tolerance/respect," 80 percent chose "independence," 72 percent chose "good manners," 56 percent chose "to think of others," 37 percent chose "imagination"—but only 8 percent chose "Christian faith."[39]

I could go on presenting similar survey data, but the point here is simply to illustrate that when it comes to the acceptance of various religious beliefs, as well as church attendance, the nations of Denmark and Sweden are among the least religious in the world. Other nations that are similarly irreligious include the Czech Republic, South Korea, Estonia, France, Japan, Bulgaria, Norway, England, Scotland, Wales, Hungary, Belgium, and the Netherlands.[40] Vietnam may also be quite secular, but due to the communist regime in power there, which severely limits personal freedom (and social science), we cannot be sure.

• • •

Now let's look at indicators of societal health. How do Denmark and Sweden—and other similarly irreligious societies—fare? This is of course a tricky matter, for just as "religiosity" is a subjective matter, so too is "societal health." One person's version of a healthy society might be another person's version of a hellish society. Take the issue of physical discipline: the spanking of children is illegal in Sweden, and has been since 1979. Is this to be considered a sign of a healthy society, or a sick society? Depends on who you ask. The same problem can be seen when considering women's rights as a sign of societal health; I might consider women's equality a good thing, whereas someone else (like a Saudi prince) might not. I also consider strong environmental regulations that heavily restrict pollution as a sign of societal health, whereas my representative in Congress, David Dreier, does not. I also consider high literacy rates as indicative of societal health, whereas someone from a strictly oral culture may not. OK, you get the idea: ascertaining societal health is an unavoidably subjective enterprise. But despite the differing value judgments that are unavoidable, I shall nonetheless proceed, and present below an array of what many would consider to be rather standard, typical sociological variables/indicators in my attempt to illustrate which countries may be said to exhibit the highest degrees of societal health.

Every year, the United Nations publishes its *Human Development Report*. Within that publication, approximately 175 nations are ranked on a "Human Development Index," which measures the average societal achievements in a given country by taking into consideration three basic dimensions of human development: a long and healthy life (measured by such things as life expectancy), knowledge (measured by such things as literacy rates and school enrollment rates), and a decent standard of living (measured by such things as GDP per capita). As of 2006, Sweden ranked fifth in the world, Denmark ranked fifteenth, and several other relatively nonreligious nations—including Norway, Japan, the Netherlands, France, and Britain—were in the top 20.

Concerning *life expectancy*, of the 20 nations with the highest rates of life expectancy—meaning that their citizens on average live the longest—Sweden ranks sixth in the world, and of the top 20 nations in this category, nearly all are nations where religion is relatively weak compared to the rest of the world.[41] Considering *infant mortality rates*, Denmark and Sweden are tied for first place—along with Norway, Iceland, Japan, and Singapore—for the best/lowest infant mortality rates in the world. And of the top 20 nations with the best/lowest infant mortality rates, most are nations in which religion is weak.[42] Concerning overall *child welfare*, according to a 2007 UNICEF report that looked at multiple factors that affect children's well-being, from safety and risk of poverty to family relations and health, the three highest ranking nations with the best scores for child welfare were the Netherlands, Sweden, and Denmark—all three being among the least religious nations in the world.[43]

When considering *wealth/GDP*, Denmark ranks fourth and Sweden ranks eighth in the world for strongest/highest GDP per capita, and of the top 20 nations with the strongest/highest GDP per capita, a majority are markedly irreligious nations.[44] As for *economic equality*, based on the standard Gini index, the country that ranks second in the world in terms of income equality is Denmark; Sweden comes in fourth. Of the top 20 nations with the greatest degree of income equality, most are weakly religious nations. And it should be noted that these high levels of economic equality do not result in stagnant economies. Just the opposite is true. For when it comes to *economic competitiveness*, according to the World Economic Forum (which ranks approximately 125 national economies), Sweden had the third most competitive economy in the world, followed by Denmark in fourth place. And of the top 20 most competitive economies in the world, only one nation—the United States (ranked sixth)—is a highly religious nation, while the remaining nations within the top 20 most competitive economies in the world are all weakly religious by international standards.[45]

How about *gender equality*? The United Nations has constructed a "Gender Empowerment Measure," which is a composite index measuring gender in/equality in terms of economic participation, political participation, and decision-making and power over economic resources. According to this measure, Denmark ranks second and Sweden ranks third in the world.[46] Other relatively irreligious nations in the top 20 include Norway (ranked at number 1), the Netherlands, Belgium, New Zealand, and Britain. Sweden comes in second in the world, and Denmark comes in fourth, in terms of having the most women in parliament.[47] And of the top 20 nations with the greatest percentages of women in parliament, a majority are relatively irreligious societies. Finally, in Sweden the female poverty rate is equal to or in some instances even lower than the male rate, making Sweden the only nation on earth where women do not have higher poverty rates than men.[48]

Several other aspects of societal health can be considered, such as *health care*. In terms of the number of physicians per 100,000 people, Denmark comes in ninth in the world.[49] Sweden is tied with Canada and Cyprus for second place for the lowest rates of tuberculosis; and Denmark is tied for fourth place on this measure—along with Australia, Netherlands, Italy, and Malta. Denmark and Sweden also have among the lowest rates of HIV/AIDs infection in the world. When it comes to *investing in education*, in terms of public expenditure on education as a percentage of GDP,

Denmark ranks fourth in the world and Sweden ranks sixteenth.[50] And of the top 20 nations with the highest rates of college and university enrollment, Denmark ranks fourteenth, with nearly all of the other top 20 nations in this category being relatively irreligious societies.[51] As for being *technologically active,* that is, how many people in a given country have access to the Internet and are regular Internet users, Sweden ranked third and Denmark ranked fifth in the world, with most of the other top 20 nations in this category being relatively irreligious. *Environmental protection* is a clear indicator of how seriously a country takes the impending threat of global warming. According to the Climate Change Performance Index, developed by nonprofit environmental protection groups Germanwatch and Climate Action Network, the number one nation in the world doing the most in an effort to improve environmental conditions is Sweden, followed by Britain in second place and Denmark in third. And again, of the top 20 nations, most are markedly irreligious. According to Yale University's 2006 Environmental Performance Index, which ranks the world's nations in terms of their approaches to protecting the environment, Sweden comes in at number two and Denmark at number seven.

When measuring a *lack of corruption* among politicians and public figures, Denmark ranks fourth as the least corrupt society in the world, Sweden ranks sixth, and of the top 20 nations with the lowest levels of corruption, the majority are relatively irreligious.[52] When it comes to the giving of *charity to poor nations,* Denmark ranks second, Sweden third, and of the top 20 countries that give the most aid to the poorest nations of the world, many are distinctly irreligious societies. These two indicators are particularly significant and noteworthy because religion is often linked in people's minds with social morality and ethical conduct; it is often assumed and argued that without a strong belief in God or a deep religious commitment, people will have no moral strivings or ethical inclinations. And yet here we see that corruption is extremely low in Scandinavia, and charity extremely high—both clear indicators of a well-developed societal morality, and yet both existing in countries that are quite secular.

What about *crime*? *Suicide*? Many people associate the latter specifically with Scandinavia. However, neither Denmark nor Sweden leads the world in suicide rates. In fact, according to recent international rates calculated by the World Health Organization (2003), of the top 20 nations with the highest *male* suicide rates, Denmark and Sweden do not even place. It must be admitted, however, that many other irreligious societies do, including Hungary, Estonia, Japan, Czech Republic, and France. As for *murder,*

Denmark and Sweden—along with many other relatively irreligious nations such as Norway—have among the lowest rates in the world.[53] But when it comes to other indicators of crime—such as rape, robbery, or car theft—fair international ranking is tricky, if not impossible, because the accumulation of valid crime statistics is often a better indicator of sound law enforcement, solid criminal justice systems, well-developed insurance systems, transparent criminal reporting procedures, and a willingness to report crime in a given country, rather than an inordinately high prevalence of crime in a given nation. That said, while the Scandinavian nations do experience their fair share of burglary and bike theft—and while such crimes have been on the increase in recent years[54]—overall violent crime rates are still among the lowest among industrialized democracies.

In sum, when it comes to *overall quality of life*, according to *The Economist's* Quality of Life Index, which measures 111 nations as to which are the "best" places to live in the world, taking into consideration multiple factors, such as income, health, freedom, unemployment, family life, climate, political stability, life-satisfaction, gender equality, etc., Sweden ranked fifth in the world and Denmark ranked ninth. And of the top 20 nations with the best quality of life, most of them—as you can guess by now—are relatively irreligious societies.

•   •   •

I realize that assembling all of this statistical information in such a short, condensed space may have been a little mind-numbing. But I feel it is necessary to do so in order to make it clear that there is simply no empirical support for the oft-touted theory that without religion—or without significant and widespread worship of God—society is doomed. For as I have sought to establish, the least religious nations on earth also tend to be the most healthy and successful nations on earth.[55] Of course, correlation is not causation. It is not that being relatively irreligious is what necessarily *causes* certain countries such as Denmark or Sweden to be such successful, healthy societies. It is simply that the *lack* of religion doesn't seem to be a hindrance.

Why, then, are Denmark and Sweden such successful societies? There is of course no one clear, definitive answer. It could be related to the relatively small size of their populations, or their historically high degrees of homogeneity, or their history of collective farming, or their centuries of successful trade with the great colonial powers of Europe, or the impressive development of their welfare states, which combine the best of capitalism with a strong safety net for the disadvantaged through progressive taxation. These are but a few obvious possibilities. It could also be related to their unique temperaments or cultural idiosyncrasies, such as their extremely passionate belief in the value of equality.[56] It could also quite possibly be related to the influence of centuries of state-sponsored Lutheranism. But ultimately, explaining why any society is more successful than any other in today's world is about as complex and complicated a matter as could ever fall within the purview of social science. What I would argue is that the reasons that some societies are marked by prosperity and peace, while others are marked by poverty and strife, are essentially historical, political, economic, geographic, and sociological. What they don't seem to be, is spiritual.

Belief in God may certainly give emotional and psychological comfort to the individual believer[57]—especially in times of pain, sadness, or uncertainty—and history has clearly shown that religious involvement and faith in God can often motivate individuals or cultures to promote justice and healthy societal development.[58] But the fact still remains that it is not the most religious nations in our world today, but rather the most secular, that have been able to create the most civil, just, safe, equitable, humane, and prosperous societies. Denmark and Sweden stand out as shining examples. The German think tank Hans-Bockler Stiftung recently ranked nations in terms of their success at establishing social justice within their societies; Denmark and Sweden, two of the least religious nations in the world, tied for first.

It is a great socio-religious irony—for lack of a better term—that when we consider the fundamental values and moral imperatives contained within the world's great religions, such as caring for the sick, the infirm, the elderly, the poor, the orphaned, the vulnerable; practicing mercy, charity, and goodwill toward one's fellow human beings; and fostering generosity, humility, honesty, and communal concern over individual egotism—these traditionally religious values are most successfully established, institutionalized, and put into practice at the societal level in the most irreligious nations in the world today.

•   •   •

I'd like to end this chapter with a bus ride.

It was a very simple, uneventful bus ride through Aarhus, on a relatively unremarkable autumn afternoon. But it was during this particular excursion that I had several personal thoughts and reflections that eventually morphed into the urge and impetus to write this very chapter.

What happened during that bus ride was this: I felt a real sense of goodness. It was a sense of goodness that stemmed not from some internal endorphin rush, but rather, simply from taking in and observing the pleasant social world around me. There I was, heading to an appointment downtown, and I felt it deeply: everything was fine. Calm. Good. The bus was clean—not dirty and grimy, like many buses in large cities can be. The bus was also on time, stopping at each stop right on schedule. And all the people on the bus were sitting peacefully. Teenagers were placidly punching the keypads of their cell phones, old ladies were holding their handbags. A young schoolgirl was absent-mindedly flicking the neon-green strap of her backpack. The bus driver was doing his thing. Outside, through the bus windows, I could see a park full of trees with leaves turning yellow and red. And people jogging. And there was not a honk to be heard, for the flow of traffic was moving right along, smoothly. As we got closer to the city center we passed ice cream stores, book shops, law offices, flower shops, banks, and bakeries. Men and women of all ages buzzed safely alongside the bus on their bikes. The city buildings were largely devoid of graffiti. Litter in the streets was minimal. Every few minutes a pre-recorded voice would announce the name of an upcoming stop. People got off, people got on. Everything was fine. Remarkably fine.

And then, amidst that goodness, I thought about the words of Pat Robertson, particularly his words concerning "God's wrath," and how when people disobey God, He gets angry, and unleashes His wrath on disobedient nations. Robertson surely isn't the only religious leader who espouses such rhetoric; nearly all religious leaders since time immemorial have warned that when God is disobeyed—or simply ignored—He gets mad, and we all suffer the consequences. Many millions of people, especially in America, sincerely believe this. And yet, on that smooth and uneventful bus ride, there were simply no signs of God's wrath. Just the opposite: all was good. Uneventfully good. Peacefully good. If ever a society could be described as "safe and sound," relatively secular Denmark would be it.

As the bus continued on its way, my mind wandered further, beyond the words of Pat Robertson, and on to the millions of people that subscribe to and support his worldview. So many millions of Americans see religion—or more precisely, their version of Christianity—as the only source of a moral social order. So many Americans assume that without strict obedience to biblical laws, society would be chaotic and horrific. *If only they could take this bus ride with me*, I thought to myself. If only my fellow Americans could see that secular society—at least the contemporary

Scandinavian version, and in Holland, as described at the beginning of this chapter by Ayaan Hirsi Ali—is not only moral and ethical but stable, peaceful, and prosperous.

Thoughts such as these continued to fill my mind, and I found myself pondering the specific Christian American obsession with abortion and gay rights. For millions of Americans, these are the great societal "sins" of the day. It isn't bogus wars, systemic poverty, failing schools, child abuse, domestic violence, health care for profit, poorly paid social workers, under-funded hospitals, gun saturation, or global warming that riles or worries the conservative, Bible-believers of America. Rather, abortion and gay rights top the bill. And yet, as I rode that bus in Aarhus, I thought: isn't it interesting, for when it comes to these "sins" of abortion and homosexuality, the nations of Scandinavia are surely the most "sinful." Abortion has been free, safe, and legal in Denmark and Sweden since 1973 and 1975, respectively. In fact, Denmark was the first nation in Western Europe to permit abortions on request for any woman during the first 12 weeks of her pregnancy. In Sweden, it is actually *illegal* for a doctor to fail to support a woman's request for an abortion in her first trimester, and he or she can face a fine or even imprisonment for failing to facilitate the request.[59] Danes and Swedes are currently among the most tolerant and supportive of abortion rights of any peoples in the world, with only 5 percent of Swedes and 13 percent of Danes condemning the practice.[60] As for homosexual rights, the nations of Denmark and Sweden are extremely open and accepting; Denmark was actually the first country to allow homosexuals to officially/legally marry, and that was back in the late 1980s. Sweden's national health-care system will even cover the costs for a lesbian couple in need of fertilization treatment. And yet, despite all of this, the "moral order" of Denmark and Sweden is stable and strong, if not downright superior to that of most other nations.

Thoughts along these lines led me to compare and contrast various aspects of Scandinavian society with various aspects of American society. The United States is arguably the *most* religious Western democracy. Denmark and Sweden are arguably the *least* religious Western democracies. Isn't it strange and rather noteworthy, then, that it is in proudly religious America that guns are plentiful (especially handguns and semi-automatic assault weapons), the penal system is harsh and punitive, the death penalty is meted out on a weekly basis, drug addicts are treated like criminals, millions of children and pregnant mothers lack basic health insurance, millions of elderly people go without proper care, social workers are underpaid and overworked, people suffering from mental illness are left festering on city streets, and the highest levels of poverty of all the industrialized democracies is here. But in relatively irreligious Denmark and Sweden—two nations that most Americans would consider fairly "godless"—guns are nowhere to be found; the penal system is admirably humane, merciful, and rehabilitative; the death penalty has long been abolished; drug addicts are treated as human beings in need of medical and/or psychological treatment; every man, woman, and child has access to excellent health care; the elderly receive the finest care; social workers are well-paid and given manageable case loads; people suffering from mental illness are given first-class treatment; and the country boasts the lowest levels of poverty of all the industrialized democracies. I wondered how and why this is so.

These thoughts led me to further examine just what it actually means to consider a society "moral" or "ethical." How are these designations constructed and applied, and just how does religion relate to the degree of morality in a given society, or the lack of it? Is a society to be considered moral if its citizens love the Bible a lot (as in the United States), or rather, if its citizens virtually wipe out poverty from their midst (as in Scandinavia)? Is a society to be considered ethical if many of its citizens go to church on a regular basis (as in the United States), or rather, if its citizens provide well-funded, highly professional care to ensure the well-being of their children, their elderly, and their orphaned (as in Scandinavia)? Questions such as these continued to fill my mind as the bus drew closer to the center of downtown Aarhus.

We reached my stop. I got off the bus.

I saw beautiful women and handsome men walking about. I saw children holding hands and chatting with one another. I walked past a falafel stand, a very stinky cheese shop, a hotel, a café, a dermatologist's office, and a small record store where a song by Donovan was wafting out of the open front door. I noticed a few seagulls fluttering above an expressive mural of a colorful mermaid painted on the side of an old building. And there were bikes parked everywhere. Further on, I saw a large sculpture of an angel-like woman with voluptuous breasts suspended over the street, hanging there by two thin wires. Walking beneath her was a university student carrying a six-pack of beer. I noticed an old woman cruising down the sidewalk in an electric wheelchair. I passed a used bookshop, a bakery, a 7-11 convenience store, and then I made it to the small restaurant where I was scheduled to meet someone for an interview. The restaurant was situated on the edge of a canal. The water was calm, moving steadily out to the nearby harbor and then on into the sea.

What is society like without God? For me, as I personally experienced it from living in Denmark for a year—as well as from several extended stays in Sweden—it was gentle, calm, and inspiring. I was often in a state of awe while visiting Sweden and living in Denmark, thinking how wonderful it is that modern societies such as these, with millions of people, are able to operate so smoothly and equitably. Of course, life in irreligious Scandinavia isn't perfect. I don't wish to give the impression that the birds don't shit in Scandinavia, or that these are nations without any problems. Every society has its shortcomings and cracks. The weather is often dismal in Scandinavia, taxes are among the highest in the world, recent waves of immigration have given rise to a variety of social frictions and cultural conflicts, the kids eat excessive amounts of candy, rates of bike theft are high, fertility rates are low, and alcohol consumption can reach unhealthy levels. I personally witnessed, experienced, and heard about a fair share of unpleasantness while living there. For example, my daughter's preschool was broken into one night (they stole some cash and a digital camera). There was also a holdup one day at my bank (the perpetrator was caught four minutes after the crime). And the property manager of the first apartment we rented lied about the condition that we left the apartment in, causing us to lose much of our security deposit. And a close friend of mine—a dentist who happened to be from Chile—had patients enter his office who then refused to let him treat their rotting teeth because they didn't trust a foreigner. My research assistant had difficulty getting a job because of her Persian name. Another friend told me of the serious injuries that his daughter had recently sustained when her bike crashed; she hit her head on the curb because a teenager had aggressively tugged at her bag in order to steal her cell phone. While we were living in Denmark, I read in the paper about elderly people who die alone in old-age homes, with no family or friends to even claim their belongings. I also remember when a small network of Pakistani immigrants collaborated in successfully murdering a young woman in broad daylight because she eloped with a man not of her family's liking. And I remember that when I stayed with friends in Sweden, one friend's father explained to me his belief that the United States was secretly run by a conspiratorial cabal of Jews. Also on the negative side, I sometimes felt like Scandinavian culture could be somewhat lonely and insular. I occasionally found people more stoic than what I am used to; demonstrative displays of affection are rare, and tears—when shed in public—can be a source of shame.

I could go on and on, mentioning other negatives about Scandinavian society. But these negatives were greatly dwarfed by the overwhelming friendliness, prosperity, intelligence, altruism, and deep societal goodness I experienced while living there. That societal goodness which I felt that afternoon in Aarhus extended far beyond that one particular bus ride. It was a goodness that I experienced on a daily basis at my younger daughter's preschool and my older daughter's elementary school. I observed it when taking my children to the doctor. Or to their ballet and gymnastics classes. Or to the mall. Or to the beach, where families could sunbathe in full or partial nudity, carefree and natural. I felt it while attending the one night a month beer and cheese men's gathering in my neighborhood. I witnessed it as I observed the (totally free) care that my wife received while pregnant and then during, as well as after, giving birth. I witnessed it at the publicly subsidized, three-story mansion in the center of town devoted to creativity, where anyone could come, and for a miniscule fee, paint, sculpt, weave, sew, etc. It was a goodness that I experienced every day eating lunch in the university cafeteria with my colleagues. It was a goodness that was evident in the humanity and civility that I witnessed while touring a large mental health-care facility. In my experiences with the tax bureaucracy and train system, during my discussions with journalists, policemen, social workers, and politicians, and while visiting public swimming pools as well as the fanciest of hotels, and through conducting so many face-to-face interviews with Danes and Swedes from all walks of life, I experienced a society—a markedly irreligious society—that was, above all, moral, stable, humane, and deeply good.

2

Jens, Anne, and Christian

IN ADDITION TO what the international surveys tell us about indicators of economic prosperity or infant mortality rates, and along with my own personal musings while riding buses through Denmark, to get a fuller, richer, and more intimate sense of life in a society wherein religion is minimal, it is necessary to sit down and talk with as many people as possible who are from those societies. That is, in order to attempt to understand people's beliefs and worldviews—which would ideally offer a glimpse into the culture and society from which they spring—you have to conversationally engage various people in open-ended interviews. In this chapter, I share excerpts from three such interviews.

Jens

I met Jens at a birthday party.

It was the birthday party of one of my daughter's friends, who was turning five. Kids were running around all over the place, chugging plastic cupfuls of soda and eating fistfuls of candy. I remember seeing this one particular two-year-old boy sauntering around the living room holding two lollipops—one in each hand—and while he was licking one, the family's shaggy dog was going after the other.

I sought refuge from the festivities by going into the kitchen, where I grabbed a beer and started talking with the three adults who had already gathered there. The topic of conversation was the "cartoon controversy." A leading Danish newspaper had recently run several satirical cartoon drawings of the Muslim prophet Muhammed, which subsequently set off massive protests around the world, leading to death and destruction in several countries, as well as the boycotting of Danish products by many Muslim nations. The participants in the kitchen conversation included a journalist, a cardiologist, and Jens.

The three of them were generally critical of the Danish newspaper. They saw the publication of the cartoons as a deliberate attempt to goad and provoke the country's small Muslim minority. They claimed that Denmark is becoming more xenophobic every day, and that the newspaper which had published the cartoons, *Jyllands-Posten*, was helping to fuel that xenophobia through anti-Muslim articles, editorials, and now these satirical cartoons. Someone did point out, however, that the cartoons had initially been published months earlier, in September 2005—and had even been reprinted in an Arabic newspaper in Egypt—yet there had been no major protests or public outcry back then. It was only after a notorious, fundamentalist, Palestinian-born Imam living in Copenhagen took the cartoons (as well as several others that were extremely inflammatory and had not even been published in *Jyllands-Posten*) on a tour through the Middle East, showing them to religious and political leaders there, that the actual protests erupted in December.

The three of them wanted to know what I, an American, thought of the whole affair. I said that I firmly believe in freedom of speech and freedom of the press, which explicitly means the freedom to satirize and even mock deeply respected institutions and widely cherished beliefs. While the publication of the cartoons may have been insensitive and even hostile in nature, so be it. If people of a given religion cannot deal with jokes, ridicule, and outright criticism of their prophets, well, then they cannot deal with life in a free, open democracy.

Jens understood what I was saying, but he calmly disagreed. Even though he of course also had a great deal of respect for freedom of the press, he said that one cannot use that ideal to smugly justify deliberate acts of provocation. He felt that the newspaper was out of line—that the publication of the cartoons was unnecessary and unkind. And furthermore, he believed that to insult people's religion just because you *can* is not the wisest of editorial choices. Satire may be an admirable and useful tool for a weak minority to employ against a powerful majority. But when a powerful majority uses satire to mock a weak minority, it is a pernicious act.

A week later, I called up the parents who had hosted the birthday party and asked for Jens's telephone number. Then I called him up and asked him if I could interview him for my book. He said that he wasn't religious, so he didn't think he would have anything to offer. I assured him that being nonreligious was fine—in fact, it was nonreligious people like him that I was interested in—and that he would certainly be a suitable interviewee. So he agreed.

I rode my bike to his house on a crisp, sunny day in early March. His house was rather unique: somewhat dilapidated, but extremely charming.

It was several stories high, made of wood, and had many windows of various sizes. I later found out that it had been built in 1908. It was at the end of a very small road, and although it was situated right in the heart of Aarhus, it felt cozily isolated by the surrounding tall trees which encircled it.

Jens is 68 years old. He has a head of completely white hair, a closely trimmed white beard, and sharp eyes. He welcomed me into his home with a smile and had a large pot of coffee ready and waiting. We sat in his living room, the high walls of which were adorned with all kinds of art, and we proceeded to talk about God, life, death, religion, morality, and Scandinavian society.

Jens was born in 1938 in a small village in central Jutland. He attended the University of Aarhus as a young man, studying literature. He spent two years teaching in Poland, and upon his return to Denmark began working with refugees from Eastern Europe. He spent the next several decades writing, teaching, freelancing on the radio, and working with immigrants. As a younger man he was a socialist, but he had moved closer to the political center in recent years. Now he is retired, and takes care of his 10-year-old daughter, whose mother died of cancer a few years earlier, at the age of 40.

I first asked Jens about his family background, and learned that his grandparents were quite religious. In fact, both of his grandfathers were pastors.

They were real believers and for them it was—to be a vicar was not just a profession to make the money, but it was a—what you call it?—a call. And they were real believers . . . My father's father, he was sometimes called a "dancing vicar," because he was in the middle of Jutland where there are lots of Pietists in from the shore, and he was pointing out the light side of the Christianity. The smiling Christianity. The joy, yeah. And the Pietists—the mission people—they said no dancing, no playing cards and whatever. No fun! So— and he was very fond—my grandfather—he organized a lot of music in the region. He was conducting and collecting people to make a choir, to make an orchestra . . . So there was a lot of music, and there was—when I was born and in all this family there was a lot of music.

And were your parents religious as well?

Yes . . . but less.

Do you know if your mother and father were believers or did they just . . . ?

They were believers, but they had the part that we are not missionaries. We are believers but we don't run around and say to people to believe the same as

we do. So they were believers. My mother would have us sing a song before go-
ing to bed and to say a prayer.

And you would describe yourself as an atheist, a nonbeliever . . . or?

A nonbeliever. Agnostic or something. . . . I would say an atheist, yes.

Okay—but just so I have a sense of the history—we can say that your
grandparents' generation was very religious and very much believers. . . .

Yes, and my parents reduced—they were still seen as believers, but not . . .
not in the same way.

Okay, and then we get to you and . . .

Yes, and we are four sisters and brothers.

Four children?

Yes, and my younger brother is a very hard atheist and my sister and my
elder brother are more—they are not practicing in the church, but they're not
against. They're more agnostics.

Jens explained to me that his loss of faith began as a child, when he
began to wonder why there were so many problems in the world, and why
doesn't God do something about them? When he was 14 it was time for
confirmation and although he already knew by then that he didn't believe
in Christianity, he went along with the confirmation process anyway because he didn't want to go against what everyone else was doing. As a
teenager he read some information about humanism—that it is possible
to believe that there is a potential for good within humanity and that although humans can of course be bad, it is a fine philosophy to believe in
the potential for goodness in human nature. When he was 19, he moved
to Aarhus to attend the university, and it was then that he decided to quit
the national church.

So then I went up to the Johannes Kirken [church]—to the vicar here—and
he knew my parents because of my mother—from the country student organi-
zations in Copenhagen—and then he said, "So, you don't want to be a mem-
ber of the church?" We had just a small talk. Then he said [imitates a stern,
disgruntled old vicar], "Now, Mr. Hansen, now it's your own problem how to
get into heaven!" [pounds the coffee table with his fist]

And he stamped the paper?

Yeah, he stamped the paper. [laughter]

Okay, well—you're 68 years old and—you've had tragedies in your
life?

Yes, I have.

You lost your wife to cancer . . . how old was your child at the time?

Four.

Tell me, how did you cope if you don't believe in heaven and God and Jesus? What was the emotional experience?

I am a rationalist, of course, so for instance when my wife died, I knew that beforehand, and I told myself: now there'll be some practical problems for you. You must be without her and there's no discussion about that, and the comfort . . . uh-h- . . . first of all, for myself and for my family and—I had a lot of very positive feelings and attitudes from all people around me, so for me it was—I never thought about any religious—I haven't had any religious feeling or something like that in connection with my wife's death. Of course, not with my parents' death because they were so old and it was a biological—natural— my father was 94 and my mother 89, so it was just the end of the story, and it couldn't be anything. My wife—it was another thing. She was only 40 years old. So it was another thing. But in none of those cases was I thinking of any God or—just—also cancer is a side of nature. It's a biological fact. So it's bad, certain evil elements in the human biology. So . . . no, I have had no religious feeling that connected . . . unless we have use for the system of the church, the rituals and everything for the funeral in all cases.

You did that?

Yeah.

And that was nice? I mean, how did you feel about it?

Because . . . in connection with the big events in the human life, you need, very often, some rituals just to say now it's done like it has to be done. And so it is . . . But, no, I've never felt anything like comfort or anything from religion.

And with your daughter, she's now 10. Has she ever asked you questions like do you believe in God or what happens after we die? And what do you tell her?

Oh . . . I tell her that people are born, are living, and after a certain amount of years we finish our life and that's that. You can see the same with the animals. We've had cats and dogs and so on, so . . . and then I say we try to have as good a life as possible. But when her mother died when she was four years old, then her day nanny, she told her now her mother is in heaven and so on. She's an angel. And I remember she told me that. Yeah okay—why not? Six years ago she was so small.

Some people, you know . . . when they hear from me or others, "Well you live, you die and that's that, there's nothing more"—they often say, well then what's the meaning of it all? So what would you say to people about what is the meaning of it all?

Yeah . . . the other meaning is to come to heaven or in the worst case, to hell. But, I think it's a long time to be here on the earth, more than 80 years

*very often, and—have a nice time, and in some cases make some difference . . .
not only for yourself but for other people, for your family. And have good relations and meet beautiful music and literature and so on—and for me—I don't
understand the people who say, "Well what else? What's afterwards?" I . . . I
think . . . eh-h-h . . . just to have a good life, even a bad life—a life is a life—
even a bad life has a lot of positive sides, so . . . just to get any—to say the
reason to live is to die and coming to heaven, for me it's [laughs] . . . it's not
understandable.*

As a nonbeliever, what are some of your morals and values?

*I remember my father saying very often a sentence which has a lot of morals
and ethics. He said, "Never do to other people what you don't want them to do
against you." It's a base sentence which can be used in most of society: to never
do to other people what you don't want them to do against you. So it's a good
rule just to go out from yourself and then from the next, then we have a sort
of . . . rule of thumb—yes—for ethics. And it's very simple. [laughs]*

As an outsider, Denmark seems to be a very ethical culture. Do you
agree with that or I am missing something?

*Uh-h-h . . . I agree in general, because there are many—most people un-
derstand because we are Lutherans in our souls—I'm an atheist—but still I
have the Lutheran perceptions of many: to help your neighbor. Yeah. It's an old,
good, moral thought. It's, of course, a problem when you—when you come from
a relaxed society to an organized society, when we live in houses, you know
your neighbor, you know the postman, in the village, in the countryside. But
when you live in a block—that stops. Then you don't know the neighbor—they
live more near in a physical way, but more distant, more far from each other in
a social way.*

It's true.

*So . . . so . . . those ethics or those morals that's coming out from the neigh-
bor, it has transferred more into a more social ideology or . . . political theory
or something like that, which says: it's rational. It's more rational that we get
all people education, because if we give all people education, then you have a
society—then it will be better for all of us. And the same with the health system. If we help everybody together, then we'll be . . . then we'll help the society
as a unit . . . as a whole—yes—and it will be better for all of us. So something
like—this is the thought—that we make it better for everybody, we will do it
better for everybody.*

Yes, yes.

*It's alright if somebody is ill. It's not his fault. So it is his right to go to the
hospital and to be treated well. And you can see the same—if people grow very*

old, then the normal . . . point of view in everybody . . . it's a right to live in a decent way, to be treated in a decent way and . . . it's not always the case that it is so, but people have the idea. . . . It's accepted by everybody. So—and you could call it moral, you could call it rationality . . . but . . . I think it's both.

I then asked Jens why he thought Scandinavians were no longer so religious. What happened? How did they lose their faith? After all, in his own life his grandparents had been very religious, his parents a little less so, and finally himself and his siblings who were all either atheists or agnostics. He spoke about the benefits of the modern welfare state, and how the nations of Scandinavia have been able to virtually wipe out poverty within their societies, which was actually quite widespread and acute in earlier generations. He said that in the old days, life was harder, and so people were more religious as a way to cope. He spoke about the life of the fishermen on the western coast of Jutland in earlier times, and how particularly hard survival was for them, and how they were consequently the most religious of all Danes. And so with the development of the welfare state—which meant tax-subsidized health care for all, free education for all, job training for all, affordable housing for all, etc.—the need people had for the comfort of religion waned. But Jens felt that it wasn't just the success of the welfare state in making life better for everyone that accounted for the loss of religion in Scandinavia. He also felt it had something to do with the mentality of the people.

I can say one thing—that the population of Scandinavia is very skeptical. And skeptical in a rationalistic way. So if somebody—some shepherd tried to get the lambs into his flock, then people will say, ah, what's his scheme? What's his idea? What's he thinking about? And—or they will say, what can we get out of it? Can we profit from it? And the Scandinavian population also is, you know, we're northern, we're not so full of expressions like the south, so . . . also that, I think the northern population is more skeptical to all those patristic expressions of feelings in connection with religion. It's not selling so good here as down to the south.

Anne

Anne works with people who are dying. She is a hospice nurse; I mentioned her earlier, in the Introduction. Day after day she tends to, comforts, and takes care of people who are experiencing their last days, their last nights, their last breaths. I wanted to interview her specifically because

I wondered what working with the dying—and working so intimately with mortality—would mean in terms of her religious faith, or as the case turned out to be, her lack thereof.

Anne was the mother of one of my older daughter's classmates. When I heard from another parent that she was a hospice nurse, I called her right away and asked if I could interview her. She was rather subdued in her response, but still open and willing. She requested that I come to her house on a weekday afternoon and that I bring my daughter along, so that the two girls could play together while we did the interview. When my daughter and I arrived, we were pleasantly awed as we entered the house. It was full of lit candles and the aroma of freshly baked rolls. Very cozy. Very warm. Very tranquil. The permeating candlelight created a very special atmosphere, and my daughter and I were both incredibly happy to be poured large cups of tea as we ate mouth-watering rolls drenched in strawberry jam.

Once the girls went off to play, we started the interview. Anne is 43 years old. She has three kids. Her husband works at a home for orphans. Anne grew up in Aarhus. As for education, she attended a few years of high school prior to attending nursing school. She is heavy-set, with a broad face and steady eyes. She expressed a real reluctance to speak in English, and insisted that hers wasn't so good. I assured her that it would be fine, and that she shouldn't worry about it.

I first asked her about her work. Like most health-care workers in Scandinavia, Anne and her colleagues are paid by the county, which is subsidized by taxes. The buildings are also tax-subsidized, as well as the food, the medical equipment—everything. And of course when people are dying and they need a place to go, they can come and stay at the hospice—for free. This is in great contrast to hospice care in the United States, which Anne was quick to point out. She was under the impression that in the United States, only the rich can afford good care when they are sick or dying.

I then asked her how she liked working with the dying.

I like it very much, because they teach me a lot of life. I get near them . . . and there is trust and love between us.

And do they have families that also come to be with them?

Yes, most have a family who stays there, and they can live there.

The family?

The family can come stay at the hospice.

Amazing.

Yes, it's very, very good.

You know, when my wife's father was dying—he had no health insurance so it was–

I'm glad I'm not in the United States.

Are you a member of the Danish National Church?

Yes.

And you pay your taxes to the church?

Yes.

Can you explain why you do that?

I think I'm a little bit afraid and perhaps I'm not—I don't know if I am Christian. But there's some fear, you know. My husband, he wants to get out of it, but not yet.

And do you ever go to church?

No, only if I'm invited to a wedding or something like that. But I don't go to church.

Do you go at Christmas?

No. But in hospice we have a priest and sometimes she is having a service at hospice and sometimes I'll go there. She is a very good priest. She talks about things I like. . . . She talks about life.

Were your children baptized?

No.

And were you married in the church?

No.

. . . and is that unusual?

No, many people nowadays don't baptize their children.

Will they be confirmed?

No, no, they didn't want to.

Okay, interesting.

We—uh—they have to make their own choice.

And do you believe in God?

No.

Always, or did you used to when you were a child?

When I was a child, sometimes I prayed. My father was sick and he died when I was a child. And I prayed sometimes.

Okay. But at what point did you think, "I don't believe in God." I mean when did you . . . ?

It was when my father died and I saw all the pains he was going through, then I thought there is no God. And all the evil in the world, I didn't understand.

So you don't believe in God and—what do you think happens when you die?

I think we die and . . . perhaps our soul will return. . . . I don't know exactly, but I think there is something about our soul. I think I've seen in hospice.

Can you tell me some of those stories?

Yes, one night we had a man who was very sick and we thought he was going to die that night. And I had just seen him and then I was going to have a cup of tea. Then I saw—and we were two who saw—his soul going outside, and we knew he was dead, and when we went he was dead. And it was cold around us when he was dead.

Wow, what did it look like?

A shadow.

And it went through the room or . . . ?

Yeah, it went through the room.

That's the only time like that, that you . . . ?

No, another night—it's always at night—we had a woman who died and she was a very strong woman. And her family, her daughter and her daughter's daughter . . . talked about her and they were very sad because she was going to die. And when they left—the family left—suddenly a bell rang and a light was blinking. We had never heard the bell ring like that. It was very strong, and we couldn't turn it out. And it rang for about an hour, and we didn't know what to do.

It was the doorbell?

It was the bell in her room.

If she wants to call you?

Yes.

Okay.

At first I was very afraid of going in there, but of course, she was lying in her bed and was dead. But I think she wanted to show us that she was there.

So, she had died?

She had died.

And then the bell rang?

Yes.

Quite a story.

I think when I'm sitting with people who are going to die, something happens . . . a few minutes before they are dying.

And you experience this so much, and yet you don't feel the need to have religion in your life?

No, no.

Can you explain that a little?

I feel . . . I'm not afraid of what I'm going through in my life. And I believe in love between people . . . and I'm very happy with my life. I don't know how to explain it, but I have a big family. I have two sisters and a brother and my mother and my grandmother and my husband's family, and my sisters have many children, and we see each other very much.

That's wonderful.

And I have very good friends. Few, but very good friends. . . . And then my job means very much to me.

So you get meaning from your life from your connections to these people . . . other people?

Yes, yes.

You don't need . . . ?

No. No. I think I will live now.

Do the people who are in your hospice, are they needing religion a lot or do many of them die without it?

Many die without.

Without religion?

Yes. We have some of the old people, they are very Christian.

Okay.

And I see it's very difficult for them to die. They are afraid of dying. They are afraid that God doesn't take them to heaven, and they are thinking of their life and have they done something wrong . . .

Feeling guilty?

Feeling guilty, yes.

And do people that aren't very Christian or aren't very religious . . . ?

No, it's the Christians who have problems.

It's so interesting, Anne. And when you said you didn't believe in God, would you describe yourself as an atheist? Do you know that word?

Yes, yes. I don't know, perhaps.

And would you say you are a Christian or not sure or . . . ?

I'm not sure . . . because I don't believe in God.

But you said earlier that you live a Christian way. What does that mean?

I'm following the rules—not to steal, be kind to all people and so on.

And do you believe in heaven and hell or . . . ?

No, no.

Were your grandparents more religious than you?

Yes, my grandmother, she still lives. She's 89 years old and she was raised up by Christians and she went to church. And then I think she's close to death, but now she doesn't think that much about God . . . but she's thinking of death, because she's old. She wants to die now because she's too old. All her friends are dead. Yeah, she's ready. You know, I took care of a homeless man who had traveled in Europe and earned his money by painting. Then he stayed in farms, and he lived that way for many, many years. And he was—he told me a lot about life and I was very fond of him. He said that when he was going to die we should play Beethoven for him. He wanted to die with music.

How nice.

He said it himself. "Now I want to lay in bed and then you must play the music," and then he died 12 hours later.

Do you ever have Muslims?

Yes, we have.

What is your experience with them?

It's very difficult to take care of Muslims, because . . . you don't talk about the illness or that they're going to die. And if there are children, we must not talk to the children about the death.

They tell you this or . . . ?

Yes, yes, they do. One night I stayed with a Muslim who was going to die and his wife mustn't be with him. There were some men who stayed in the room. His wife was very sad and she mustn't be there. It was very hard to see and they didn't want to listen to what was told them. But, of course, I had a respect of their religion.

Christian

Christian works in law enforcement. He is a prosecutor for the city of Aarhus, where he has been convicting criminals for some 15 years. As with Anne, I made contact with Christian through my older daughter; his daughter was one of her classmates. Christian had a very busy schedule and it was difficult to arrange a time to meet. But we finally did. His home was one of the largest and most expansive of the many homes that I visited over the course of the year. It was in the same neighborhood as Anne's, but its size and grandeur made it feel much more affluent. The interview took place in the "sun room," a recent addition of glass walls that protruded out into the back yard.

Christian is 39 years old. He is in great shape: fit and muscular. He has two children and his wife is an assistant nurse. He grew up in a small town in a remote area of northwest Jutland. Unlike Jens and Anne, Christian supports the *Venstre* political party, which is one of the more right-wing, conservative parties in Denmark. Before getting into religion, we talked a bit about his work. I said that Scandinavia was known for its high levels of gender equality, and I wondered if that was true in his line of work.

Yeah, it's true.

Well, let's take your work for example. How many prosecutors in your office?

Twenty.

How many are women?

Eighty percent.

Eighty percent? That's amazing. And . . . of the judges, how many are women?

Seventy percent.

Seventy percent?! So most of these people are women?

Yeah, the main issue is in my profession—working hours for private lawyers are long, you know, and it's a male job. So . . . people want to be in the public service, you know—judges, prosecutors—so we can leave at 3:00 and go home. The wages are lower, but we have the security and we can keep our family intact.

So if you're a public attorney or a judge, it's good for family life?

You can't find anything better. I get to work at 8:30 and I'm back at 3:00, you know.

The first thing that stood out for me when we moved here was I did not see a police officer for one month . . . and I mean I didn't see a police car, I didn't see a policeman or woman walking, nothing. Are there many police out on the streets? Are they in plain clothes or something?

No, they are in uniform. Well, we have the criminal detectives, they are in civil clothes and then we have the normal police and they have uniforms. We're trying to improve the patrols on the streets because it's what the public wants.

But I saw the lack of police as a nice thing. I like that.

Yeah, but in Denmark we like to see the police and it's one of the primary things for the police to keep people safe. Try to keep them safe, keep the public safe, that's one of our most important things. So we want to be more extroverted, or to get out, but we have resource problems, just like everybody else. But there's not as much police here as in United States, that's for sure.

And is prostitution illegal?

Prostitution . . . oh, it depends. It's not illegal as long as you pay taxes. It's illegal if you—if you're a pimp and make money—take money from the prostitutes. But if you're just a prostitute and you put a sign on your door—"I'm a hooker, come and visit me, 500 crowns for ½ hour" and you pay taxes, it's alright. As long as you pay your taxes, it's legal.

What sorts of violent crimes do you have?

Well, we have ordinary violence—street violence, you know, mugging people and robberies. And I think it's getting worse, really getting worse. We have this large group of people from other countries and they are really doing a lot of crime. It's a big problem, especially because they're not educated and they don't want to adapt to the Danish society, so we have, I think, if they represent in Aarhus about 15 percent of the population, they represent about, in my job, over 50 percent of the crime. So a lot of the problem comes from them.

The crime is from immigrants . . . ?

It is. It is.

Mostly men?

Mostly men, yeah. Young men between—from 10 years old, and we only take them from 15, otherwise it's the social authorities. But from 15, it's the primary age of the crime age in Denmark—from 15 and up to 30 years old. That's the main part.

What are the most typical cases you prosecute? I mean in a given week or month, like the most common?

It's violence.

Like fights?

Like street fights, yeah, people in a disco they get into a fight and—yeah, it's violence, and then we have a lot of burglars, you know. We have tax evasions, we have everything.

Any rapes?

Yeah, you know, you probably heard about it from in the festival . . . the Aarhus festival there was a serious rape, a 16-year-old girl was raped right outside her door. She was in town, took the bus home, to get off where all the immigrants live, and then just when she was outside her front door she was taken from behind from an immigrant and he almost killed her and raped her.

Did they catch him?

Yeah, we caught him. From surveying the bus, we could see the picture and then we got him after 24 hours. And then I took him to, you know, within 24 hours we have to put him in front of a judge. So I had the week-end where they caught him, so I was down on duty.

If he's found guilty, what penalty will he receive?

Between 2½ and 4 years.

That's it?! In the United States that's nothing.

I know, I know, but one or two years ago—normally from one or two years ago, a rape, just an ordinary rape without any severe violence, would be around 1½ years. So now—and then the government said we had to do something about it and then they said we had to add one more year to these crimes. So in Denmark, 4 years of prison is pretty severe.

What do you think he should get?

Well, I think . . . I think . . . I don't think it's enough . . . 5–6 years I think would be . . . but I'm a product of my society, so when I hear sentences in the United States where it's 20, 15, 100 years, I say . . . gotta be kidding.

In the United States you would get that for pot . . . I mean—forget rape—just drugs you'll be put away for life.

In Denmark, if you smuggle heroin or cocaine or something like that, then you . . . 2 kilo of heroin costs 18 years. So compared to rape, it's hard to say what's worse. I think rape is worse than smuggling heroin in some way, but in another way it's not as bad. But I think maybe 6 to 8 years for a rape would be nice. But we will never, never, never get that sentence.

Can I switch topics . . . to religion?

I'm a total atheist.

Okay, tell me about that.

Well, I'm not a member of the Danish church. Mainly because I don't believe in God. I was baptized and I also, when I was 14, you know, I said yes and was confirmed. But I never believed. I have never believed one single minute in my whole life. So when I turned 18 and I started to pay taxes, I said no I won't pay taxes to something I don't use. But then again, I was married in a church, and my children are baptized in the church, and I use the church, but it's just a part of society, you know . . . but I don't believe anything. I believe in people and I believe in the goodness in people, but I don't . . . I don't think there's a God somewhere that controls everything.

And when you stopped being a member of the church, what is the process one has to do? Do you have to . . .

Oh, you just have to fill out a form at the priest's office. Just get a form from them that says I don't want to be a member any more . . .

And that's that?

That's that. [laughter] Oh, they threatened me.

What'd they say?

You are not allowed to be buried in the sanctified ground or something like that.

The priest said that?

Yeah—no, it was written down below, but I don't care [laughter]. So we laughed a little about that, if that should be a threat. [laughter]

And when you were 14 and you did this confirmation, tell me why did you do that?

It's the presents. [laughter]

And nothing else?

Well, it's the group pressure, you know, you're 14 and you don't want to stick out from the others and everybody did that. Well, in Denmark I don't think a lot of people believe, but it's a tradition like walking around the Christmas tree. It's just like that. It's just a part of Danish society, you know, and it's a good way for the family to get together and have a nice time. Yeah, we had a great party and I got a lot of presents, and that's the main issue. [laughter]

Yeah, the only reason I'm asking these questions is because that's one of the things that stands out about Denmark and Sweden in the statistics is that they do seem to be so low in religion compared to other countries. In fact, some recent surveys have Denmark and Sweden at the very bottom of the whole world.

I read somewhere back in the '70s and '80s when Russia still was a strong nation, and the iron curtain went down, they were studying how we did in Denmark to get the religion so low and interest in religion, because we are very unique in that field, I think.

It's interesting. Why do you think that is?

We have too few problems, I think. The standard of living is so good and if people believe in something, it has to be an exotic kind of religion, you know, something spiritual. I think it's more like that. I lived in the United States for a year and I went to church over there every week, and that's different.

Why did you do that?

Well, my family did that, so . . .

When you were younger?

Yeah, I was in the United States for one year from 15 to 16. So I stayed with a family and they were normal Christian people in the United States, meaning going to church once a week and saying prayers at tables. But I couldn't relate. I sat there and said this is interesting. I'm here to learn and so I just blend in.

Where was that?

In Minnesota.

Were they Scandinavians?

No, they were plain Americans, you know, coming from Germany a hundred years ago or something like that.

Before, when I asked you why Danes and Swedes are so not religious and you said we have so few problems, do you mean because of the welfare state?

Yeah, I think. Well . . . I think it's, you know, everybody's busy and I think religion, if you really had a bad life and poverty and something, I think it's . . . it's a simple way to get an explanation for something. But we're pretty educated people and just . . . well, everybody knows about Darwin and how can you put those two things together? You have an explanation problem, as I see it.

And you were taught about Darwin in school?

Yeah, everybody knows about it.

Were your parents religious?

My father was the son of a priest.

Okay.

But you know, my grandfather was a priest and—obviously he was a believer and my father, he had a very strict childhood . . . going to church, being a choir-boy, and all that kind of stuff. Actually he never believed and always made fun of all the Christian things, so of course, I listened to that at home. And he was very aware of telling me about the other side, you know, that there might be another explanation for it than just being a God up there controlling everything. So . . . no, and my mother, she was . . . I think she's a more typical Danish Christian. She thinks it's cozy and nice and it's a good way to celebrate Christmas, and then we use it for the ceremonies, and if we want to use it for the ceremonies, we have to pay for it. And that was her opinion. And I said okay I can just take the cheap way. I get all the good stuff and I don't pay for it. [laughter]

Okay, and you have two children?

Yeah.

You did get them baptized?

Yeah, we did.

Was that because of your wife or . . . ?

No, I think . . . um-m-m . . . I think it's the Danish culture. We baptize our children and then I'm not the one who has to make the decisions for them, so . . . it's easier to follow mainstream and then do as everybody else and then when they get old enough they can say, "Oh, I don't want to do this," and then it's up to them. But doing as everybody else, it's easier for them. That's something I really try to do in my life . . . that's to make life as simple as possible for my children.

How would you feel if they grew and when they were 18 or 20 or 25, they became like a real Christian fundamentalist and they found Jesus and they became extremely Christian and extremely religious . . . how would you feel about that?

As long as they accept other people, they can do whatever they want. I don't have a problem. The only thing I really hate, it's when you try to force your own opinion onto somebody else. But . . . I don't like . . . if I want to drink a beer and they said it's not Christian to drink a beer, well, I don't like that but they can say, "Oh, no thank you, I don't want to drink it because I am," but they don't have to force their opinion onto me.

Sure.

Otherwise we . . . I don't think we are . . . it would influence my relationship to other people as long as they keep it to themselves. I think that's a typical Danish thing, you know, you can do whatever you want, just you keep it to yourself. [laughter]

Okay . . . What do you think happens after we die?

Nothing, I just think it's over.

Are you afraid to die? Do you worry about it?

No . . . well, I worry in the sense that I won't be able to see my children grow up and I think I have so much that I need to do. But I don't think I have to go to a test, you know, and getting burned up in hell or something like that . . . no. No, I just think when you die, you're dead and that's that.

Have you ever had a personal tragedy?

Well, both my parents are dead. They died of cancer. Both of them.

When you experienced the death of both your parents to cancer—it didn't make you turn to God or anything like that?

No, no, well . . . I think the church was nice at that moment in the sense that we could get the ceremony and . . . get . . . people together. My father wasn't a member of the church, so there was no priest there. But, you know, his burial or funeral was just as good as my mother's, I think, because then we just . . . I made the prayer, the speech, you know, and then my mother did. And that was good. That was just as good as for my mother, the priest was the one saying the prayer and talking about my mother. But she did a really good job. I think it was very good what she did. But . . . there wasn't really any difference between my mother's funeral or my father's . . . with or without the church service. So . . . but it's nice, you know, just to get people together and say, "Look at all these people, they loved that person." But I think it was . . . in some way it was nice in my mother's funeral because the priest was very good, and she had a meeting with us and she said all the right things, you know, how my mother really was. She did a very good job, but I could have done it myself. But it was nice just to lean back and hear it from somebody else.

Sure, sure. Um-m-m . . . of your closest friends . . . are they also kind of typically not religious or do you have any friends that are real Christians?

No, they are . . . well, we share the same feeling about—I think we get our children baptized and we get married in the church, but . . . and we dance around the

Christmas tree—but we're very similar and I . . . no, actually one of our friends up there, and that surprised me a lot, we've known them for some years and suddenly one night we had a few drinks and then he said to me, "I have a confession to make." "Okay," I said, and then he told me that he believed in God. And I was quite surprised. I never thought in my whole life that . . . well, he was getting pretty loaded, you know, and then he had this urge to tell me.

But he's unusual?

Yeah, he's unusual. I never expected anybody to tell me something like that. That was—I almost fell down off the chair. I said—[pantomimes an expression of shock]*—and I didn't know how to react, and then he said to me, "I hope you don't feel I'm a bad person." So he said that to me and I said, "Oh, of course, you can believe whatever you want as long as you respect me," I said to him. But it was something he had kept for a long time, and finally he got the mood, you know, and it was after a few bottles of red wine, you know. It was a confession . . . "Now we are so good friends, I can tell you this because this is my inner secret," you know.*

· · ·

One of the remarkable things about doing this type of research is that you get to have deep, thoughtful conversations with people that you don't even really know. They are virtual strangers, and then, after an hour or two, you leave their home feeling as though you have just had a very deep connection with another human being. And you have. After every interview, I felt I had grown somehow. I didn't know Jens, Anne, or Christian. And yet in the brief time that I spent with them, they talked to me about their beliefs, their opinions, their families, their work—their lives. (Of course, I have presented only excerpts from each interview.)

I was struck by different things during each conversation.

With Jens, I was struck by how much he seemed to love and appreciate life, and yet how matter-of-factly he simultaneously talked about death—the untimely death of his young wife, the death of his parents, and death in general. It just is the way it is, he said. We live and we die, just like other animals. And I was moved when he said that to think otherwise—to think that after this life there is something more—is simply unimaginable. Jens is living evidence that it is possible to live in the here and now, to find this life in and of itself satisfactory, and to not obsess about one's impending mortality.

With Anne, I was struck by the fact that even though she believed in the existence of souls—or something supernatural of sorts that emanates from the body upon death—this in no way caused her to feel religious, to be involved with religion, or to even believe in God. Anne is evidence that one can believe that there is more to this existence than that which is empirically provable—recall the shadow that she saw which passed through the hospice, or the ringing bell, or the simple feeling Anne described of coldness around the recently departed—and yet remain somewhat of an atheist. What also struck me about Anne was her deep altruism, her genuine compassion. It was clear that she found great meaning in her work—in taking care of those in need. And it was also apparent to me that working with the dead made Anne that much more in tune with her day-to-day life and appreciative of the fragile beauty of her family and friends. What years of working with the dead did not do, however, was cause Anne to question her lack of Christian faith.

As for Christian, the story of his good friend confessing his belief in God one night after having had a bit too much to drink, was incredibly noteworthy. "I hope you don't feel I'm a bad person," his friend had said! For secretly believing in God! To me, this anecdote reveals just how secular Danish culture can be. It was only after years of friendship—and several bottles of wine—that this man felt comfortable enough to "confess his sin" of theism! Also from Christian—as well as Jens and Anne—there was evidence of a real loss of religion over time in each of their family histories. All three of them described their grandparents as much more religious than their parents or themselves.

•   •   •

Many scholars of religion argue that being religious is simply part of what it means to be human. For example, Dean Hamer describes spirituality as "hardwired into our genes," as "one of our basic human inheritances. It is, in fact, an instinct."[1] Rodney Stark (along with various co-authors) has argued that all humans need and thus seek out answers concerning the mystery of death and will subsequently develop faith in God as a sort of "supernatural compensator," and that the human demand for religion remains more or less stable in all societies and at all times.[2] Such a view echoes the position of Andrew Greeley, who argues that there are simply "basic human religious needs"[3] that have remained unchanged since the late Ice Age. According to Greeley, these religious needs are "inherent in the human condition."[4] Justin Barrett and others have argued that belief in God is actually part of the wiring of the human brain, and therefore innate, and that a lack of religious belief is "unnatural."[5] Christian Smith has argued that humans are simply driven to have faith in religious ideas and postulates, and as such, "secularization will probably never get very far."[6]

After spending a year in Scandinavia, and conducting nearly 150 interviews with people like Jens, Anne, and Christian, I have come to seriously question the innateness or naturalness of religious belief. Belief in God may be widespread the world over, but that does not make it natural or somehow a necessary or inherent part of the human condition. Ubiquity must never be mistaken for biology. There are currently millions of men and women in Scandinavia living rich, meaningful, sad, lonely, and lovely lives without much religion or faith in God. Such people actually constitute a majority in that Nordic part of the world, where Jens, Anne, and Christian—three nonbelievers—are not deviants. They are not random, iconoclastic "village atheists." They are typical, average, common. Mundane.

3

Fear of Death and the Meaning of Life

IT IS OFTEN stated that religion is so enduring and widespread because it deals with death as well as existential matters concerning the meaning of life. Because people fear death, they turn to religion for comfort. Furthermore, people are deeply concerned about the ultimate meaning of life, and so they turn to religion for existential answers. To me, these propositions always made sense. Of course people are afraid to die. Of course people wonder about the meaning of life. And so as long as religion claims to offer solace or insight concerning these presumably eternal, universal problems, people will be religious.

And then I spent a year in Scandinavia.

That year made me rethink my understanding of religion in the contemporary world, specifically certain taken-for-granted assumptions about human attitudes toward death and the meaning of life. What I found through my research was that it is possible for a society to exist in which most people don't really fear death all that much, and simultaneously don't give a great deal of thought to the meaning of life. In Denmark and Sweden, death is widely accepted as natural and inevitable, and most people don't think there is some grand meaning to life, other than what you make of it. Death and the meaning of life may thus not be such eternal, universal human problems after all. Millions of contemporary Scandinavians are proof of this. Their general lack of fear or worry when it comes to death, and their overall lack of deep curiosity or existential concern for the ultimate meaning of life, has fascinating sociological and theoretical implications, not only for our understanding of religion, but for our understanding of its absence.

Death

Two of the first Danes that I interviewed while living in Denmark were Arne and Agnethe. They live in a very tiny village on the east coast of

Jutland. For most of their lives they were farmers, but they stopped farming several years ago and turned the 300-year-old farmhouse on their property into a vacation rental house. When my cousins came to visit us during our first summer in Denmark, we found Arne and Agnethe's summer house advertised on the Internet and subsequently rented it out and stayed there for a week. One afternoon, I persuaded Arne and Agnethe to let me interview them. They were initially reluctant, claiming that their English wasn't good enough and that they surely wouldn't have anything of interest to say. But I politely persisted, and they acquiesced. So on a breezy summer afternoon we sat at a wooden table beside their house, surrounded by undulating wheat fields, and as soon as Arne brought out the beers, the interview began.

Arne is 67 and Agnethe is 65. They have been married for 43 years. They are a short and stout couple, with wrinkled faces and worn hands. Arne was the more laid back of the two, while Agnethe was a bit more feisty. They both grew up in the same small village, they both attended school until the ninth grade, and they both always vote for the same conservative, right of center political party (*Ventsre*). They have two grown children, a daughter who is a secretary and a son who lives in Thailand. Arne and Agnethe attend church much more regularly than most Danes, about once a month. However, when I asked them if they believed in God, Arne replied "Oh, not so much" and laughed. Agnethe said the same thing: "Not so much." When I asked them why they go to church if they don't believe much in God, they said that they go because it is a nice tradition, that they like to see their friends from the village, and because they like the pastor—a woman who they find very knowledgeable and friendly.

But it was their reaction to my question about death that struck me the most. It was the part of the interview that made the deepest impression on me and was what I most wanted to talk about with my wife later that day. I wish I had the interview on video, because it will be difficult to convey Agnethe's response in words. But I will try. When I asked her what she thought happens after we die, she paused, looked right at me, and then with her right hand she swiped her neck as though slitting her throat and made a verbal "swish" sound and then with the same hand she quickly made a fist and stuck her thumb out and pointed downward toward the ground and made a sort of verbal farting or squashing noise. It was very succinct and to the point. A sort of "no nonsense" gesture that basically said: You die and then you go to the ground and that's that. I looked at

Arne to see his reaction to his wife's starkly matter of fact take on death. He laughed and said, as if to agree with her:

I don't think I come in the sky.

So you don't believe in heaven?

No.

Hell?

No. [laughter]

They said these things very casually and frankly, as though not believing in life after death was normal. And I came to find that in Scandinavia, it most certainly is.[1] The overwhelming majority of people that I interviewed—when asked what they think happens after we die—basically said, "nothing." Or, as in the more specific words of Tina, a 39-year-old chemical engineer from Stockholm:

Absolutely nothing!! I think we are gone. I really think that's it.

Jakob, a 35-year-old preschool teacher from Copenhagen, put it this way:

I think that we're put down in the earth.

According to Isak, a 69-year-old retired physician from the Stockholm area:

We cease to be. That's it.

In the words (conveyed through a translator) of Mads, a 52-year-old man from Aarhus who works in a slaughterhouse:

My body will dissolve and be part of the natural cycle of nature.

Adam, a 28-year-old sales manager for a computer company who grew up and still lives in southern Sweden, calmly replied:

Our energy goes through exactly the same process as anything that dies in nature.

Bent is a 59-year-old retired high school teacher who grew up and lives in Copenhagen. In his words:

We're chemically dissolved . . . the worms and the bacterias and viruses will come and make me to chemical substances.

Alva, a dental technician, is 61 years old and grew up in a small town in Sweden, but now lives in a suburb outside of Stockholm. She said:

I think when it's over, it's over.

When you are dead, you are dead?

Yeah.

Karen, a 34-year-old nurse who grew up in Copenhagen but now lives in Aarhus, answered:

We die.

That's it?

Yeah.
When we die . . . ?
We die.
Lasse, a 25-year-old medical student from central Sweden, replied:
I think nothing happens. The ultimate nothingness. Just like before life, you know. When it's finished, that's it. When you're dead you're dead.

The individuals that I have quoted here accurately reflect the attitude of most of the people that I interviewed. Although I didn't explicitly ask Arne and Agnethe—or the others above—if they worried about death or feared death, I got the distinct impression from all of them that they did not. This impression was conveyed by their demeanor during the part of the interview dealing with death, their tone of voice, and the look in their eyes. However, since I didn't ask them directly, I can't say for sure.

But I did ask many others.

Kim is 55 years old. He grew up in Copenhagen, but now lives in a small village outside of Aarhus. He works as a technical administrator at the university. He doesn't consider himself a believer, but eschews the designation "atheist" as too strong, too negative. When I asked him what he thought happens after we die, he answered, "I don't know" and seemed decidedly uninterested in the topic. When I asked him if he was afraid to die or if he worried about death, he succinctly replied:

Um . . . I don't worry about it because—normally I don't worry about things that you cannot avoid.

Tommy is 38 years old. He grew up and still lives in a small town in Sweden. He owns a small business dealing antiques. When I asked him if he believed in God, he sighed and said that it just wasn't something he actually thought much about. But then he off-handedly remarked, "I believe in something, but I don't know what it is, really."

What do you think happens when we die?
Rotten. [laughter] *It's over.*
That's it?
Yeah.
And does that thought worry you? Are you afraid to die?
No.
Have you ever been afraid to die at any point in your life?
No, not really. Not ever. No. If it happens, it happens.

Jonas is 25 years old. He grew up on the west coast of Jutland, but now lives in Aarhus where he works at a grocery store. He looks almost exactly like Christian Slater. He doesn't believe in God, per se, but he also wouldn't call himself an atheist. Like Tommy, he said he believes in "something," but was unable to elaborate much on that belief. As for death and what might or might not come after death, he said:

I really don't think too much about that, really.

It's not something you worry about?

No . . . right now I have a lot of other things to worry about, really . . . I think 90 percent of all sane people don't worry about what happens when they die. They worry about how to pay their bills, how to feed their family, how to put clothes on their backs . . . even if they're rich—that's what you worry about.

Mia is 34 years old. She grew up in Copenhagen but now lives in Aarhus, where she is one of the directors of a science museum. Mia said that she does not believe in God, but she wouldn't label herself an atheist because she sees that designation as too extreme. She says that she believes there is "something that makes us want the best for our neighbor," although she recognizes that this "something" could very easily have a biological explanation and need not be supernatural or divine in nature.

What do you think happens after we die?

Nothing.

Nothing?

Yeah . . . just I'm buried, I become earth if I'm buried without being burned, and I return to the . . . yeah.

Does that cause you worry or dread or fear, or you can accept that?

Um-m-m . . . oh, I can accept it. It would worry me if it didn't end.

So . . . I mean . . . it's not like you're walking all day terrified that one day you won't exist?

No, no, no.

Anna is 50 years old. She grew up in Gothenberg, but now lives in a small fishing village about 60 miles north of the city. She works as a graphic designer. When I asked her what she thinks happens when we die, she replied:

Oh, we die.

That's it?

Yeah.

And do you worry about death? Do you fear death?

No, not at all . . . we live and we die and that's the same thing for all creatures . . . whether you're an ant or a microbe or a human being or a zebra. [laughter]

Preben is 50 years old and grew up in Copenhagen. He owns a small hotel in Aarhus, where he now lives. He said that he does believe in God, and when I asked him what that meant, he said, "I think there's more be-tween earth and—uh . . . I think the big boss is watching us, you know," followed by convivial laughter. When I asked him what he thought about life after death, he said:

There might be something after. If it's heaven, I don't know, but maybe there is. Sometimes I think it's important for many people to have a wish that there is, but maybe they are just telling stories to themselves, you know. I mean it can be okay sometimes.

But for you personally . . . ?

No.

Do you worry much about what happens after we die, or you don't think about it so much?

Oh, I don't worry about it.

There was also Jarl, a 41-year-old submarine officer who lives in Stock-holm. Although he does believe in God, his views on life after death were decidedly secular.

What do you think happens after we die, Jarl?

I think that's it. [laughter]

When we're dead, we're dead?

I think so, yes.

Okay, so you don't believe that . . .

I don't go on . . . I don't believe in reincarnation. I really don't know what happens when we die, but I don't really want to have too many high hopes on death. I haven't really analyzed or thought about it too much, yet . . . maybe I should, but . . .

It's not something you think about . . . ?

No, I don't.

Kai is 44 years old and lives just outside of Copenhagen, where he works as a radio journalist. Like Jarl, Kai also said that he does believe in God, who he described as loving and forgiving. But when I asked him what he thinks happens after we die, he replied:

Well, I couldn't say [chuckles]. *I don't have—I don't have a specific—I think I'm very much like the Danes that you have spoken to . . . I'm not really occupied with this. I think it's not our—I think we shouldn't worry about this. If there is a God and if there is an afterlife, we'll find out by then . . . but if not . . . I mean we have no way of knowing anything about it and we have to focus on our life here and our relationship with other people. That's the most important point.*

Hedda is a 66-year-old high school teacher from a small town in Swe-den. When she has had close loved ones in her life die, such as her brother and father, she finds solace not in religion, but by going out into nature. She thinks that after we die there is "nothing." And she's not worried about dying—but her grandmother, who was religious, was:

No. It's not a big deal. But I remember my mother saying that my grand-mother—she was religious—and when she was going to die, my mother said that she was quite scared of what was going on. Perhaps she thought about a God that was not so good and he should punish her because that was not good or something. Yes—my mother said that.

Leif is a 75-year-old book publisher who was raised in Gothenburg, but now lives in Stockholm. Although he identifies as a Jew, he is a self-designated atheist.

What do you think happens after we die?

Nothing.

And how does that make you feel?

Well, not very sorry. It is as it is. Really, I don't feel anything about it especially.

You're not worried or scared?

No, I'm not. I'm not very well in health anyway, but I'm not worried.

Leif's resigned acceptance of his own imminent death stayed with me for quite some time after I interviewed him. "It is as it is," he had placidly stated. There is almost a transcendent or spiritual quality to this sentiment. One can easily imagine a priest or rabbi uttering the same words in a sermon beside a fresh grave. But for Leif, there is nothing mystical, spiritual, or religious about it. For him, after death there is nothing, that's the way it is, and even as a 75-year-old man in poor health, it is not something to fear or worry about.

Imagine having similar conversations and similar exchanges as those quoted above over and over again, hundreds of times—literally. That was my experience. And I interviewed people who had lost loved ones to illness, suicide, or old age. I interviewed people who worked with the sick and dying. I even talked with people who were sick and dying themselves, such as Sigrid, a 53-year-old Aarhus native who was battling cancer at the time of the interview. When I asked Sigrid about death and what happens after, she calmly said:

I think we will be earth, you know. I don't think anything will happen.

When you come face to face with this baldly secular orientation to death over and over again, person after person, it can really be a powerful experience. It was for me. Not only did it cause me to reflect rather deeply on my own feelings concerning my own mortality, but it caused me to ponder the very nature of death anxiety. Does it affect everyone? Clearly not.[2] Is the denial of death and the refusal to come to terms with mortality a human universal, as argued by Ernest Becker in his well-respected book *Denial of Death*? Clearly not. Is it possible to find a culture in which the majority of people therein do not worry so much about death, accept the inevitability of death, and are not all that devastated by the knowledge of their own mortality? Clearly yes.[3] Thus, when sociologist of religion William Sims Bainbridge asks, "How can humans deal . . . with the crushing awareness of mortality?"[4] I think he is committing a mistake that many scholars of religion commit: assuming that his own fears and worries about death are universal, when clearly they aren't. Not everyone's awareness of his or her own mortality is all that "crushing," as Bainbridge suggests.

Of course, not everyone that I interviewed exhibited a serene acceptance concerning their own eventual demise. While variations were relatively minimal, there were some people who deviated from the typical orientation illustrated above. For example, there was Jeppe, a 64-year-old retired physical education teacher who grew up in Odense and now lives in Copenhagen. Jeppe is a self-described atheist who thinks that "there's nothing after death." But in terms of worrying about dying, he did admit that as he gets older, he ponders his own demise with some degree of concern:

I've noticed that the older I am, I'm thinking about it. How many years in average have I back now? How old was my mother? How old was my father? How are my genes? And how long can I live? and so on.

There was also Tora, a 54-year-old laboratory worker who grew up on a small island but has lived in Copenhagen for several decades. Like Jeppe, she describes herself as an atheist and said that after she dies she thinks "there will be nothing." But when I asked her if she was afraid to die, she replied:

If someone came to say that I was sick and I would die in a few months, I would say yes I am afraid—I can't know—but I know that if someone said in three months you are going to die, I would be scared. . . . Of course I'm afraid in that way. And maybe I'm more afraid because I know there is nothing.

Admittedly, not all Danes and Swedes have such secular outlooks on matters pertaining to life after death. They certainly don't all believe that "nothing" happens after death. I did interview some people who had more religious orientations and believed in some form of life after death. For example, with the help of two graduate student assistants serving as translators, I interviewed eight elderly Danes at two different old age homes in the city of Aalborg. Six of them were women, two were men. One was 74, another was 97, and the rest were in their eighties. Whereas five of them were nonbelievers, three of them were definitely believers. One that stood out was Ebba. She sat in her chair with a sweet smile throughout the course of the interview, and all the while clutched a cute white teddy bear. When I asked her what she thinks will happen after she dies, she confidently declared:

God will be waiting for me in heaven with open arms.

On a different day I interviewed Rikke, a 57-year-old retired social worker from Aarhus. Rikke was nonreligious for most of her life, but when she spent several weeks in the hospital the previous summer, struggling to survive a serious operation, she developed a new orientation. Although she doesn't necessarily believe in God, she does believe in "something higher," which she further described as "a distant dignity." When I asked her what she thinks happens after death, she said:

I think something happens. I don't think it's over. In a way I think our souls are going away and maybe coming again, yeah, kind of reincarnation. Yeah, maybe. I'm not quite sure about it because my . . . logic tells me that it can't be that. But in some ways I think it might be something . . . yeah.

There was also Aina, a 56-year-old office clerk from Gothenburg. As a believer in God, this was Aina's take on life after death:

The soul will go somewhere . . . the soul will be somewhere . . . but I don't know where and I don't think about it. I had—my mother died when I was young—my father found another wife and she died this past summer . . . and when I think of it now, I'm looking up in the sky somewhere, and I know she can see me . . . I can't answer your question really, but she's up there, but where— the place—I can't put a name on it. It's just somewhere . . . just somewhere.

Though people such as Ebba, Rikke, and Aina certainly exist in Denmark and Sweden, they are in the minority. They are atypical. And that makes Danish and Swedish culture distinctly unusual as quite possibly the only culture in the world (and perhaps even the history of the world?) in which most people don't believe in life after death, most people don't fear death, and the overall degree of worry about death is relatively minimal. As stated at the outset of this chapter, the sociological and theoretical implications of this fact are numerous. I shall discuss three.

First, we must consider the relationship between the level of belief in life after death in a given society and the level of despair/happiness there within. One might be tempted to think that if most people in a given country thought they had about 70-odd years to live and then everything was over, that such an orientation would lend itself to a general state of sadness or despair. Life might seem somehow futile for the majority of the population. After all, if one has only a few decades left—or maybe only a few years—and then that's all, with no hope of a future existence, wouldn't such a belief lead to feelings of emptiness, depression, or despondence? What I found in my research, however, was just the opposite. A widespread lack of belief in life after death does *not* manifest itself in high levels of despair among contemporary Scandinavians. Rather, the Danes and Swedes I interviewed were, for the most part, a happy, satisfied lot. They generally live productive, creative, contented lives. They pursue careers, travel, surf the net, build homes, raise children, get involved in politics, art, technology, music, charitable foundations, entrepreneurship, cooking, and so on. Sure, some of the people I interviewed had bouts of depression, loneliness, illness, and the like. No human population is entirely immune to these things. But still, the people that I interviewed, and the people that I lived among for a year, were generally in good spirits, more or less. And my own findings have been supported by additional research. For example, Ronald Inglehart and his associates[5] asked people from over 40 countries the following survey question: "During the past few weeks, did you ever feel on top of the world/feeling that life is wonderful?" The nation with the highest percentage of people who responded "yes" to this survey question was Sweden, with 77 percent of respondents saying yes. Denmark came in third with 64 percent. (The United States trailed both, at 56 percent). Concerning general life satisfaction, another question was posed: "All things considered, how satisfied are you with your life as a whole these days, on a scale of 1 (dissatisfied) to 10 (satisfied)?" For this survey question, Denmark came in first place with 86 percent of Danes choosing between seven and ten, and Sweden came in sixth. (The United States again trailed both, coming in eighth place.) In sum, societies in which most people don't believe in life after death are not characterized by widespread despair, but just the opposite. The typical Scandinavian orientation to death is a relatively positive, life-affirming one. It is articulated well by Anders, a 43-year-old father of two from Aarhus who owns a corner market. When I asked him what he thinks happens when we die, he replied:

I think we just die. That's why we have to have our lives when we've got it . . . before I know—it's over. So you just have to live every day . . . and make nice days. And I try to do that, actually. I have a good time here and I've got a good family. I've got some good friends, and . . . I'm a very lucky person.

A second matter to ponder, in light of Scandinavians' atypical orientation to death, is the underlying source of death anxiety. As has been stressed in this chapter, death anxiety is relatively low in Scandinavia. Why? Is the answer to be found by looking into the unique minds or distinct personalities of Danes and Swedes, or rather, into the nature of their modern society? Put more broadly, is the fear and/or worry about death (or the lack thereof) something innate—something that originates and develops in the psyche—or rather, is it something that is ultimately social or cultural at root? Of course the answer is unavoidably both. Death anxiety surely has a psychological component as well as a cultural or sociological aspect. But I would argue that the latter—the cultural or sociological aspect—may be more significant in this particular instance. After all, one can easily hypothesize that the level of death/disease/disorder in a given society would greatly affect the general level of death anxiety within the population. In a society that is wracked with disease, poverty, and warfare—where sickness and death dwell in every other household and around every other corner—anxiety and fear about death will probably be much greater and more ubiquitous than in relatively safe and secure societies, where disease, poverty, and warfare are minimal or nonexistent, and sickness and death are marginal or successfully sequestered aspects of social life. Since Denmark and Sweden are among the most societally healthy countries in the world, where poverty, disease, warfare, crime, and famine are minimal if not downright nonexistent, then anxiety about death—and the concomitant belief in life after death—are low. The source of Scandinavians' atypical orientations toward death, I would argue, is not to be found in the peculiarity of their minds, brains, or neurological wiring, but simply in the atypically successful nature of their modern society.

A third and final matter to consider is this: how does the relative lack of death anxiety and general acceptance of mortality among contemporary Scandinavians relate to our understanding of religion, or the lack thereof? As mentioned earlier, many scholars have argued that the fear of death is one of—if not *the*—most important source of religiosity. According to Bronislaw Malinowski, "of all sources of religion, the supreme and final crisis of life—death—is of the greatest importance."[6] For Malinowski, because humans are condemned to live life in the shadow of death, and because all who enjoy life must simultaneously "dread the menace of its end," humans turn to religion because it offers them hope of immortality and quells the haunting fear of personal nonexistence. For Sigmund Freud, humans cannot avoid the "painful riddle of death"[7] and thus our impending, imminent demise contributes to a general state of helplessness, for which people turn to religion or God for solace. Robert Hinde[8] also argues that the fear of death and the desire for life after death are major reasons as to why people hold religious beliefs. Charlotte Perkins Gilman describes concern over life after death as the "key note" of religion.[9] Dean Hamer argues that without religion, humans would simply be "incapacitated by our dread of mortality."[10] And finally, in the poetic words of Peter Berger:

> The power of religion depends, in the last resort, upon the credibility of the banners it puts in the hands of men as they stand before death, or more accurately, as they walk, inevitably, toward it.[11]

What my research into contemporary Danish and Swedish views on death indicates is that the theories summarized above may very well be correct, at least to a certain extent. But if the direct implication of Malinowski, Freud, Hinde, Berger, and others who support this perspective is that *all* people fear death and that death anxiety is somehow a *natural* or *given* element of the human condition, then contemporary Scandinavians' lack of high degrees of death anxiety clearly suggests otherwise. Not all people dread the coming of their own personal annihilation, nor are all cultures characterized by the same degrees or levels of death anxiety.

The Meaning of Life

If it isn't a fear of death that causes people to be religious, perhaps it is a deep concern over the very meaning of life. This is a widely accepted theory in its own right, namely, that people turn to religion because it provides the "ultimate answers" for life's deepest existential mysteries. In the words of Stark and Bainbridge:

> [S]ince time immemorial, humans have desired to know the meaning of existence. Why are we here? What is the purpose of life? Where will it all end? Moreover, people have not just wanted answers to these questions; they have desired particular kinds of answers—that life have meaning.[12]

For Stark and Bainbridge, concerns over the meaning of life have troubled humans for thousands of years, and the deep desire for answers to these existential questions is a common human need—a need that causes people to become religious. Andrew Greeley has argued that "man (by which I mean most men at many times of their lives) need some sort of ultimate explanation" and thus turn to religion for a sense of meaning.[13] Peter Berger has similarly argued that humans "cannot accept meaninglessness" and that the "need for meaning" is possibly humanity's strongest need, which religion exists to address.[14] Kenneth Pargament has argued that the search for meaning and significance is "the overarching, guiding force in life."[15] Justin Barrett posits that humans are simply "compelled" to ask, "What does it all mean?"[16] Max Weber's entire discussion of theodicy is predicated on the notion that people need to feel as though there is some deeper, ultimate meaning to the bad (and good) things that befall them.[17]

Since Danes and Swedes are the least likely of contemporary humans to be religious, I wondered what they thought about the ultimate meaning of life, particularly given their common attitude toward death—that it truly is the end. I wondered: If we are merely the products of natural selection and biologically bound evolutionary developments, if this world of ours is nothing more than a conglomeration of physical properties, and if death is truly the end, what is the meaning of it all? Aren't contemporary Scandinavians vexed by the existential mysteries of life? I asked this question over and over again. Below are some responses.

Preben, quoted earlier, is a 50-year-old owner of a small hotel. When I asked him if he ever pondered the meaning of life, he succinctly replied:

Do I wonder about the meaning of life? [pause] No, I don't go that deep.

Katrine is a 43-year-old elementary school teacher who lives just outside of Copenhagen. She doesn't believe in God, she says, and she wouldn't necessarily identify herself as a Christian. When I asked her what makes life meaningful, she said:

There are good forces and bad forces and you have to fight the bad forces. But it's individual and it's in groups. You have to fight against the Nazis, you have to fight against the fundamentalists, you have to fight against many different groups. And also individuals—as a person, you have to fight against the bad things. . . . Yeah . . . not just for yourself, for your own sake, but for others too, and for your family's sake. So . . . .yeah, that's it.

As for Jonas, quoted earlier, he explained:

Eh-h-h . . . yeah, the meaning of life. I don't know if I think about the meaning of my life. The meaning of my life, I think, is just to have a good life for myself and the people I care about. All this making the world a better place—I don't know. Because we as humanity really just screw it up so bad. Society is just so way, way out—in my point of view, anyway. You've got people in Africa who have got absolutely nothing, and you've got people in Denmark who have just got everything. And as long as that problem is there, we're going to have the threat of war and . . . those wars are probably going to be fueled by religion, if you want to say that. As you've seen so often before. But . . . I don't know . . . the meaning of life? I don't know.

Tina (also quoted earlier) is from Stockholm, age 39. She told me that religion simply doesn't interest her, and when I asked her if she believed in God, she said "No, not really," and again made it clear that the whole God issue just isn't all that interesting to her and it just isn't something that she ever really thinks about ("Not ever!"). As for the meaning of life, she said:

But there is meaning everywhere . . . I mean, I think the very idea that there is a God up there telling us what to do and playing with us like pawns is absolutely horrible. It's another thing: I don't think people really need meaning. I think you work out your own meaning. . . . And if you can't do that, you'd really better get yourself a better life. [laughter]

Tyge is a 62-year-old retired shop steward who worked at a Coca-Cola plant in Copenhagen for most of his life. When I asked him what he thinks happens after we die, he said, "End—you're dead." So I asked him, if that is the case, then what is the meaning of life?

It has no special meaning. People try to find some special meaning. We are born, we live, and we die. Somebody has a good life, somebody has a bad life.

Uh-huh. And for you, what are the things in your life that you enjoy or give meaning for you personally?

First of all, my wife and my daughter—my family. My friends are dead, but my family is the most important thing.

Maja is 28 years old, and lives in a very small town outside of Aarhus. She graduated from law school, but is currently staying at home taking care of her new baby. On the day of our interview she was wearing a small cross, but when I inquired about it she said she only wore it because she thinks it is pretty—not because it has any religious significance to her. Maja is not a believer, but she said that she does think about existentialist questions more now that she has had a child. As for the meaning of life:

I'm not sure that there is a meaning. There doesn't have to be really. No, I don't think there's a meaning. It's just . . . something we're going to go through. I don't know why.

When you think of that, how does it make you feel?

Um-m-m . . . in a way relief, because then . . . because then you don't have to think about it—has to be a meaning—it doesn't matter if there's no meaning about it.

Lars is a 43-year-old journalist who was raised on the island of Fyn but now lives in Aarhus. A self-described atheist who refused to get married in the church because he simply could not go along with the things that the pastor says in such ceremonies, he does acknowledge that perhaps sometimes he thinks that there might be "something bigger" out there. As for the meaning of life:

[long pause] . . . I don't know, I think . . . the meaning is to be with other people . . . be nice to other people, nice to your family, have an interesting job, and I really have an interesting job, I think. But sometimes you can ask yourself, now you are here what are you going to do? Do something, you know, so that when we get to the end you can say I did something good for other people.

Kjerstin is a 24-year-old engineering student at the University of Gothenburg, on Sweden's western coast, where she grew up. She doesn't believe in God and sees herself as "very science oriented." When I asked her what she thinks happens after we die, she replied,

Nothing. We just disappear. We're just living for a short amount of time and then there's nothing.

But if we just live and we die . . . then what's it all about?

Well, it's not something I've thought a lot about. But I basically think that life is about what we do now, and whatever makes us happy and feel like we're achieving something. That's the meaning of it. Because if you think of it, look at animals. They just live and they're happy. I hope, at least.

For Jeppe, the 64-year-old retired P.E. teacher I quoted earlier, who doesn't believe in God or life after death:

I think there's no meaning with life. The meaning is what you set yourself putting in to it.

For Vibeke, a 33-year-old unemployed biologist living in Copenhagen:

The meaning of life is living your life and having a good life, and you should not be living life waiting for something afterwards.

Hjordis is a 68-year-old widow who lives outside of Copenhagen. She worked most of her life as a cook in a small restaurant. Although a tax-paying member of the National Church, she never actually goes to church. Not ever. She does not believe in God, and as for what happens after we die, she replied, "nothing." As for the meaning of life (conveyed through a translator):

There is no meaning.

Then what keeps you living?

Good neighbors, friends, music, computer, everything—flowers, the garden.

Isak is a 69-year-old retired physician who was raised and still lives in a suburb just outside of Stockholm. I quoted him earlier, stating that after we die, we just "cease to be." Isak is somewhat of an agnostic; he believes that there are aspects to existence that simply defy rational comprehension. Possessing intimate knowledge of the biology of human life, and having worked for years with people who have gotten sick and died, I asked him about the meaning of it all:

I would say that it's been a pleasure to live. I mean my whole life, it's a long time, I had a lot of very pleasant feelings and experiences and a lot of . . . yes, of course, you can be sad and be in bad situations and some people even take their life because they think that the life is not worth living. But in principle, the life is a gift to everybody and it's nice to have it. You don't need to have a sort of continuation of it, and I also have difficulties in understanding what would then be the next life? If after this life, what would happen and how would that be? If everybody that had lived on the earth suffers and also this question of eternal life. I mean, eternal life is really something the worst that would happen to everybody. They never have the possibility to die, I mean for all time to be living. That is horrible.

Earlier I quoted Leif, the 75-year-old book publisher from Gotheburg. When I asked him about the meaning of life, he replied:

I don't think—I don't know if there's any meaning in life. I enjoy life. I enjoy making the things I do. I made a dictionary—English-Swedish-Yiddish—a half a year ago. It's very good, if I do say so myself. And I work as a publisher still . . . my wife, 16 years ago she got a stroke and she was in a coma for a year or something like that . . . I always thought that I was a very weak person, but when my wife went ill, then I got stronger, in a way—so I got some strength—I don't know from where. I even wrote a book—I had a diary for the first year of when my wife was ill. So I didn't get depressed. And I even published it and it was a success.

One might think that Leif, who doesn't believe in God, doesn't believe in life after death—and doesn't believe that life has any special or grand meaning—would perhaps feel unconnected to the world, or despondent, or utterly depressed, especially as an old man with a wife in a coma. And yet quite the opposite is the case. He enjoys life and is able to find meaning in his work, among other things. Many people I talked with cited the raising of children as the thing that makes life meaningful. Others talked about hobbies, such as elk hunting. Others talked about living in the moment, and not waiting around for an afterlife. Some spoke of the meaning of life in strictly genetic terms; that we are here to pass on our DNA. But many others actually had very little to say on the matter. These individuals found the whole question of the ultimate meaning of life something that they just didn't think too much about. An example of this perspective is Henning, a 76-year-old retired engineer who lives in a suburb outside of Copenhagen. He is a nonbeliever. When I asked him what he thinks will happen after we die, he replied "nothing." And this was our subsequent exchange concerning the meaning of life:

Okay, now Henning . . . I talk to some people and they say, "Well, if I think that when we die, we die and there's nothing, then what is the meaning of it all?" So how do you answer that?

Ah-h-h . . . um-m-m . . . I don't think I can answer it . . .

But you like to live?

Yeah.

So what do you enjoy about life or what gives you meaning in life . . . for you?

[long pause] . . . *uh-h-h* . . . [unable to answer]

You don't think about it so much?

No, I don't.

Having conversation after conversation like those excerpted above led me to some deep thinking. Some serious pondering. But not about the meaning of life. Rather, I deeply pondered *the deep pondering* of the meaning of life. Put simply: I began to seriously question just how important and significant "knowing the meaning of life" really is for people, after all. Is it truly such a burning matter? Is it really such a deep, universal concern? I started to think that perhaps for maybe a very small, select proportion of humanity existential questions of the ultimate meaning of life are of constant, visceral concern and that these types of people perhaps do ponder the matter deeply and for long periods of time. And they probably go on to get degrees in philosophy or religious studies. And they are probably not like most people.[18]

Based on my research among Danes and Swedes, I have started to theorize that most people, most of the time—at least in certain cultures—don't actually worry too much or actually even care about the "ultimate meaning of life." What probably concerns most people most of the time are things like their job (or lack thereof), their family life, what they are going to eat, their friends, sex, the neighbor's barking dog, etc. While living in Scandinavia, I found credence in the sentiments expressed earlier by

Jonas, who had said he thinks that 90 percent of people don't worry too much about religious or existential questions, but rather concern themselves with things like "how to pay their bills, how to feed their family" or other such mundane, this-worldly matters. This position has also been broached elsewhere, by Zygmunt Bauman, who put it this way:

> [T]he sole things that matter to humans are the things humans may take care of. Such a premise may be perceived as sad and reason to despair, or on the contrary—as a cause for exhilaration and optimism; both perceptions, though, are decisive only to the lives devoted to philosophical reflection. . . . The organization of daily life is by and large independent of philosophical sadness and joy, and evolves around concerns which seldom, if ever, include worry about the ultimate limits of things which humans, as humans, could reasonably (and effectively!) be concerned about.[19]

I just don't think that wondering about the ultimate meaning if life is a human constant or universal. Sure, every human who has ever lived may, from time to time, wonder why we are here and what the point of it all is at certain special moments, now and then. Call them fleeting moments of existential pondering. But I would argue that these fleeting moments of existential pondering come and go, and are not necessarily the moments that people construct their lives around, or devote inordinate amounts of energy to. At least not contemporary Scandinavians, who are living proof that the quest to know the ultimate meaning of life need not be a deep or vexing human obsession.[20]

As I conclude this chapter, it is important to stress that, just as with low levels of belief in life after death discussed earlier, the observably low levels of deep concern for the ultimate meaning of life in Denmark and Sweden do not breed widespread apathy or indifference. Danes and Swedes do not believe that since life is potentially meaningless, it thus is something to be wasted or uncared for. Danish and Swedish culture is not characterized by widespread nihilism. Danes and Swedes care about politics, for instance, as evidenced by the fact that their rates of election participation are among the highest of any democracies in the world. They also care deeply about their fellow human beings, as evidenced by the fact that their charitable donations to poor nations and disaster relief are among the highest rates in the industrialized, democratic world. Danes are also inclined to join organizations and associations; on average, a typical Dane is a member of 3.5 voluntary associations, and one-third of working-age adults regularly perform some kind of voluntary work.[21] Additionally, they enroll in universities, they travel, they raise children, they make movies, they pioneer advances in medicine, they make love, they develop technologies—in short, the markedly irreligious societies of Denmark and Sweden are characterized by an admirably committed and involved citizenry. Clearly, meaningful lives can be lived even within societies where concern for the "ultimate" meaning is relatively minimal.

4

Lene, Sonny, Gitte

IT WAS NOT always so easy to get people to agree to be interviewed by me. It wasn't like I could just stand on a street corner or walk into a grocery store and stop strangers and ask them to sit down with me for about an hour to discuss their personal beliefs—with a tape recorder running, no less. For the most part, I had to have some "in" with people before I felt comfortable asking them for an interview. This "in" was usually established through friends, neighbors, relatives, colleagues, or people I met through my daughters' schools and extra-curricular activities. However, there was an added difficulty. Many people were simply put off by the topic: religion. More often than not, if a person heard that my research had anything to do with religion, they expressed various levels of reluctance. They would either say that they weren't religious themselves—in which case I would say, "That's OK, I am also interested in people who aren't religious"—or they would say that they honestly had nothing to say about religion one way or the other, and that their indifference would surely not be conducive to a good interview. One telling example was when a friend of mine in Aarhus asked around at his office if anyone was interested in taking part in my study. His co-workers initially expressed a willingness to participate, but as soon as they heard that my research involved questions about religion, their interest evaporated. He eventually did recruit two people who agreed to an interview with me, but these were atypical people who actually had a fair amount to say on the matter. The majority of my friend's colleagues simply bowed out. How I wished I could have interviewed them.

This was a constant theoretical and methodological question for me during my time in Scandinavia: how to study the relative *absence* of something. How do you investigate a pervasive *lack* of something? Specifically, how does one study the absence or lack of religion? For the typical, average, or "normal" person in Denmark or Sweden, religion just isn't all that significant an element in their lives. They don't think about it much and they have relatively little to share/offer. How, then, was I to find people and get them to talk about something for which they have little interest and relatively little to say? Part of the answer—as I stated above—was that I had to have some sort of "in." Without question, most of the people that I interviewed actually only did the interview because they knew me—or they knew someone who knew me—and otherwise probably would have had little or no desire to sit down for an hour-long conversation about religious issues. The three people that comprise the heart of this chapter fit this description: they are all relatively uninterested in religion, but agreed to do the interview anyway, almost as a favor.[1]

Lene

I was able to set up an interview with Lene because she is the long-time friend of a second cousin of mine who lives in Copenhagen. So on a very sunny fall morning, I interviewed her in her third story apartment in downtown Copenhagen. Lene is 32 years old and works as a graphic designer. She is single. Her hair is very blonde—almost white-blonde—and she speaks English fluently. She offered me some tea and a few chocolate candies as we began the interview.

Are you religious at all?

Not at all. [laughter]

And do you ever go to church?

Uh-h-h, well, I do actually. It's funny because I was baptized and I was— confirmation, yeah. And I did sing in a church choir for 3 or 4 years or something. But I was paid to. [laughter] *And we had cookies and tea and stuff afterwards and all my friends were there so it was lots of fun. And then I just go whenever someone gets baptized or married.*

But you never go on a Sunday?

No.

Did your parents?

My dad absolutely does not go into a church. My mom goes for Christmas Eve sometimes.

Tell me about your dad.

He is an old communist, [laughter] *and now he also votes for the Social Democrats and he just doesn't believe in any of that—at all. He would probably go if I decided to get married or something in a church, but he would never go on his own.*

If you were to get married, would it be in a church or . . . ?

Probably not, actually.

Do most of your friends—are they the same as you, would you say—your closest friends?

Yeah, most of them are probably the same like me, but some of them do get married in churches—just for the romance, I think. . . . Yeah, and there's probably something about it when you get married—many people think that it is something that should be in the church or something, but if you ask them, most of them won't believe in God anyhow, so . . . .

If I asked you do you believe in God, what would you say?

No . . . but I do believe that maybe once there was this guy called Jesus or something like it, and that Jesus had some special things that he could do like some people do today, also—or maybe he was just a good speaker. Maybe he had some nice thoughts or something. And then someone decided to write down something and it all explains something and they made up this God or something like that . . . but I don't believe in God.

Would you call yourself an atheist?

Yeah.

And most of your friends also, you think?

Yeah. I have a few friends that say they believe in God, but they don't talk much about it . . . and I also have some family members that do. Like my favorite nephew was brought up in a very Christian—well, his mom is very Christian and they go to church a lot and he believes in it. It really hurts me. [laughter]

Why?

Because I think they're telling him stories that are not true. They're making him believe things that are not true.

And when you were growing up, were your parents very clear, like: "we don't believe this stuff"?

No. It was just something that we didn't really talk about.

So if your dad was a communist and didn't believe and your mom wasn't so religious, why did you have the baptism and the confirmation?

Because my Granny started to cry when my brother decided not to go to church. [laughter] *My Granny—she believed in God and my mom actually said that she does, but then she's not really that religious, but she's become maybe a little bit more . . . but she never prays and stuff. I don't think it's like that.*

Do you think we have a soul?

Uh-h-h . . . that's a difficult one. I do believe in things like supernatural things, but I don't believe that they have anything to do with a God, maybe. I do believe that people have sixth senses and that we might have a soul and that if we're really lucky, maybe there's one more life. There's probably not, but if we're really lucky then there's one more. But you'd better get the best of this one because there might not be one more.

So what do you think happens when we die?

I'm not sure, actually. [long pause] I'm not sure. But you hear stories sometimes about people seeing lights and all these things, and there might be something to it, but I don't know what happens. No, I don't know because I also believe a little bit in ghosts. [laughter] Mostly because I have stories—like I have a girlfriend that had ghosts in her old house, and I believe that she's not telling lies. They had two different people come to the house, like those kind of people with sixth senses that can see things and hear stuff. They had two different ones come to their house without them knowing about the other one. And they said the same things about this ghost, and her daughter was actually able to see the person.

This is your friend?

Yeah, this is one of my friends. They called these two people in because the daughter was seeing things and she was scared all the time, and so they had these people come and examine the house. And they said the same things about this person—about how he looked and what he was doing and stuff. And then they also—both of them said that her father, who is dead, was in her bedroom. And she always had this feeling that she was being watched by him when she was in her bedroom with her husband.

Your friend's daughter?

No, no—my friend said that there were like two ghosts in her house. Her father was sitting in a chair in her bedroom and then there was another guy that the daughter was afraid of—who was a nice guy mostly, but then he would sometimes put on a mask and then he would scare the little girl. That's what she sometimes saw—the girl would go like something was there, and there was nothing. Emma couldn't see anything, so they had these people come in and tell exactly the same things as the daughter said.

And what did they do?

She moved. [laughter] They sold the house and moved away.

And then?

And then—nothing. They got divorced, but in the new apartment there's nothing there. I don't know where he's living.

That's incredible. Have you ever had any experiences like that?

No, not myself, no.

But you just heard about it?

Yeah, I heard about it and then I figure, yeah, why not? It could be something to that. But still, to me that doesn't have anything to do with a God or religion or anything. That's something different.

Do you ever check out or look into Eastern religions or anything like yoga or . . . ?

Yeah, because I do travel a lot in Asia. And if I were to choose a religion, like if I was forced to choose a religion, it'd probably be Buddhism. Not that I know actually too many details or anything about it and I haven't really read about it, but it just seems like a really nice—more like a philosophy than a religion.

Do you, like, meditate ever, or do the practices?

No. I do yoga sometimes, but I never meditate. I don't seem to be able to do it. [laughter] *My brain goes a little too much around everywhere.*

If you had kids, how would you raise them? Would you have them baptized and would you tell them they were Christian?

I might have them baptized . . . but . . . I wouldn't raise them in any religious way. I would just try to raise them to be good people. Because there's some nice things in Christianity and in many other religions about how to treat other people and stuff like that. With my nephew, I think that's fine that he learns all these things and when he reads the Bible if he can get some nice rules for living or something. But that he actually believes that there was a person that created this world in seven days and stuff like that. I hate it when he believes in that. But there's some nice living rules and stuff.

Will you ever tell him that you think it's a bunch of nonsense?

My nephew?

Yeah.

When he gets bigger, probably, yeah, but now I'm not sure he's—it's a bit annoying because he's actually very like—he thinks he knows better than us and that we're not religious and he will sometimes scold his grandparents, for example, and other people for not believing. He will say, "Haven't you even the read the Bible? Everyone has to read the Bible," and he's very, like—and then when he does that sometimes I'll say something like, "Not everyone believes in the same things and that's okay, you don't have to". . . . And I don't like it when he does that. [laughter] *It's seldom, but he actually does it sometimes. But he's entitled to have his beliefs and stuff. I just think it's a pity when someone takes a child and teaches them these things because he really doesn't get a choice—or it'll be more difficult for him to make a choice, I think, because he has to disown something when he gets older instead of taking something. It'll be difficult for him to put it aside, because this is what he learned all through his childhood.*

Why do you think Danes and Swedes are so secular or nonreligious? If you had to come up with something . . .

We weren't always, were we? I mean, many, many years ago we were religious. I don't know . . . I don't know why actually . . . what happened. Um-

m-m [long pause] . . . *maybe our brain works different. Maybe we're eating too many fish or something, I don't know* [laughter]. . . . *No, I don't know. I haven't got a clue what happened.*

Sonny

Sonny was a substitute teacher at my oldest daughter's elementary school. I told him about my research one day and he agreed to an interview. In addition to working as an on-call sub for elementary schools in the Aarhus area, Sonny also works as a part-time casting agent for Aarhus's small film and television production industry. It was at his office at one of the production buildings, down by the shipyards, that we met for the interview. It was a few days before Christmas, and his office was quiet and almost empty. Outside the large windows behind his desk the sky above the sea was gray and still.

He made me a cup of coffee and then we got to talking. Sonny is 31 years old. He was raised in a small town about an hour's drive south of Aarhus. He is currently engaged. We talked about movies for a while before I turned on the tape recorder.

Could you tell me a little bit about—your growing up—brothers, sisters?

Yeah, I have a brother, and my father died when I was four, actually.

Wow, what happened?

He got some sort of a kidney—what do you call it?—some sort of infection, which shut down the one kidney and then the other kidney had to work harder and then it also shut down and then . . .

Ah, that's hard.

It is. He was in the military at that time and—he got, you know, one of the exercises—it was quite cold and then he got the infection and . . .

When you were four—whew. And did your mother remarry?

No, she never remarried. But she got other men, yeah.

And what did she do for a living?

Yeah, it was quite tough, because in the 1970s in Denmark, you know . . . women were not—they were allowed to work, but it wasn't common, so the salary for my mother was very, very low. It was very uneven for men and women, so she did some cleaning and she did some—she worked in a kitchen in a cantina, so she had two jobs and she had two kids, and we were not easy. I'm told that we were not easy.

Did she get any support from the government because her husband died?

Eh-h-h . . . she did get something. We have child benefits here. But not much extra, I don't think so, so she had to, you know, make sure that she could pay the rent and bring us to nursery school, kindergarten, and she had to get a driver's license and buy a car without money.

She struggled?

Yeah.

And she's doing okay now?

Yeah, yeah. She just got a new car. [laughter]

Well, we've got to talk a little bit about religion, if that's okay.

It's okay. Not that I'm prepared.

Are you a paying member of the church?

Yes I am.

And tell me why.

You know, that question I have asked myself many times. Actually, two weeks ago it was in the news—it was if you choose to sign out of the church, then you can actually save a million within 30 years.

From your taxes?

Yeah, from your taxes, and it differs how high a percentage from where in the country you live. I think the highest is 1.7 and the lowest is 0.4 or something. But if you have a normal, an average income of 250,000 Danish crowns, then you will save a million within 30 years. And to put that million on your pension, that's quite good, because it adds up. You save the one million becomes four million within 30 years because of interest.

So this was in the news?

It was in the news.

And were people talking about it?

Yeah.

You discussed it with your fiancée?

Yeah, but we are supposed to be married, and my girlfriend wants to be married in the church. Now we have a kid and we want her baptized and everything, so it sort of conflicts, you know.

Well, maybe after you baptize her?

Yeah, and then we sign off. Because you know I have paid to the church for 15 years. I do pay my taxes—not that I'm cheating or anything. But it sort of conflicts because you want all the things the church has, but you don't want to pay. You know that's—even though I go every Christmas to church.

Oh?

Yeah, actually back home, because that's where we have Christmas, but that's—it's cozy—it's tradition. Not that I'm religious—but it's just . . .

Nice to go?

Yeah.

And what's the service like? What happens? Just mostly singing or is there a sermon also?

There's a sermon also, but it's very low key. It's very, "Then Jesus said blah, blah, blah" and then we sing a song and then "blah, blah, blah" and there's lot of kids and people want to go home to their Christmas duck or whatever. It's just for the façade, I think . . . because, as you probably know, if you go to church on a common Sunday, there'll be 5 or 10 people.

Do you ever go on a common Sunday?

No, no, never. Actually, I don't think I have ever been, besides my confirmation preparation . . . maybe Easter—yeah.

And you will get married in the church?

Yes.

And is that mostly because your wife wants it? I mean would you—or you also kind of would like it?

Yeah, you know, that's the picture of me getting married is to be in a church and not in the city hall. Actually, and that's a conflict again. Actually I don't believe in marriage. I could just as well not be married, but when you are married you gain some rights. And when you have a kid, you have to have those rights, otherwise you—because if you go away somehow, you know, like my dad did—then you need those rights . . . for your child and for the wife.

Would you say you believe in God?

No . . . um-m-m . . . but the tricky thing is I want to believe . . . I want to believe that there's something higher, something bigger than us, but all reasons say there's not, and I've never had that confirmation ever in my life. And, you know, I'm more like a science kind of—I know—I think I know how things started and I believe that, so that's quite a huge conflict with God as an almighty saying what—my belief is that God was created because when people experienced something tragic or couldn't explain stuff, then they would make up some sort of almighty thing that could explain things that they couldn't explain, because they weren't wiser, but now we are wiser, now we can explain things.

Did you ever believe in God, even when you were a kid?

Yeah, I did actually pray a lot when my grandmother died. I was 10, I think. Uh-h-h . . . yeah, I did. But that again, I do think about why I did that. But when you are in sorrow, I think you sort of—you approach God, but when you're not, you forget him. If I was in some sort of a trauma and I couldn't find a reason why she had to die, then I would go because I didn't have the answer, then I would start believing in something . . . because I didn't have the answer.

Was your grandma religious?

No.

Grandparents?

No.

How about your mom?

No.

When your father died, did your mother turn religious at all?

No, not that I know of. She should have.

It would have helped?

Yeah. But then again if there isn't any tradition in the family, then it would be weird. Maybe if my grandparents had gone to church or something.

But it just wasn't part of her upbringing?

No.

So your mom wasn't religious, your grandparents weren't religious, both sets?

Yeah. And my dad wasn't either.

Interesting, okay.

It is interesting, because—why did I pray to God? Of course, I had been to church, I actually went to Sunday School. Yes I did.

So at some point you heard . . . ?

Yeah, yeah, I heard and we were told in school . . . we had religion in school, as well.

But at what point did you say, "Okay, I definitely don't believe this stuff"? I mean, were you a teenager, was it in your 20s, like—when did you say, "I just don't believe there's a God"?

I think, actually, I never believed it. Not that I—I don't recall me thinking, "That's it, He doesn't exist". . . . But the stories are good.

The stories are good, okay. Do you have a favorite?

Um-m-m . . . yeah, about the—I don't know what you call it in English . . . the samitan . . .

The Good Samaritan?

Yeah. I think that's a good story. Yep, the thing about religion is even though I'm not religious, all my values are based on religion. So that—what do you call these stories in English?

Bible stories?

Yeah, because those Bible stories are fundamental for the values we have, and for the laws that we have made. So that's why they're interesting because they say a lot about society and how it's built.

Yeah, for sure. And so—like, if you're growing up in Denmark and your parents aren't very religious and your grandparents aren't religious . . . is it sort of that no one really thinks about these things or were other kids religious and you had, you know, conversations in the schoolyard, "well do you believe in God or don't you?" . . . or was it just kind of not part of your life?

Actually . . . um-m-m . . . if you did believe in God, then you were sort of pulled out—"you're weird, man, you believe in God."

Okay, that was uncommon?

Yeah, really.

So you were more typical?

Yeah, I was typical.

Can you remember kids in school who did believe–tell me some of those stories?

Actually once we—as a class—we went to a religious school and we had to speak about the religion issues . . . they have to speak to us about God.

How old were you?

I believe we were about 12 at that time, and we saw a play about Jesus and stuff. And we, you know, we were laughing at that because—Jesus—how stupid can you be believing in that stuff? I mean, it's a good story, yes, but believing it . . . it's like . . . and we had a discussion and there were two students and the teacher telling us about the play and what it meant . . . symbolic. And we came to the discussion about God . . . "and God created the earth." And we came to the discussion, "But we all know how the earth was created, it was not God, how can you believe that there is an Almighty?" And they came up with some sort of answer and we just started laughing. It was quite mean, actually.

So most of you were just laughing at the few?

Yeah, yeah . . . "Jesus loves us." [laughter]

When you say we know how the earth was created or the world—how is that? What is your answer?

You know, with the big bang and the creation of the solar system.

Okay, and now if someone were to say to you, "Well, what created the big bang?" what would you say?

Actually I have—my answer would be that I think I believe that the universe expands and implodes, and that's the bang.

But where does the universe come from—in the beginning?

Yeah . . . that's a question we . . . you know the theory of being that there are other universes. I had a wild theory, not that I believe it, but it's just a theory. Because, if you have atoms the core is stable and around there are some sort of electrons that sort of orbit the center. That's a fact with the solar system and that's actually if you see the galaxies—the formation of the galaxies, it's the same way. So if there are universes, other universes than what we know of, that spin around other universes, then you actually have—you know, you have planets in the solar system which are moons. They circle. It would be funny, though.

That's the pattern?

That's the pattern.

And that is easier for you to believe than God?

Yeah, if I had to choose, I would choose that way.

Some people might say—if we're just atoms spinning around another universe, spinning around another universe—so what's the meaning of it all? Have you ever wondered about that?

Yeah, yeah, yeah. I think everyone is philosophic in some things. Uh-h-h . . . but I don't think there's a meaning. The meaning is that there is no meaning. I think the meaning is for yourself. I have to create meaning in my life with the values I sort of stick to. And I think family is the meaning of life. You know, it's quite simple, actually, to get—to be fed and have children.

To be fed and to have children?

Just like—flies—small flies, you know. What do they call in English? The "day fly," you know—24 hours they die. There's a South American fly that only lives 24 hours—no actually it's 48 hours, but they call it the day fly because it comes to earth, it comes to life from this pupa thing, the egg, and it—and it's fed by the mother, it starts flying, it gets more food, and it sort of gets in contact with another sex, it has kids, it dies, and the female lives 1 or 2 hours longer and it sort of, lays eggs and then she dies and then there's a new generation within 48 hours. That's quite amazing . . . I think that's the meaning of life.

And how about—do you think inside us there's a soul or a spirit or do you think we're just bodies?

I would really like to hope that we have spirits . . . uh-h-h . . . because I cannot imagine me being dead and then I'm gone . . . like whoosh. But once in a while you have the feeling that you have lived before . . . um-m-m . . . actually I just studied and got my driver's license . . . it's quite unusual at my age . . . um-m-m . . . and the first time I went driving it was so easy. I mean, I just spoke with my teacher and we just went, and . . . at some point I had the feeling I'd been driving a car before. It was weird, it was really weird. And then you have all these people who think they can see in the past and see in the future, but there is actually—there was a show, I know it's a show and you don't believe everything you see—but there was a show where you could sort of be hypnotized back in a previous life. And this woman, who I know now—I didn't know before that show—she gave a detailed description in France where she lived in a little city with a castle and river and forest and a graveyard, you know, how the local church and city hall were made, you know, stone by stone and what the inscription said—very, very detailed, and then she went down there—she'd never been in that city before, and it was exactly as she described in that hypnotic state. That was amazing.

So you believe there's something possibly . . . ?

I don't think I believe—I think I have to experience it personally to believe it—but I want to believe it.

Gitte

My "in" with Gitte was knowing her husband, Martin. He was a colleague of mine at the University of Aarhus. One evening in May I drove out to their home on the outskirts of town. Martin was gone—playing music with his rock band. Their two children were asleep, so the house was quiet and peaceful and the aroma of herbal tea filled the living room. I had never met Gitte before, but we hit it off quite well as we began by talking about Martin, his research, kids, the birth of my new baby, etc. Gitte is 40 years old. She grew up in Aarhus. She works as a preschool teacher. I began the interview by asking her about her upbringing.

My mother died like 25 years ago, I think, and she was a nurse. And my father, he's retired now. He's 67 years old, and he was a printer.

And they were both from around Aarhus, your parents?

No, they were from a small island here in the bay, Samsø. You told me you went there?

Yes. I think it's my favorite place in Denmark that I've been. What do you know of your grandparents? Do you know what they did and where they were from?

Yeah, yeah. My mother's parents, they were farmers, and he was also—I don't know the English word, but I can explain it. Like if farmers have problems with the—not a doctor, but he walked and said, "This cow is good for making small cows, and this male cow—bull—is good for making that." And also about the corn, the different kinds of corn. My grandfather was advisor supervisor for farmers in that way.

Okay, so that was your mother's side. And your father's . . . ?

He had a farm and he was ruined in it because of the war, and then in the next seven years, he had several different jobs—and they lived seven different places in Samsø. And then he died, and my grandmother—she continued cleaning in the school and jobs like that.

Do you know if any of your grandparents—I mean—were they believers?

The only one I know most about is my grandfather on my mother's side. He was a nonbeliever, but he was part of the National Church. But often he told me that when he was young, he had a grandmother who lived in the western part of Denmark where they're very religious, and he said often he—he—I'm sorry, it's been a few years since I have spoken English. He invited her—because she said, "When I'm dying I'm going to God and He takes care of me." He often told me this. He died when he was about 90 years old, and the last few years he often told me, "I admire so much that she believed in that because I would like to do that now."

But—did he?

No, he didn't.

And do you know about his wife? Was she a believer?

I don't know.

Tell me about your parents. Were they believers?

Um-m-m . . . I'm not sure. I think no. Still like maybe most Danes—members of the National Church. And when my mother died—yeah, it's 23 years ago—my father started going to church. Like, not every Sunday but once a month or something like that.

More than when she was alive?

Yes, and for maybe 1 year, 2 years—and then he shut down and he stopped again.

Did you ever ask your parents if they believe in God?

No.

Never had that conversation?

Maybe as a child, but I don't remember—either the questions or the answers. And maybe I have never been so interested. My parents never went to church, for instance, and I have never—I know some people, they—every night when they go to sleep, they pray a prayer to God and they teach their children the same. And they never taught me that. When I was a small girl, maybe six or seven years old, my great-grandmother died, and from her I had a small book made of glass and there was a prayer on it, and I learned it because I was interested in reading.

Yeah, okay, I understand.

But still they were married in a church and I'm Christian and my brother's Christian, too.

And was your mother, if I may ask, was she ill or was it an accident?

No, she was ill. She had cancer.

Okay, so she knew she was going to die?

Yes, and she was a nurse, so of course she knew.

And how was that? Did she cope okay or was it—I mean, you never saw her turn to God or pray?

No, never.

So she just did it without religion?

Yes.

And your father, you said he did go to church after a bit, maybe?

Yes, but later—now when I think about it—maybe he was just seeking and didn't find what he wanted to, maybe.

I'm curious—how did your parents and perhaps you cope without thinking—you didn't think your mother was going to God or—what did you think?

I don't know what I thought. I thought it was—really bad luck, [nervous laughter] and why does it happen to us? Why not the others, but I didn't blame it on any—I didn't blame it on God or anything. It was just like—"okay, it's not always the neighbors, sometimes it's you also."

Would you say you're a believer?

No. I'm not a believer. But I still am a member of the National Church, and our children, they're baptized.

Okay, and would you call yourself an atheist?

No. [laughs] I don't know why. Because if I was an atheist I would say no to the National Church, I think. It's for me—when you do that you go out of the community or—not community, but—how can I explain? I don't believe in God, but for me—I would like to keep the church and to keep it so that if people want to go there and keep it for culture.

Yeah, okay. So if you said you were an atheist, you would feel that you would also have to quit the church?

Yes.

But even though you don't believe in God, you like the idea of the National Church being there for people and . . .

Yes, and I think it's a part of the Danish culture. And also because of— for being there with my children when they—I don't know what you call it—confirmation.

So you expect them to do that?

Yeah, I think, especially our boy. He's now 11 years and he now tells us that he wants to do that.

Why would you want—I mean, if you don't believe in God and your parents didn't believe in God and perhaps even your grandparents didn't believe God, what does it mean for you? Why would you want him to confirm that he believes in God?

Yeah, it's strange . . . [laughs]

It does seem to be a really important tradition for Danes.

Yes . . . and I was confirmed myself, too. And maybe at that time—I think I believed in God. Yes, I think when I was 10 or 12—in some ways, yes.

Do you remember, like, praying or . . . ?

Yes, I do. When going to bed—making up my own prayer—for being good friends with this one and this one or—yes. Maybe half a year, one year, something like that.

When did you really realize you didn't believe in God? I mean, do you remember? Were you a teenager, were you in your twenties?

No, no.

You don't remember when?

No. I only remember that earlier period when I really—maybe I hoped, and it didn't succeed.

Have your children ever come home from school and asked, "Do you believe in God?" or . . . ?

No.

You haven't had that conversation?

No. We have talked about it sometimes and Sophie, our daughter who is eight years old, she sometimes said, "I don't know if I believe in Jesus or Buddha," and it's because of Martin's work also, of course [Martin studies Buddhism]. *We don't discuss our personal opinions, but more about different kind of religions. Also because Rasmus is going to school with two Muslims, and he asks what is this and what is that, and we try to explain to him . . . so I think they know a lot about different kinds of religions, but not personally—more theoretically.*

What do you do on a typical Sunday?

A typical Sunday I have a nice breakfast and read my newspaper. We don't go anywhere, we just stay here and the children play around . . . we relax.

Okay. And so—I guess, do you feel as though you're missing something by not being religious?

No.

That there's a hole in your life?

No. I thought of sometimes if I'm getting old and getting lonely, then I maybe would look to the church—can they give something to me, yeah.

• • •

Earlier, back in Chapter 2, I noted that many social scientists see religion as something natural or innate. They argue that all humans have basic, unalterable religious needs. I countered this position by arguing that societies like Denmark and Sweden, rare though they may be, suggest otherwise. This point bears repeating. For when David Hay states that religion is a "biologically natural phenomenon" that is "built in to us,"[2] or when Robert Bellah asserts that religion is a part of the "species life of man" and is "central" to his self-definition,[3] we must always keep people like Lene, Sonny, and Gitte in mind. Religion is quite far from being central to their self-definition. Religious concerns, concepts, ideologies, participation, and beliefs are quite marginal to their sense of self. And even though it might be tempting for skeptics to suggest that maybe there is something abnormal, idiosyncratic, or otherwise "unnatural" with Lene, Sonny, and Gitte which might account for their marked secularity, it is difficult to maintain such a position given the fact that they are absolutely *not* oddballs in their cultures, but rather, fairly typical representatives of what millions of their fellow countrymen and women think and believe. When you consider such modern societies in which millions of people are indifferent to religion and generally uninterested in God, it is hard to conceptualize religion as something intrinsically, naturally human. Whatever it is that compels the majority of the world's humans to be religious must be something cultural, social, political, psychological, emotional, economic, or philosophical—*and then some*. But what it clearly cannot be is something "innate," or "natural." Societies without God may be nothing more than rare, unusual, or atypical cultural phenomena—fleeting, flickering blips on the screen of human civilization—but they are there nonetheless, and their existence poses a strong challenge to any theory that would posit religion as something essential, inborn, or universal to humanity. As Zygmunt Bauman astutely proclaims, "the case of the 'innateness,' of the 'natural' presence of the religious drive in the universal human predicament . . . has not been proven."[4]

I'd like to conclude this chapter with some specific observations concerning Lene, Sonny, and Gitte.

First, what struck me after talking with Lene and Sonny was that although they are both nonbelievers, they both still seemed open to the possibility of supernatural or paranormal phenomena. Lene spoke of her good friend whose house was haunted (I did subsequently interview this friend, by the way, and got all the eerie details). And Sonny spoke of watching a television show in which a woman was able to describe details from her past life. While he remained somewhat skeptical of the show's claims, he also seemed to be clearly open to the possibility that it could still be true. Although most people that I interviewed did not believe in or have any experiences with the paranormal or supernatural, many did—even those who are more or less nonreligious. For example, one woman told me that at her boyfriend's grandmother's funeral they were all singing her favorite song about a butterfly, and just then, a butterfly entered into the church and flew around. Another woman told me that when she was a teenager drinking vodka in a cemetery with a friend one night, she saw what appeared to be two ghosts (men without legs) floating by. One woman told me how when she was a teenager alone in her room, she experienced a strange darkness at just the exact time that her mother was dying of cancer in the nearby hospital. One man told me that his mother is certain that she once saw an angel. Another woman told me of how a close friend died in a boating accident, and that a few weeks after his funeral she felt his presence very strongly one day and somehow heard his voice telling her that everything was OK. Another woman told me that she was at her mother's bedside as she was dying, and that she actually saw light come up and out of her body at the precise moment of her death. One man told me a beautiful story about when he took his dog for a walk on a cold winter's night and suddenly stopped and looked up at the moon, which was shrouded in a strangely beautiful circle of clouds, and felt a deep sense of "something."

The point of all of this is to simply make it clear that although Denmark and Sweden are societies without much in the way of strong religious beliefs, and although Danes and Swedes are an extremely well-educated, rational, and skeptical lot, their worlds are not totally disenchanted. Ghosts and the like have not completely evaporated from Scandinavian culture. Yet the discourse surrounding supernatural phenomena is one that is almost completely divorced from a traditional religious worldview. Of the people that I interviewed who had some sort of beliefs in or experiences of the paranormal, most did not in any way see their experiences as relating to God, nor did the experience make them feel "religious" in any way. They spoke of these experiences as interesting, moving, or memorable—and they framed these experiences as being examples of there being "something more" out there—but they rarely characterized these experiences as causing them to be more Christian or to take more seriously the possibility of God's existence.

A second noteworthy detail from the interviews above was the fact that both Sonny and Gitte said that they prayed and somewhat believed in God—*as kids*. Sonny remembered that when he was 10 he prayed a lot following his grandmother's death, and Gitte recalled that when she was around 12, she also prayed for a stint. I highlight this because their dabbling with prayer and/or belief in God as children was actually quite common among many of those that I interviewed. A majority of the people that I interviewed said virtually the same thing: that at some point in their childhood, they took a stab at believing in God and praying. Sometimes they prayed to God asking for help in winning a girl's affections, sometimes they prayed in the wake of the death of a grandparent, sometimes they prayed "just because." And almost every one also said that this religious phase didn't last very long, and that their eventual loss of belief in God and prayer was simply a matter of growing up. Whenever people told me that they had believed in God as children, I always wanted to hear the story of how they actually lost their faith. I rarely got that story. Hardly anyone could ever recount some dramatic moment when their faith was shattered. Few could ever recall some specific event or instance that caused them to become a nonbeliever. No one could ever cite reading a certain book, or learning some fact about history or science, or coming under the influence of a teacher or friend, which led to a loss of faith. Instead, what I heard—time after time—was that their belief in God simply withered with age, undramatically, and without much to-do. Tyge from Copenhagen and Sigrid from Aarhus are typical in this regard. When I asked Tyge, a 62-year-old retired shop steward, about how he lost his childhood faith in God, he replied:

It just happened.

When I asked him if there was a decisive factor in his transition to a nonbeliever, he struggled for a moment and then said:

Common sense.

Sigrid, a 53-year-old artist who runs a small bed and breakfast, said that she believed in God as a child, but has considered herself an atheist all her adult life. I asked her when it was that she became an atheist, and she replied.

When I grew up.

I then asked her if something specific happened to her that led to a loss of faith. Her response:

You get mature and think about things.

The notion that religious belief is somehow childish, that earnest prayer is something that only children engage in, and that faith in God is just something that one dabbles with in childhood, but eventually grows out of as one becomes a mature adult, would strike most Americans as offensive. But for millions of Scandinavians, that's just the way it is.

5

Being Secular

In my world, I don't know anyone who is religious.
> —Britt, age 37, works at a music recording company in Stockholm

WHAT DOES IT mean to be secular, and what does the term "secular" actually connote? Dictionaries will offer a variety of definitions, including "of or pertaining to the world," "of or pertaining to the temporal rather than to the spiritual," "not pertaining to religion," "not overtly or specifically religious," "not having any connection with religion," and so on. As with any adjective, there is no single, definite, or absolute meaning of "secular" that everybody can agree on. Rather, its meaning is nebulous and fuzzy—and changes over time and in different contexts. But generally, when we speak of something as being secular—be it a person, song, or government—we basically mean that it is not religious. OK, well, then what does "religious" mean? Answers to that question are abundant—to put it mildly. Tens of thousand of articles and books have been written on the subject of what it means to be religious. An impressive plethora of magazines and academic journals are devoted to the topic of religiosity. Thousands of colleges and universities throughout the world contain departments and institutes that are devoted to the study of religious people, religious practices, religious scriptures, religious history, etc. In sum, oceans of ink have been spilled, and legions of keys have been typed upon, describing and explaining what it means to be religious.

But what about those humans out there who are not religious? They have been sorely neglected. As Benjamin Beit-Hallahmi recognizes, "those who have shaped the modern human sciences have been preoccupied with explaining the phenomena of religion and religiosity. Accounting for the absence of religious faith has never been of much concern to them."[1] As Talal Asad notes, social scientists "have paid scarcely any attention to the idea of the secular."[2] I do not know of a single academic journal that is devoted to the study of secularity. Books on being secular are markedly few and far between.[3] I know of only one institute in the entire United

States devoted to the study of secularity, and that is The Institute for the Study of Secularism in Society and Culture, housed at Trinity College, in Connecticut. And that was only established in 2005.

The truth is, if there has been any chunk of humanity that has been ignored or under-examined by social scientists, it is the secular chunk. And contrary to what many Americans may think, "chunk" is an appropriate term to use when denoting the number of humans alive today that can be considered secular, or at least, nonbelievers. A few years ago, in an attempt to determine just how many atheists and agnostics there are in the world, I carefully looked through as many international surveys as I could find concerning people's religious beliefs—or lack thereof. After assembling a country-by-country tally, the estimate that I came up with was that there are somewhere between 500 million and 750 million atheists, agnostics, or nonbelievers in the world today.[4] Given such numbers, this means that there are approximately 58 times as many nonbelievers as there are Mormons, 41 times as many nonbelievers as there are Jews, 35 times as many nonbelievers as there are Sikhs, and twice as many nonbelievers as there are Buddhists. "Nonbelievers in God" as a group actually come in fourth place—after Christianity (2 billion), Islam (1.2 billion), and Hinduism (900 million)—in terms of global ranking of commonly held belief systems. That is a whopping chunk of humanity.

To be sure, a lot has been written about secularization[5]—the historical process whereby religion weakens, fades, or loses its hegemonic or public significance. Many scholars have been aggressively debating secularization for years, and yet despite all of the books and articles that have been written on the subject, all of them—at least that I am aware of— are generally theoretical or broadly historical in nature, and don't examine secular life as it is actually lived by nonbelieving men and women in the here and now, or the nuances of the secular worldviews of actual individuals who are irreligious. Then there are of course many books that have been written which polemically advocate secularity over religiosity, such as the recent best-sellers by Sam Harris, Richard Dawkins, and Christopher Hitchens.[6] But again, these are not books about secular life or secular people, per se. The fact is, shockingly little research has been undertaken that simply attempts to describe and understand men and women as they go about living their religion-less lives. Secular cultures, secular approaches to life, death, sex, politics, love, child-rearing, government, etc., and the varieties of the secular experience have simply been given short shrift by the social sciences. Why have irreligious people been so grossly ignored? Given that most people in the world are religious, wouldn't that make the study of secular men and women all the more pressing? Since most societies are permeated by people who claim to hold strong religious beliefs, doesn't that make the study of societies whose members don't hold much in the way of strong religious beliefs all the more necessary?

• • •

Prior to living in Scandinavia, I knew quite a bit about the low levels of religiosity there. I had done a fair amount of book-worming and was familiar with what the published surveys revealed: that such-and-such a percentage does or does not believe in this or that, and how such-and-such a percentage doesn't attend church once a month, etc. But had I limited my study of the lack of religiosity in Scandinavia to reading such articles and surveys, I would have missed quite a lot. As stated in an earlier chapter, surveys can only tell us so much. They can give us snapshots of information—useful information, to be sure—but it is often information that amounts to little more than quick and partial glimpses of various aspects of a given population. In doing ethnographic research—that is, by living with and among the people I was attempting to study—and by conducting face-to-face, in-depth interviews with as many people as I could over the course of a year, I was able to get a much richer, subtler, and more nuanced understanding of what it means to be secular in a relatively secular culture than any statistical survey could ever reveal.

Through my qualitative research, I ended up "discovering" aspects of religion and irreligion in Scandinavia that I had never anticipated or expected. There were so many interesting and compelling contours to their secularity that I had never even considered before, had never experienced, had never pondered, and hadn't even really known were possible—until I did my research.

In this chapter, I would like to present three specific aspects or contours of being secular in Scandinavia. The first I call "reluctance/reticence," the second "benign indifference," and the third "utter obliviousness." I present this material for two reasons. The first is that I simply want to show that secularity comes in more than one form; there are various shades and degrees of secularity, just as there are various shades and degrees of religiosity.[7] Second, I seek to clearly illustrate the degree to which certain segments of Scandinavian society are about as secular as is sociologically possible.

Reluctance/Reticence

The most common orientation to religion that I experienced among Danes and Swedes was reluctance/reticence. People were often disinclined or hesitant to talk with me about religion, and even once they agreed to do so, they usually had very little to say on the matter. Taciturnity was the most common disposition. You may recall that I mentioned this reluctance to talk about religion at the beginning of the previous chapter—how it was often difficult for me to find people willing to sit down and talk to me about the subject.

But I am not the only one who has had such an experience.

Just ask the National Church of Denmark.

In 2003, the National Church of Denmark decided to hold a weekend retreat. The idea was to get people together from all over the country to spend a day or two on a given weekend to discuss the state of the church and religion in Denmark: how do people feel about the church? What do they like? What do they have problems with? What could be improved? What aspects of religion are important to them? Things like that. The weekend retreat would be an all-expenses paid affair (transportation and meals provided), and the location of the retreat was purposely selected in the center of the country so as to be as convenient as possible for all who were invited. The church sent out 6,000 invitations to randomly selected men and women all over the country. The fact that these individuals were randomly selected is sociologically significant, because it means that a truly representative sample of Danish society was solicited. After the invitations went out, almost nobody registered. The National Church became so worried about low attendance that they subsequently placed ads in various newspapers with an open invitation to anyone who wanted to attend. Eventually, the retreat did take place, but with only 80 participants. Out of 6,000 people invited—plus thousands of others who were informally invited via the ads for the event in their morning paper—only 80 people were willing to spend their time one weekend discussing the state of the church and the role of religion in their society. With 80 people attending out of 6,000 invited, we're looking at a response rate of approximately 1 percent. This makes a very clear statement about the dramatically low level of interest in religion and church affairs among contemporary Danes—or at least their striking unwillingness to spend much of their free time thinking and talking about it with others.

That was exactly what I found, too. And even when the initial reluctance was overcome and I was able to get people to agree to an interview, once it was under way, the topic of religion rarely generated much elaborate conversation, strong opinions, interesting details, personal diatribes, idiosyncratic confessions, thoughtful arguments, compelling stories, or provocative musings. Most of the men and women that I spoke with had precious little to say about it. For many or even most contemporary Danes and Swedes, religion is not something to be discussed or analyzed, nor is it something to be debated or debunked, nor is it something to be resisted or feared. Rather, it is something quite altogether different: *a non-topic*. And when religion becomes a non-topic for significant segments of a modern society, we are dealing with an extraordinary social reality: secularity, par excellence.

Of course, it is quite possible that the reluctance/reticence that I so often encountered was not necessarily the result of a deep cultural secularity. It may be due to two other factors, the first being language, and the second being the fact that religion is construed as a "private matter" within Danish and Swedish culture.

Concerning the matter of language, nearly all of my interviews were conducted in English. This certainly rendered my Scandinavian informants at a linguistic disadvantage; they could not express themselves as clearly, comfortably, or colorfully as they could have had the interviews been conducted in their native tongue. It is possible that much of the reticence on religion that I encountered in my research was partially a result of people feeling less able to express themselves in English. And this is especially plausible concerning religion specifically, for it is a topic which is often very philosophical and existential in scope and involves nuanced meanings, personal feelings, and subtle distinctions that would render anyone without an expanded vocabulary at a conversational disadvantage. However, the reticence on religion that I experienced cannot be entirely chalked up to the language factor. I say this for several reasons. First, the majority of informants that I interviewed were quite fluent in English, and they were able to converse freely and colorfully about many other topics that I broached with them, including politics, childhood, education, work, taxes, sexuality, gender roles, immigration. I consistently noticed a distinct taciturnity, however, when it came to religion—a taciturnity that was not nearly as overt or manifest when discussing so many other topics or issues. Second, I did conduct 12 interviews in Danish with either a graduate student or colleague serving as an interpreter. In nearly all of these interviews, reticence when it came to religion was still quite overt. For example, while interviewing several elderly Danes at an old age home in the city of Aalborg with the aid of an interpreter, the discussion of religion merited very little response—just a few yes's and no's, really. The lack of conversation was awkward for me (and my interpreter), as I just couldn't get them to say much, no matter how hard I tried. Finally, at one point, when I asked them why they had nothing to say about religion, one of the older men said, "Because it is bullshit." I asked for clarification: "Religion is bullshit, or talking about religion is bullshit?" "Both," he succinctly grumbled. Third, one semester I led a seminar on secularism with eight university students. They all were required to do interviews with several people on their religious identities (or the lack thereof). These interviews were all conducted by Danes in Danish, and yet the students also reported how difficult it was for people to talk about religion, and just how little they had to say on the subject. Finally, concerning this matter of language as a possible source of reticence, I am not the only one to find a lack of loquaciousness concerning religion among Scandinavians. In 1971, Per Salomonsen, a Danish sociologist, published a book based on research similar to mine: face-to-face, in-depth interviews about religious identity.[8] And although Salomonsen's interviews were conducted in Danish, he still found a similar reticence among the men and women that he interviewed. The terms he used to describe how Danes discuss common religious matters included "inarticulate" and "vague," and he concluded the English summary of his study by noting a "low level of communication and information about religious matters among the respondents."[9]

In short, the fact that my interviews were conducted in English definitely affected the content of my interviews, in terms of both quality and length. But I don't believe that is the sole or even main reason that people were reluctant to talk about religion with me, or were reticent once the interview was under way.

A second possible factor to consider when trying to explain why so many people had so little to say about religion—and were often reluctant to do an interview with me—is the fact that most Danes and Swedes consider religion to be a personal, private matter. Throughout my year of research, people told me this, over and over again: religion is a very personal, private thing. One of the pastors that I interviewed, Jokum, a 36-year-old head of a small congregation in a little village outside of Aarhus, put it this way:

In Denmark, the word "God" is one of the most embarrassing words you can say. You would rather go naked through the city than talk about God.

Rikke, a 57-year-old retired social worker from Aarhus, said:

Danes are very open. You can talk about sexuality and you can talk about a lot of problems. But when it comes to what you believe, we just never talk about it. Even with very good friends, it's very seldom you share those things. That's a bit funny, I think, but I think it is—it is very private.

Hans and Trine are both in their early forties. They are married, have two daughters, and live in one of the nicest neighborhoods in Aarhus. They both described themselves as irreligious, and when I asked them if they were typical in this regard, Trine replied:

I think I am very typical, but actually, I can't really answer that because, like—it's not something you talk about. I think for Danish people, love and sex are easier to discuss than religion. It's—it's a bit intimate, isn't it?

Hans: Yes, and there are no words for it. I mean—

Trine: We have no language for it—it's not usual to talk about it. It's just not a thing that you discuss. I think people make up their mind about religion and it's a very private thing. It's just not something you talk about.

I asked Hans if his grandparents were religious, and he replied:

I don't know. But they went to church. Not every Sunday, but every second Sunday, like that.

You say you "don't know"—is that because you didn't really know them too well, or because religion wasn't talked about?

We never talked about it. I knew them very, very well. But religion was never a subject. No. I could quite easily have talked about sex with them. I mean, I was very close with them—it was not a subject—and it would be strange for me to talk to them about religion. I had a very close relation to my grandpa on my mother's side and we talked about a lot of things. But we never talked about religion.

Given these statements from Jokum, Rikke, Trine, and Hans—and similar sentiments expressed by many others that I talked with—it is incontrovertible that religion just isn't something that is talked about much in Scandinavian society. This was made more than evident by the sheer majority of people who told me that they never discussed religion with their grandparents, couldn't really remember discussing religion with their parents, and seldom or never talked about religion with their friends, co-workers, lovers, or spouses. But what about the persistent claim that religion is a private, personal matter? After many months of conducting interviews, I began to question and, well, become skeptical about that assertion. And the more people that I interviewed, the more skeptical I became. After all, the insistence that "religion is a private matter" in Danish and Swedish culture actually implies that people *are* religious, deep down, but that they just don't make it public and don't like to talk about it with others. This is the argument made by a leading Bishop in Denmark, Jan Lindhart, who has likened Danes and their religiosity to lottery tickets: you may not see much religiosity on the surface, but just scratch that surface a bit and you will find their religious hearts revealed, underneath a veneer of secularity.

I spent a year scratching. I scratched and I scratched and I scratched.

And what I found was that religion wasn't really so much a private, personal issue, but rather, a *non-issue*. The reticence that most people exhibited when answering many of my questions about religion wasn't, in my experience, so much about religion being too personal or private. Instead, it seemed to stem from a basic disinterest or sheer lack of thought on the topic of religion. How could I tell? One big indicator was body language and general demeanor. What I rarely experienced with an informant was a guarded nervousness—what one usually encounters when broaching a private or personal issue. Far more typical was something more akin to what might be termed *comfortable blankness*. By that I mean that most people seemed comfortable with the subject when it was broached—not nervous, embarrassed, or guarded—and they were generally quite open to my questions. They just didn't have much to say in response to them. They tended to draw blanks.

Let me give the example of Mette, who is 24 years old and worked at my younger daughter's preschool as an assistant teacher/day-care provider. The interview took place at a café at the university. We began the interview by talking about her work—and she had a lot to say. She talked about my daughter, the other kids at the preschool, the other kids' parents, the other teachers, etc. Then we talked about her boyfriend—a truck driver—and his nationalistic political sentiments. We also talked for some time about immigrants, and her opinions on racism within Danish society (she felt that it was the immigrants who tended to be more racist than the Danes, an opinion that may have been shaped by an unpleasant experience she had recently had with some immigrant men at a disco). We also talked about the recent death of her grandmother. Throughout this section of the interview, Mette was a thoughtful, lively, and fairly animated conversationalist, and she embellished her narrative with anecdotes and opinions. But when it came time to discuss religion, things just went flat. She became noticeably taciturn. Almost bored. And it wasn't as if she somehow became nervous or embarrassed about religion and her own (private) religious beliefs. Rather, it was more as if the topic of conversation had just suddenly—and unfortunately—switched to the price of cardboard boxes. I plodded on with my questions, but her answers tended to be succinct and un-dynamic, at least when compared with what she had offered on previous topics. I asker her if she or her parents went to church when she was growing up.

Nope.

Did your parents talk about religion ever when you were growing up? Teach you to believe in God or . . . ?

No, they never told me to—that there was a God. Of course, of course, you hear it as a child that there's a God . . . but they never talked about it like that.

It wasn't a big part of your life?

No, no, no, no.

Like—was sports more talked about?

Yeah.

When your grandma died, did you or your parents become—turn to religion at all for . . . ?

No, no.

Did you talk about it with your parents? Like—is there a God and all this?

No.

And how about your friends, do you ever have conversations about God or . . .

Not at all.

Why do you think it is that Danes are not interested in religion?

I don't know, because . . . we just don't care.

And that is basically the tenor and tone of the interview that went on for another 20 minutes or so: short answers, without much in the way of elaboration, pondering, or mulling over. And certainly no anecdotes or strong opinions. Just sort of comfortable blankness.

In short, while it is definitely possible that the reluctance/reticence that I experienced so often among the people I interviewed was due to having to speak in English, and it can also be reasonably explained by the fact that religion is considered a very private and personal matter within Danish and Swedish culture, I think there is something else at play, some additional underlying cultural factor: bald secularity. I suspect that for many people, their reticence was due to the simple fact that religion is such a marginal aspect of their culture, and such a minimal element in their daily lives. In the words of Callum Brown, they lack a "narrative structure" when it comes to religion simply because it is a topic that they rarely think too much about, and talk about even less.[10]

Admittedly, I did on occasion interview people who were illustrative of the "religion is a private matter" notion. There were a handful of men and women who acted noticeably uncomfortable with the topic of their religious beliefs in a way one might expect: they got nervous, slightly embarrassed, fumbled to express themselves, etc. For instance, when I interviewed a 60-year-old secretary from the university, she grew somewhat anxious as soon as the topics of God and religion came up. She kept her arms firmly crossed throughout that part of the interview. When I asked her if she had ever had a religious experience, she said yes, but said that it was too personal to talk about. However, this sort of exchange was extremely rare. Indeed, I never had any other individual tell me that a given subject concerning their religiosity was "too personal" or "too private." And it was very seldom that anyone's body language, facial expressions, or demeanor revealed such a feeling. Most people were more like Mette in their overall demeanor and orientation to religion: not nervous or embarrassed, just flat and sort of disinterested, with relatively little to say.

Benign Indifference

A particularly interesting orientation to religion that I had not anticipated prior to my year of research in Scandinavia—an orientation that I would say was expressed by about half of my sample—is what I would call "benign indifference." The people in this camp are not especially anti-religion. In fact, they actually think religion is OK. Nice. Fine. Good. So their feelings about religion are, if anything, slightly positive (hence the "benign"). They think the church buildings are beautiful and peaceful, or they can at least appreciate them as venerable architectural symbols of their cultural and religious heritage. They think the church services at Christmas and Easter are cozy, even if they don't always go. They think that most pastors are kind, thoughtful, and decent men and women, even if they don't interact with them all that much. They see religion—at least the Scandinavian Lutheran brand—as basically a harmless, innocuous enterprise that even does a bit of good now and then. As for religious people who do believe in God? Well, that's fine for them. That's OK. Who can say for sure if there is or isn't a God, right? As for this fellow Jesus? Well, maybe he didn't walk on water or raise people from the dead, but surely he was a nice man who taught some nice things. And the Bible? Well, it is full of nice stories and good morals, isn't it? And that about sums up their views on religion. Aside from such commonly held sentiments, religion is just not something that really interests many Danes and Swedes. They don't know much about it, they don't think or talk much about it, and they certainly don't have much to say about it.

"Benign indifference" is definitely not an orientation to religion that I have experienced much in the United States. In America, even when a person is nonreligious, he or she usually has quite a bit to say on the topic. Most nonreligious Americans can articulate what it is about religion that they don't like, or they can carefully explain their reasons for not believing in God, or they can offer their skeptical views on current religious issues and debates, or they can relate a story about how and why they broke with religion, or they can give thoughtful explications of their lack of religious belief and/or participation. Many nonreligious Americans are also somewhat *anti*-religious—they generally find religion distasteful, dogmatic, hypocritical, ignorant, or threatening. Not Danes and Swedes. Although there are some exceptions here and there—such as Lene of the previous chapter who didn't like that her nephew was so religious—the general irreligion of most Danes and Swedes is not *anti*-religion at all. It is mere disinterest. Religion is simply not a part of their world and they just don't really give it much thought—not even enough to be "anti" it. After all, to be "anti" something is to still be concerned about it, to still be engaged with it, to still be dancing with it. To care. What I found in my research was that many people were simply and utterly—and even benignly—indifferent to religion.

Rasmus is a 32-year-old researcher at the University of Copenhagen. As he explained:

I don't believe in God . . . but I've got nothing against religion. I think religion can be very comforting. It can be good for many people . . . religion—in some modest or reasonable way—I'm supporting that. I can't believe myself, but . . . yeah.

Trine, who I quoted earlier, is a nonbeliever, but doesn't mind at all if others are believers:

I'm not repulsed by religion as such. It just doesn't have any meaning to me.

And Lasse, a 25-year-old medical student from Sweden:

I don't know anyone in Sweden, except my aunt, who believes in the Bible. And I know hundreds of people—hardly anyone believes the Bible. And maybe a bit more sort of believes in God. But most of my friends are atheists.

Definitely—one hundred percent. But they still respect those believing. And— you know—it doesn't matter that much.

This benign indifference is a fascinating incarnation of secularity, and is arguably only possible—let alone conceivable—in a society where re- ligion is truly marginal and relatively powerless. For in a society where most nonreligious people are simultaneously anti-religious—as is the case in the United States—that indicates that religion is still a social or cultural force to be reckoned with. But when millions of people are just benignly indifferent to religion, we can thus truly characterize religion as being somewhat insignificant in that society. Or, if not insignificant, then merely quaint.

Utter Obliviousness

Another surprising aspect of being secular in Scandinavia that I came upon in the course of my research that I never anticipated—and that I didn't even know was possible—was this: utter obliviousness. This orientation was certainly rare, but it was nonetheless present and discernable among a minority of Danes and Swedes. It is similar to benign indifference, but qualitatively more extreme. Let me start with one illustration: three Swed- ish women on a train.

One night I was on a train from Copenhagen to Aarhus. It is a three- and-a-half hour ride. I happened to be sitting in a compartment with three women who appeared to be in their mid-thirties. They were Swedish. They were talking amicably among themselves and it was obvious that they were good friends. Although I was very tired—having just spent the day giving a lecture and meeting with colleagues at the University of Copenhagen—I couldn't pass up the opportunity to interview these three Swedish women about their religious identities. So I waited for a good moment, and then struck up a conversation with them. I asked them where they were from (the city of Malmö), what they did for a living (they were all physical ther- apists), and why they were headed to Aarhus (for a physical therapists' conference). They were very gregarious and eager to talk with me. They asked me what I was doing in Denmark, about how my wife and kids were adapting to Danish living, and then when I eventually explained to them the nature of my research in Scandinavia, they all agreed to do a group interview. So I whipped out my pen and yellow pad of paper and began what would become over an hour-long discussion.

The first noteworthy part of the "group interview" came when I asked them if they believed in God. Two of the women immediately said no. But the third, Katarina, hesitated before answering. She sat there, paused in thought. We quietly awaited her reply. She looked out the window, at the night blurring by. And then she said that *she hadn't really thought about it before.* She didn't know whether she did or didn't believe in God—not because she was philosophically agnostic, per se, but rather, because she found it somewhat of a novel question. She asked for some more time to think it over. Finally, after several moments, she came to her conclusion: no, she didn't think so. What struck me as so remarkable about her response was not that it was in the negative (I was quite used to that), but that she had needed time to mull it over, having admitted that it just wasn't something she had pondered much before. This was a slight shock to me. Never thought about belief in God before—come again? How is it possible to be in one's thirties and not yet have formed an opinion on God?

But Katarina wasn't the only such person I met for whom religious questions were not all that pressing or even much a part of their reality. On another occasion, I spent a long day interviewing Swedish medical students (individually, not as a group). I asked these young men and women in their twenties about their experiences in medical school, and honed in on their dealings with dead bodies. Yes, they had all dissected dead bodies and had performed various procedures on cadavers. I then asked them what they thought humans were, that is, did they think that humans were nothing more than a collection of bones, muscles, tissue, chemicals, amino acids, etc., or did they perhaps think that there was something more to us, something else, something beyond the mere biological components— perhaps a soul—that was part of our being? When it came to this question, one of the female medical students replied similarly to Katarina from the train. She paused at my question, thought for a bit, and then said:

Hmm . . . I've never really thought about that before.

Again, I was somewhat taken aback. How can a person be in the midst of medical school—spending time cutting up cadavers—and yet never ponder such a question? Not that there is anything wrong with that; it is certainly well and good if a person never ponders the existence of a soul, or the existence of God. I am making no value judgment here. But it simply strikes me as quite remarkable. There was another Swedish medical student that day, Astrid, age 23, who also had a hard time answering basic questions such as whether or not she believed in God, in life after death, or in the divinity of Jesus; almost every response of hers was in the negative, but it was almost always followed by the phrase, "I don't think much about it," a response which permeated her interview. I asked another Swedish medical student, Göran, age 28, about his belief in God, the Bible, and Jesus. He mustered some brief responses, but then confessed that it was a very unusual conversation for him to be having. As he explained:

It's not a very typical conversation . . . I don't really know, for myself, how to really address these questions. I haven't really thought about them.

Another Swede that I interviewed, Tina, is 39 years old and works as a chemical engineer in Stockholm. When I asked her about God, she said that she just wasn't interested in the topic and that she never gave it much thought. When I asked her if she thought humans possessed a soul or spirit, she replied:

I've never really thought about that before.

Another Swede of a similar ilk was Erik, a 26-year-old submarine officer raised on the island of Gotland. An irreligious man, Erik said that he "didn't have a religious bone in his body." But he then had difficulty when I asked him if he was an atheist or agnostic; when I asked him how he identified himself in terms of his lack of religion, he replied:

I don't know. I haven't paid too much attention about it, really.

It's not something you think about too much?

Not at all.

Later on in the interview, after I had asked him about his beliefs concerning life after death, the meaning of life, and whether he might consider anything in his life to be holy or sacred, he succinctly confessed:

These are issues I don't think very much about. So I don't know.

Nana is a 16-year-old Dane who attends high school in Aarhus, where she recently moved, having spent most of her life in a small town in the countryside. She was markedly irreligious. I asked her if she ever talked about religion with her friends.

No.

How about at home?

No. Not at all . . . it's just like—we don't really talk about it. Not in school, not with our friends, not with our family.

Lise is a 24-year-old computer technician. She said that the topics of God, Jesus, or religion simply never came up in her family, and when I asked her if her friends from high school were religious, she said that she honestly couldn't answer, because as she succinctly explained:

We never talked about it.

Annelise, a 47-year-old manager at a telecommunications company, who lives in Aarhus, stressed just how much of a nontopic religion is in her life:

We never talk about it.

Did your Mom and Dad believe in God?

Well, I actually don't know. We never, ever discussed religion. So actually I don't know . . . it's never been discussed.

Why do you think Danes are so nonreligious or not so interested in religion?

I don't know . . . I really don't know, actually . . . I really have never thought about that. . . . It's been fun to get these kinds of questions that I never, never think about.

Bente is a 71-year-old woman who grew up in Copenhagen, and worked most of her life as an office clerk. She had very little to say about religion during the interview. When I asked her about belief in God, she said no, but had little else to say other than to succinctly explain her orientation thus:

I'm just not interested in God or the question of whether he exists or not.

Other people—not many, but about 15 percent of my total sample—expressed similar sentiments: a sober disinterest in religion, characterized by not only a lack of religious beliefs, but even *a distinct lack of thought given to even the most basic religious questions.* Although such individuals were clearly a small minority in my sample, they do exist, and their utter obliviousness to religion speaks of the notably extreme tributaries of secularity that currently flow through contemporary Scandinavia.

How is it possible that these people—in a world that is overflowing with religiosity—can be so disinterested or indifferent to religion? What is it that makes religion in Scandinavia so weak—to the point of it being a veritable non-issue for many people? Why are Danes and Swedes among the least religious people on earth?

It is to these pressing questions that I now turn.

6

Why?

Strongly felt religion has always been around; what needs explanation is its absence rather than its presence.   —Peter Berger[1]

IN CERTAIN COUNTRIES today—many of them in Western Europe—religion isn't doing so well.[2] Sure, one can occasionally read about a successful Pentecostal church springing up here and there,[3] but the overwhelming trajectory for religion in most Western European nations over the past century has been that of unambiguous decline. In Germany, for instance, most people aren't going to church anymore, and church buildings that were regularly frequented by Germans for hundreds of years are now being converted into restaurants, coffee houses, discos, and apartments. One study predicts that in the coming years, 50 percent of Germany's churches will meet such a secularized fate.[4] But it isn't just a drop in church attendance that illustrates the poor health of religion in Germany—religious beliefs are also withering there, with far fewer people today believing in the supernatural tenets of Christianity than in earlier decades.[5] A similar phenomenon is discernable in the Netherlands. Whereas nearly 100 percent of the Dutch belonged to a church 100 years ago, today only 40 percent are church members, with the majority of men and women in the Netherlands being religiously disaffiliated.[6] And only a small minority of the Dutch now maintain a strong faith in God and basic supernatural Christian teachings.[7] In France, whereas 91 percent of babies received baptism in 1958, that percentage had fallen to 51 percent by 1990.[8] In Britain, Christianity may very well be on its last legs: church membership has plummeted over the course of the last 100 years, and as for traditional Christian beliefs—in God, that Jesus was the Son of God, in an afterlife, the holiness of the Bible, etc.—they have eroded substantially, with a marked decline in recent decades.[9]

And, of course, the decline of religiosity over the course of the twentieth century is evident in Denmark and Sweden, too.[10] Palm and Trost describe Sweden as "one of the most secularized countries in the world."[11]

Andrew Buckser describes Denmark as "one of the sociology of religion's type cases in the secularization of modern society."[12] Indeed, over the last five decades, belief in God among Danes and Swedes has dramatically declined,[13] as has church attendance.[14] As this book has attempted to illustrate, the state of religion in Denmark and Sweden is remarkably weak.

The question is: *why?*

It is the most pressing of questions, and yet unfortunately, the most difficult to answer. That is because any and every major characteristic, trait, trend, or aspect of any and every society is inevitably the result of a frustratingly complex and highly idiosyncratic combination of historical developments, economic dynamics, cultural peculiarities, political formations, gender constructions, creative expressions, geographic realities, weather patterns, family structures, etc.—all affecting one another and acting upon one another in a myriad of ways. However, that said, I shall nonetheless press forward and do my best to offer a sociological explanation of Scandinavia's marked irreligiosity, or rather, offer *explanations*, for there is no one single answer or sole explanation to this puzzle. Rather, there are numerous possible theories, all of which may illuminate our understanding to varying degrees, but none of which, on their own, solves the puzzle completely.

Lazy Monopolies

This theory comes primarily from the work of Rodney Stark and his associates.[15] I am paraphrasing here, but the theory basically goes like this: when there are many different religions in a given society—with none of them being state-subsidized—interest and involvement in religion will be high. Conversely, when there is only one dominant religion in a given society—and it is subsidized by the state—interest and involvement in religion will be low. Why would this be the case? According to Stark, when there are many different religions—again, none of which are state subsidized— a "free market" competition arises; religious organizations must compete for members if they are to stay afloat. Religious organizations thus become good at marketing themselves, and are able to successfully stir up interest and involvement in religion by offering alluring products and services.[16] However, when a religious organization is the "only show in town," that is, when a given religious organization has a state-subsidized, hegemonic dominance in a given society akin to that of a monopoly—without any competition—it grows lazy. Because it doesn't have to market itself, it becomes boring, stale, or unappealing, and people eventually lose interest in it and, by default, in religion. We can thus explain levels of religiosity by looking at the "supply side" of a given society's "religious economy": how many religions are out there? Are there a lot of different religions in a given society in competition with one another, or only a few? Or maybe only one? And furthermore, what role does the state play? Does the government stay out of the religious economy as a neutral entity, or does it take an active role by perhaps favoring, or even financially supporting, one of the religious organizations? Stark argues that societies characterized by a high degree of religious pluralism with no state interference experience healthy religious competition and wider "consumer" choice, and in such a societal situation with such a diverse and "unregulated" religious economy, the net result will be an overall heightened interest and involvement in religion, as is the clear case in the United States. However, if the religious economy in a given society is that of a monopoly—and a state-subsidized religious monopoly, to boot—the result will be an overall weakening of interest and participation in religion.

The situation in Denmark and Sweden seems to fit this Lazy Monopoly theory quite nicely.[17] For many centuries, Lutheranism has been the overwhelmingly dominant religion in both countries. And furthermore, this Lutheranism has been consistently state-enforced and state-subsidized. Today, 83 percent of Danes continue to voluntarily pay annual membership taxes/fees to keep their national church afloat, and while the Church of Sweden officially split from the Swedish government in 2000, nearly 80 percent of Swedes are still subsidizing members of their national church.[18] Thus, the "religious economy" of Denmark and Sweden is one in which there is very little serious competition. The national Lutheran Church holds a virtual monopoly. It isn't an absolute monopoly, of course. About 4 percent of Danes[19] and 5 percent of Swedes belong to independent, so-called "free" Christian churches, be they Baptist, Pentecostal, Methodist, or Jehovah's Witnesses.[20] And another 1 percent of Danes and 2 percent of Swedes are Catholic.[21] And there also exist smaller religious movements within Denmark and Sweden, such as the Baha'i Faith, Judaism, Scientology, not to mention the new and ever-growing influx of Islam. However, when compared to other Western nations, the overall dominance of Lutheranism over the centuries has been markedly pronounced. And since the Lutheranism of Denmark and Sweden is largely state-subsidized through taxes, what that ultimately means is that the churches will all be nicely painted, the gas bills will be paid, the lawns will be mowed, and the salaries of the pastors will be regularly ensured—whether five hundred people come to church every week, or only five. It doesn't really matter. Since the state is subsidizing the enterprise, there has been little motivation for pastors to "market" their congregations. If people come on Sunday, swell. If they don't, oh well. And there is little motivation for the national Lutheran Church to make itself attractive or inviting, since it is basically the sole religious option. It is thus very possible that the national churches in Denmark and Sweden have simply grown lazy.

Although there are several criticisms of this theory[22]—most important, it doesn't seem to hold true throughout much of the rest of the world[23]—it is still very plausible that because the churches haven't needed to compete much for members they have not marketed themselves much, and people have subsequently come to take them for granted. Danes and Swedes have thus generally lost interest in religion over the course of the twentieth century.

Secure Societies

This theory comes from the work of Pippa Norris and Ronald Inglehart.[24] Their explanation for why some societies are much less religious than others essentially goes like this (and again, I am paraphrasing): when the bulk of people in a given society experience a low degree of security, they tend to be more religious. Conversely, when the bulk of people in a given society experience a high degree of security, they tend to be less religious. What do we mean by security? The term refers to questions like: do most people have enough food to eat? Do most people have access to stable housing? Uncontaminated water? Jobs? Do most people have access to medicine? Are they vulnerable in the face of natural disasters, such as droughts or floods? Do most people find their personal or communal survival precarious? According to this perspective, when a given society is riddled with poverty, disease, and disorder, we can say that the bulk of its people live relatively insecure lives—and they will tend to be more religious. And conversely, if a society has very little poverty, disease, and disorder, we can say that the bulk of its people live relatively secure lives–and they will tend to be less religious. In the words of Norris and Inglehart:

> People who experience ego-tropic risks during their formative years (posing direct threats to themselves and their families) or socio-tropic

risks (threatening their community) tend to be far more religious than those who grow up under safer, comfortable, and more predictable conditions. In relatively secure societies . . . the importance and vitality of religion, its ever-present influence on how people live their daily lives, has gradually eroded.[25]

This of course is not a new theory: when life is hard, people turn to religion for comfort, as Karl Marx argued back in the 1840s.[26] What is new here is the rigor and depth of Norris and Inglehart's social science; their theory is supported with excellent data that take into account numerous possible variables and rely upon extensive international comparisons. In short, their systematic analysis is quite convincing. And more important for our purposes here, their theory of high levels of security correlating with low levels of religiosity is directly applicable to the situation in Denmark and Sweden.

In past centuries, Denmark and Sweden were poor, impoverished countries, where poverty, epidemic diseases, and starvation were constants for most of the population. Neil Kent describes the Nordic region of the Early Modern period as "one of the least healthy in Europe," marked by high mortality rates and lives lived "close to the existential minimum."[27] Donald Connery describes nineteenth-century Scandinavians as "a poverty-stricken mass."[28] But over the course of the twentieth century, Denmark and Sweden became not only among the wealthiest nations in the world, but also among the most egalitarian. Due to the success of the most well-developed welfare systems within the democratic world,[29] the wealth in Scandinavia is shared to an impressive degree throughout the nations' populations; the gap between the rich and the poor in Denmark and Sweden is smaller than in any other industrialized democracies. They are countries where "wealth" is envisioned as a communal condition in which, in the famous words of Danish national and cultural icon N.F.S. Grundtvig, "few have too much and even fewer have too little." Poverty and starvation have been almost completely eradicated in Denmark and Sweden; famines are the stuff of history. And nearly everyone has access to decent housing, health care, food, education, and shelter from nature's harsher manifestations. As was discussed in Chapter 1, life expectancies in Denmark and Sweden are among the highest in the world, the percentages of infants born with low birth weight are among the lowest in the world, rates of HIV infections are among the lowest in the world, the maternal mortality ratios are among the lowest in the world, rates of tuberculosis are among the lowest in the world—to mention a few indicators of the excellent societal conditions one finds in Denmark and Sweden.[30] Additionally, we can consider the recently published Global Peace Index (2007),[31] which ranks 121 nations on an international scale according to the degree of peace and security in each country. This index takes into account such factors as homicide rates, levels of violent crime, levels of disrespect for human rights, likelihood of violent demonstrations, political instability, levels of distrust among citizens, etc. According to this index, Denmark ranks third as being among the most peaceful societies in the world, and Sweden ranks seventh. (First place went to nearby Norway; the United States ranks 96th.)

When it comes to the levels of security and insecurity that Norris and Inglehart discuss, Denmark and Sweden are, without question, among the most "secure" nations on the planet, and perhaps in the history of modern, industrial democracy. And this may very well explain their markedly high degree of irreligiosity: with such secure lives and healthy societies, the demand for the balm and comfort that religion often provides has waned.

Working Women

This theory comes from the work of Callum Brown, a British historian who has attempted to explain the decline of Christianity in British society over the course of the twentieth century.[32] By his account, what has occurred in Britain is that "a formerly religious people have entirely forsaken organized Christianity in a sudden plunge into a truly secular condition."[33] The explanation for this drastic decline in religiosity among the British is to be found, according to Brown, by looking at women. He argues that it was women who historically kept their children and husbands interested and involved in religion. And then when women opted out of religion, their husbands and children followed suit. As Brown states, "women were the bulwark to popular support for organized Christianity . . . and . . . it was they who broke their relationship to Christian piety in the 1960s and thereby caused secularization."[34] According to this theory, a major cultural shift occurred in the 1960s that changed the way women perceived themselves, their lives, and their possibilities in the world. Traditional Christian femininity was problematized—or, in Brown's words, there was a "de-pietization of femininity"[35]—and subsequently new forms of feminine identity were forged. A key ingredient of this cultural shift in feminine gender construction was that British women became less interested in religion, Christian faith became a less central or essential element to their identities, and when this secularized generation of British women stopped going to church or caring about God, so too did men.

If there is one thing we know about religion, it is this: women are more religious than men, on all measures.[36] Whatever indicator one wants to look at—whether in terms of church attendance, frequency of prayer, or faith in God—women always score higher than men.[37] And this seems to hold true in all societies, including Scandinavia.[38] So, if women are in fact the ones who push their husbands and children to get up and go to church on Sunday mornings, if women are the ones who keep their husbands and children dutifully praying at night and studying their Bibles, if women are the ones who instill piety in their families and keep the candle of faith lit in their homes, then it would make sense that if women were to themselves become less interested and involved in religion, a general loss of religion would occur throughout society— just as Brown argues. But what might cause such a change in women's religiosity? Although Brown doesn't offer too much here, one could easily argue that a major reason would be women's increased participation in the paid labor force. As Ole Riis acknowledges, drawing from much previous research, "women in paid employment are less religious than women working at home."[39]

Prior to the 1960s, the vast majority of Danish and Swedish women were engaged in unpaid domestic work as mothers and housewives. But over the course of the last four decades, there has been a dramatic change in terms of women's involvement in the labor force. By one count, in 1960 over 800,000 Danish women worked at home as housewives; 20 years later, that number had dropped to 250,000.[40] Put another way, in 1969 just over 43 percent of women worked outside the home in the paid labor force, but by 1990 that had increased to over 78 percent.[41] Today, the vast majority of Danish and Swedish women work outside the home.[42] In fact, Danish women currently have the highest employment frequency in the labor market in the world.[43] And according to a recent report by the Confederation of Danish Employers, the percentage of women in the paid labor force is actually on the verge of surpassing the percentage of men in the paid labor force![44] Thus, it is quite possible that the remarkably high degree of women in the paid workforce in Denmark and Sweden helps account for the low levels of religiosity there. As Bradley Hertel has concluded:

The lower level of membership, attendance, and religious identity of men and women in families in which the wife works full time may in turn—and probably does—lead parents to place less emphasis on religious training for their children. If so, then the work-related declines in married women's involvement in religion may impact negatively on the long-term future religious involvement of their children.[45]

An influx of so many women into the paid labor force may not have caused the secularization of Danish and Swedish society, but it most certainly helped accelerate or deepen it. Once women became occupied with the duties and concerns of paid employment, their interest in—and energy for—religion decreased. And their husbands and children followed suit.

Other Possibilities

I consider the above three theories to be the most plausible sociological answers in attempting to explain why Denmark and Sweden are so relatively irreligious. I think that when taken together—a lazy church monopoly, secure societies, and working women—much of the puzzle of secularity in Scandinavia is explained. But there are other possibilities.

The first additional factor to consider when accounting for secularism in Scandinavia comes from the work of Steve Bruce[46] and David Martin.[47] It concerns what can be described as *the lack of a need for cultural defense.* Bruce and Martin recognize that religion is often a key ingredient in national, ethnic, or cultural identity. And whenever national, ethnic, or cultural identity is threatened, the religiosity of the threatened group will typically be strengthened. That is, whenever a society or nation feels threatened or oppressed—either by a dominating foreign power or a neighboring menace—religion often serves as a pillar of ethnic, communal, national, or cultural defense. The classic illustration for this phenomenon would be the case of Ireland, where Catholicism and Irish nationalism have strongly reinforced each other over the centuries.[48] Another fine example would be the case of African Americans, who have historically turned to the Black Church for refuge and support against an often hostile and oppressive white majority culture,[49] which greatly helps to explain why black Americans are far more religious on all measures than white Americans.[50] How might this relate to Denmark and Sweden? Simply in the sense that there has been a noticeable *lack* of a need for cultural defense concerning Danish and Swedish society. Over the course of the last several centuries, Danes and Swedes have never been extensively oppressed or dominated by a foreign conqueror, especially one of a different faith. Although Denmark suffered humiliating military defeats at the hands of the Prussians in the 1860s (which resulted in a significant loss of land and people), and although Denmark endured several years of German occupation during the Second World War, it is safe to say that neither Denmark nor Sweden has been extensively threatened, dominated, or oppressed in the past several centuries by a foreign culture with a different religious tradition. In the words of sociologist Benton Johnson:

> Ecclesiastical laziness and public detachment from religion are most likely to set in when the culture/religious monopoly isn't threatened by alien powers. When it is threatened, as Irish Catholicism was for centuries at the hands of the British, or as Poland was under centuries of alien rule, then a religious monopoly can serve as a reinforcer of a people's identity and an institutional center of resistance. Lutheran Europe, with the possible exception of Finland under Czarist rule, hasn't felt itself culturally or religiously threatened for a long, long time, maybe as long ago as when the Swedes stopped being a Protestant military giant in Europe's religious wars.[51]

And this situation very well might change in the decades ahead, with the ever-increasing presence of deeply committed Muslim immigrants in Denmark and Sweden. Their presence could result in an increase of Lutheran piety as a contemporary expression of Scandinavian cultural defense. But this remains to be seen. It is equally possible—and perhaps even more likely—that if Scandinavians feel the need for some sort of cultural defense in the face of the new immigrants' strong Islamic religiosity, it will be in the form of an increased embrace and celebration of rational, democratic secularism—rather than traditional Christian belief and practice.

Another possible factor that may help explain the marked irreligiosity of Danes and Swedes would be simply the matter of *education*. Denmark and Sweden were two of the first nations to successfully push for widespread literacy among their populations. In fact, Denmark was the first nation in the world to legally enact free compulsory elementary schooling for all children throughout the country, regardless of social status, and that was back in 1814.[52] Sociological studies have consistently shown that the more educated a person is, the less likely he or she is to accept supernatural religious beliefs. For example, a recent Harris poll found that of Americans with no college education, 86 percent believed in the resurrection of Jesus, 77 percent believed in the Virgin Birth, and 74 percent believed in the existence of hell. But belief in such things was noticeably lower among those highly educated Americans possessing postgraduate degrees, of which 64 percent believed in the resurrection of Jesus, 60 percent in the Virgin Birth, and 53 percent in the existence of hell.[53] A recent Gallup poll found that of Americans with no college education, 44 percent consider the Bible to be the actual word of God to be taken literally, but of Americans with graduate degrees, only 11 percent maintained this view of the Bible.[54] International rankings further strengthen the correlation between strong education and weak religiosity. For instance, a 2002 UNICEF report[55] shows that of the top ten nations ranked highest in terms of their teenage students' abilities in reading, mathematics, and science, all—with the exception of Ireland—are relatively irreligious nations such as South Korea, Japan, Britain, and the Czech Republic (Sweden ranked ninth). Both Denmark and Sweden have very well-funded and well-organized school systems and highly educated populations. According to a 2000 report by the Program for International Student Assessment, teenagers in Sweden and Denmark rank in the top 20 in the world regarding reading literacy, mathematical skills, and scientific knowledge.[56] Furthermore, Denmark and Sweden have among the highest adult literacy rates in the world (assumed to be at 99 percent).[57] It is thus quite possible that some correlation does exist between having a very well-educated population and subsequently low levels of religiosity.

A final possible factor in accounting for secularism in Denmark and Sweden is the significant governmental influence the *Social Democrats* have had in constructing Danish and Swedish society for much of the twentieth century. More than any other political party, the Social Democrats have dominated the parliaments of Denmark and Sweden, with their nearly hegemonic strength only diminishing in recent years. The Social Democrats have always been relatively anti-religious and anti-clerical and have sought at times to weaken or dilute religion's influence throughout society. Examples of this abound and include, for example, changing the public school curriculum so that Christianity is not taught in an evangelical or confessional manner, but in a more "social science" vein which teaches "about" Christianity as one among several religious traditions. Additionally, the Social Democrats have had the power over the years to appoint liberal, progressive, nonfundamentalist or "modern-thinking" men and women as bishops or to other upper-level positions within state-linked religious institutions. Thus, it is possible that the secular and often anti-religious agenda of the Social Democrats over the years has influenced or perhaps accelerated secularization in Denmark and Sweden. The only problem with locating the Social Democrats as a source of Danish and Swedish ir-religiosity is that it begs the question: why would Danes and Swedes allow the Social Democrats to dilute or weaken their religion? After all, if religion was so important to them, surely they wouldn't have elected and re-elected the Social Democrats, year after year, decade after decade. Perhaps the secularity and relative anti-religiosity of the Social Democrats, rather than *shaping* the will and sentiments of the people, actually just *reflected* them.

Religion and Irreligion in the Past

Throughout my year in Denmark, there was one matter that kept pestering me; one issue that I continually wondered about. As I pondered the question of why Danes and Swedes are among the least religious people in the world, I found myself often wondering about a specific historical possibility, namely: *maybe Danes and Swedes have simply never been all that religious.* OK, perhaps "never" is a bit of a vague designation. But what I mean to put forth is the important question of just how deeply religious Danes and Swedes have been over the course of previous centuries. It is widely assumed that everyone was very religious in the past, and that this religiosity has waned or weakened in modern times.[58] But maybe this is an assumption without strong evidence to support it—at least concerning Scandinavians. Perhaps the typical Dane or Swede never really believed all that much in God, never quite bought the whole Jesus thing, never really believed in or fully understood sin or salvation, and only went to church in centuries past because of social obligation or pressure from the local authorities. And if this is perhaps the case, then the low level of religiosity among Danes and Swedes is not some new development brought about by various sociological aspects of modernity. Instead, it may simply be an extended manifestation of Danish and Swedish culture that has been relatively secular for many centuries.

Of course, this raises the key question of all historical speculation: how can we know? How can we know just how religious Danes and Swedes were in the tenth, thirteenth, or sixteenth centuries? How can we be sure

just what religion or spirituality meant to the Danish and Swedish peas-
ants of the past several centuries? The fact is, we can't. Because there were
no sociologists or anthropologists roaming the villages of Denmark and
Sweden way back when, interviewing people about their religious identities, and because the vast majority of Danes and Swedes were illiterate
until the nineteenth century, leaving us little in the way of troves of letters
or diaries attesting to the state of religious beliefs 500 or 700 years ago, we
just can't know for sure.

We do, of course, know a little about religion in the distant past, thousands of years ago, and there is a fair amount of evidence to make at least
some limited characterizations. We know, for instance, that over a thousand years ago the Scandinavians had their own beliefs, rituals, legends,
and practices that could be considered religious.[59] By interpreting archeo-
logical finds (stone carvings, amulets, runic inscriptions, art, graves, etc.),
by analyzing the sagas from Iceland which were written in the eleventh
and twelfth centuries, and by examining the writings of early Christian
missionaries to Scandinavia, we get fairly good glimpses of various aspects of the old religion of the ancient Nordic peoples, which included
the presumed worship of various gods and goddesses (Odin, Thor, Freja,
Tyr, etc.), imaginative accounts of the world's creation and eventual end,
beliefs concerning an afterlife and otherworldly realms, reverence of nature, concern for ancestors, along with various sacrificial rites and seasonal festivals. We also know that several temples were built throughout
Scandinavia, presumably in honor of various Nordic deities—the temple
at Uppsala, Sweden, being one of the most important and ostentatious.
We can also surmise that certain pagan gods had significance in ancient
Nordic culture given the survival of various place names (such as the city
of Odense in Denmark, which literally means "Odin's Sanctuary"), or the
survival of the names of the gods in the Danish/Swedish names for certain days of the week ("Wednesday" in Danish/Swedish is *Onsdag* from
Odin's day, and Thursday is *Torsdag* from Thor's day).

And yet, despite the relative abundance of materials that has been accu-
mulated concerning the ancient religion of Scandinavians, we still cannot
really say just what this religion actually meant to people in their hearts
and minds, nor how truly significant it was in their daily lives. We can
never know just how deeply they "believed" in Odin or Thor, or if that belief was similar to—or maybe markedly different from—the way in which
certain Christians today believe in Jesus, or Muslims in Allah. And we can
never know just how "religious" the ancient assemblies and festivals were

to the participants; perhaps these gatherings were as much social, political, economic, and recreational as they were spiritual. As for ancient amulets and jewelry, such as the Hammers of Thor worn around the necks of the Vikings, it is impossible to know if these hammer necklaces were imbued with deep religious significance, or if they were superstitious talismans, or simply considered fashion.[60] As Richard Fletcher argues, "we know so little" about the pre-Christian religion of ancient Scandinavians that we ultimately remain "in the dark . . . about belief, ritual, organization, [and] the whole functioning of pre-Christian religious life and the degree of loyalty it commanded."[61]

It is certainly possible that ancient Scandinavians were a deeply religious lot, that they strongly believed in and worshipped various pagan deities and saw their will and hand behind every incident, that they strongly believed in life after death, that they regularly engaged in sacred rituals and rites which they interpreted in a strictly spiritual fashion, that their daily lives were steeped in supernatural beliefs and religious practices. But, it is also quite possible that ancient Scandinavians were only mildly religious, that their belief in deities was weak and amorphous, that their pondering of existential matters was minimal, and that the rituals and rites which they engaged in were more to be understood as social, cultural, or traditional endeavors—perhaps superstitious—but not necessarily "religious" in our modern sense.

And then Christianity came to Scandinavia. Christian missionaries initially began trying to convert the Danes in the 800s, but with very little success. The first Christian conversion of major significance was that of King Harald "Bluetooth" Gormson. According to a seemingly reliable account, Harald's conversion from pagan to Christian was caused by a magic trick; a Christian priest by the name of Poppo was somehow able to hold on to a hot iron with his bare hands without sustaining injuries, and King Harald was so impressed by this miracle, that he subsequently converted.[62] This was sometime in the 960s. Harald then "united" Denmark into a single Christian entity—or so the story goes. By 1150, there were some 2,000 churches in Denmark. As for the coming of Christianity to Sweden, missionaries also attempted to set up shop there in the 800s, but with no success. Eventually one Swedish king, Olof Skötkonung, was baptized a Christian in 1008, but this had little effect on the vast majority of Swedes. His attempts to impose Christianity within several regions of the country only bred resistance, and set off a series of pagan uprisings.[63] Swedes were ultimately the last Germanic people to come under the influence of

Christianity, remaining "firmly heathen" until the beginning of the twelfth century.[64] The great pagan temple of Uppsala was eventually destroyed in the early 1100s, and a Christian church was built upon her ruins. By 1164, Sweden had its own archbishop, who oversaw the building of many new churches throughout the country.[65]

In short, Christianity was first introduced to Denmark and Sweden by missionaries in the 800s, but it took hundreds of years to become dominant, and then, in the words of H. R. Ellis Davidson, by the twelfth century, "Christianity was firmly established."[66]

But was it? Really?

What does it mean to say that Christianity was "firmly established"? It seems to me—given my limited reading of Scandinavian history—that what it actually means is that some kings in Denmark and Sweden became Christian, thereby allowing their authority to be linked with the power and wealth of the Catholic Church in Rome. But there is very little evidence indicating that the majority of Danes and Swedes actually became "Christian." Danish historian Palle Lauring argues that, throughout the Middle Ages, there was a definite "gap" between the Church and the townspeople:

> The peasant settlements continued to pursue their own lives . . . relics of ancient heathen cults were still to be observed at spring and harvest festivals and parish life bore the mark of ancient peasant-settlement beliefs that refused to disappear. Rome was far away. On "wakeful nights" the young men and girls of the village went to the church taking their beer-casks with them and danced and made merry. Night life in the church was thus not exactly Christian.[67]

The fact is, Scandinavia's Christianization was not popularly initiated by the people themselves, out of a deep or widespread love of Jesus or comprehension of the Bible, but rather, it was accomplished through the will of chieftains and kings. John Flint explains that Christianity did not spread throughout Scandinavia through "the conversion of individuals in the modern sense of personal, subjective conviction," but rather, "the shift was made by the decision of chieftains."[68] As P.H. Sawyer acknowledges, "In all areas the lead was taken by rulers; there is no evidence that conversion was ever the result of popular demand."[69] And as for this initial Christian conversion undertaken by various kings, deep spirituality or heart-felt religious beliefs don't seem to have been major motivating factors. A lack

of deep theological passion also seems to be the case concerning Scandinavia's embracing of Lutheranism in the 1500s. This was clearly done—
again, not by the popular will of the masses—but by those in power: the
chieftains, the nobility, and the kings. And again, it seems that this major
"religious" transformation—the Protestant Reformation in Denmark and
Sweden—was not so much theologically motivated, but rather, was undertaken because it was politically and economically advantageous.[70] For
instance, prior to the Reformation, the property of the Danish Crown represented one-sixth of the total area of the country, but after breaking from
Rome and confiscating the Catholic Church's lands, the Danish Crown's
land holdings grew to well over half of the total area of the country.[71] In
Sweden, the Lutheran Reformation was the single-handed work of Gusta-
vus Vasa; his break with Rome resulted not only in a marked consolida-
tion and strengthening of political power, but also in a lucrative transfer of
ecclesiastical wealth to the Swedish Crown.[72] To be perfectly clear: it was
the power elites that embraced Protestantism, not the illiterate masses of
Danish and Swedish people themselves. As T. K. Derry suggests, during
the Scandinavian Reformation, "it would be unrealistic to suppose that
Lutheran teaching on justification by faith or even on the nature of the
Sacrament meant very much to the average layman."[73]

What I am attempting to suggest here is the possibility that even though
the nations of Denmark and Sweden became nominally or officially Christian some eight or ten centuries ago, that does not mean that the average or
typical Dane or Swede was very devout or strongly believing back then, or
in subsequent centuries. It is quite possible that for most of the time after
Christianity was nominally introduced into Northern Europe, the actual beliefs of Christianity didn't seep too deeply into the hearts and minds of the
majority of the men and women who lived in rural villages throughout the
countryside. According to B. J. Hovde, "until the late 18th century, the mass
of the Scandinavian population never experienced a true religious awaken-
ing. Christianity had been introduced by compulsion ... [not] from a deeply
felt popular need for religious expression.[74] H. Arnold Barton argues that
well into the late 1700s, the Christianity of most Danes and Swedes wasn't
theologically or biblically grounded, but simply part of a larger worldview:

> In the peasant world the Christian God and Devil coexisted with their
> predecessors, a host of supernatural beings—trolls, elves, watersprites,
> fairies, ghosts—and ultimate concern for salvation through the church
> was balanced by immediate needs to propitiate the spirits of farm, for-

est, and stream. "Wise" old men and women were charged with the cure of man and beast, and undertook a variety of other transactions with the unseen world.[75]

Matters become even more complex when we find that Christianity in previous centuries was often forced upon the common people through a system of government-imposed sanctions and punishments. For instance, we know that many of the early churches built throughout the country in Denmark were financed mainly through land tithes imposed upon the populace by those in power.[76] And in Denmark over the centuries, failure to attend church could result in fines, corporal punishment, and even exile; participation in church rituals such as baptism and confirmation was compulsory for one wanting to attain citizenship.[77] A Danish law in 1683, for instance, required every person to attend Sunday church services.[78] In Sweden, the failure of a man or woman to recite the Lutheran catechism could result in the authorities refusing them permission to marry.[79] Furthermore, receiving Holy Communion at least once a year was mandatory, and those who abstained could not be full citizens.[80] While there is ample evidence that Danes and Swedes in the 1600s and 1700s were certainly a superstitious lot—believing in ghosts, persecuting witches, revering holy springs, seeking the assistance of "cunning folk" for help in removing curses, and assuming that demons caused illness[81]—the extent to which they were true believers in the Christian faith is uncertain. The words of Bryan Wilson are particularly relevant here:

> We simply do not know of the past what proportion of men actively subscribed to, passively acquiesced in, or quietly dissented from the formal belief system institutionalized within the societies in which they lived. Occasionally we know something of those who actively challenged official beliefs, and even in some periods, of those who simply refused to conform; we know of them because officials, whose business it was to ensure that ideological and ritual conformity prevailed, recorded something of the time, energy, and resources they spent in seeking to induce or coerce acceptance of the faith, and in cataloguing the evils of heretics. Of the actual incidence of unbelief, however, we know very little.[82]

That said, by the time we come to the late 1700s and 1800s, there is no question that heartfelt, faithful Christianity was discernably pervasive in various parts of Denmark and Sweden at this time. Many devout, grassroots religious movements blossomed, particularly various popular forms of Pietism. Strong veins of Christian ascetic fundamentalism spread through the countryside, wherein church attendance was routine, Bible study was common, fear of the Lord's wrath was earnest, and earthly pleasures such as gambling, dancing, and drinking alcohol were fiercely condemned as sinful. But I wonder if this period of religious revival and evangelical piety in Scandinavia actually represents what might be conceived of as a fairly contained flare of Christian faith and fervor, bracketed by a relative lack of widespread religious enthusiasm during the many centuries prior, and a distinct decline in religiosity in the century after, taking us to the relatively secular society of today.

Admittedly, the question of just how religious people were in the past—in Scandinavia, or elsewhere—is a vast and complex topic open to lengthy speculation and debate. I'd like to just put it this way: Although I am simplifying greatly here, it is possible that one can imagine two "stories" about the history of religion in Denmark and Sweden.

One story goes like this: Way back when, Danes and Swedes strongly believed in and adhered to a Nordic pagan religion which was rich in spiritual beliefs and sacred rites. Then Christianity arrived, and over the many subsequent centuries Danes and Swedes came to strongly believe in the specific teachings of Christianity, devoutly worshipping God, and piously participating in many Christian rituals. And then, in the twentieth century, thousands of years of widespread religiosity suddenly weakened and withered, apparently almost overnight.

A second story goes like this: Way back when, Danes and Swedes relayed legends of various pagan deities and heroes, and they engaged in seasonal rites and harvest festivals, but were never really all that devout or deeply committed to an ancient Nordic cultural enterprise which we today might characterize as religion. And then came Christianity, which was introduced by kings, generally for political and economic gain. The actual tenets of Christianity were never really believed in all that deeply, and most people participated in various Christian rites and rituals and attended church because to not do so could bring trouble from the authorities. And it was only during a brief period—mostly throughout the late 1700s and 1800s—that a deep and faithful Christianity was ever all that popular, a period in Danish and Swedish history to be best characterized as an exception or anomaly in an otherwise relatively irreligious trajectory.

I don't know which of these stories is more accurate. Perhaps the "true" story of religion and secularity in the Nordic world lies somewhere between these two extremes. But I do know this: ever since sociologists began collecting data on religion in Denmark and Sweden—which, admittedly, wasn't that long ago—the clear pattern has been that of decline, in both belief and participation. And nearly all of the people I interviewed described their grandparents and great-grandparents as much more religious than themselves. Granted, most people often assume that folks were more religious "in the old days," and so there may be a tendency for people to attribute a degree of piety to previous generations that may not necessarily have been so. But I was aware of that possibility, so when people described their grandparents or great-grandparents as more religious than themselves, I pushed them for details and examples. And, much more often than not, I got them. People would describe their grandparents and great-grandparents as praying often, studying their Bibles regularly, attending church on a consistent basis, and simply expressing a more faithful worldview. One fine example is that of Kirsten, who is a 35-year-old professor at the University of Aarhus. She is a nonbeliever, but her grandmother, who lives on a small island off the northern coast of Denmark, is a firm believer. Or perhaps, as Kirsten explained to me, "believer" is too weak a description:

My grandmother—she's not a "believer." She KNOWS that God exists. I mean, the firmness of her belief is so: "Don't do that or God will punish you." Obviously she's a believer, but it's even more—it's more that "I KNOW" . . . I mean, I think there's sort of a whole difference of the firmness or the strength of belief.

Kirsten's insight concerning her grandmother's religiosity is very important, for there is certainly a significant range within the continuum of religious belief. One can perhaps "believe" in God, or, as in the case with Kirsten's grandmother, one can "know" that God exists. The former (to believe) somehow implies a choice or perhaps small leap of faith. The latter (to know) is more akin to a solid orientation of firm understanding based on a perceived incontrovertible truth and reality.

Very few people in Denmark and Sweden today *know* that God exists. This chapter has attempted to explain why.

7

Dorthe, Laura, and Johanne

IF I WERE to give the impression that there are no religious people in Denmark and Sweden today, or that the only religious people are the elderly—such as Kirsten's grandmother—I would be presenting a very false impression indeed. There most certainly are men and women of all ages in Denmark and Sweden who can be readily characterized as religious—or if not religious, then certainly spiritual.[1] These individuals are people who believe in God, or who find solace in religious or spiritual teachings, or who consider Jesus a holy man, or who believe that the Bible is full of sacred wisdom, or who think that it is important to teach their children the basic tenets of Christianity, or who enjoy a nice church service now and then, or who simply see a religious or spiritual orientation to the world as good, sound, and fulfilling. I spoke with many such individuals over the course of my year of research. I would say that about one-fourth of the people that I interviewed were either religious or spiritual, in varying degrees. Of course, most of these people were not Christian fundamentalists of the American variety.[2] That is, most did not believe that the Bible was the actual divine word of God, and very few believed that Jesus was literally born of a virgin and that he actually rose from the dead, or that when we die we will either go to heaven or hell. Unlike strongly religious Americans, the vast majority of religious or spiritual people that I spoke with in Scandinavia did not consider homosexuality a sin, had no objections to abortion, believed in evolution as a more plausible explanation of human origins than the Genesis creation story, and often spoke of God and other basic religious concepts in metaphorical or idiosyncratic terms. And yet, they weren't exactly without any form of religion or spirituality, either.

This chapter is devoted to recognizing the many people in Denmark and Sweden who are definitely not secular, but rather, find religion or spirituality to be a meaningful part of their identities. For example, there was Jesper, a 38-year-old psychiatrist who was raised in northern Jutland. A few months after he was married, he found out that his wife was having an affair. This discovery was devastating, and he found solace by turning to religion.

I was so desperate. I was so far out mentally that I think the only hope I could cling to was to like pray to God, you know, that he would help me through. So often when I felt very depressed and sad and frustrated and in despair, I prayed . . . often I pray when I go to bed. And I still do that because I think—well, I don't really know if God has answered my prayers—but I feel that life has really embraced me quite a lot. So I kind of feel grateful now. It has really been comforting for me to pray . . . I think, for me, God has to do with love and with order, you know. That we should try to treat each other nice, otherwise we would be barbarian. I think for me, God is like order founded on love.

There was also Dag, a 36-year-old Swedish military recruitment officer who lives in southern Sweden. Although he never attends church, thinks that Jesus was just a human being, and believes in evolution, his orientation is not completely secular. He explained to me that the time he spent as a peacekeeper in Bosnia and Lebanon helped to solidify his beliefs in a higher power:

I believe there must be some kind of purpose and meaning and something behind it, and whether you call it a God or something—another force—I don't know, but there must be something because strange things happen . . . I've seen totally unbelievable things—very much kindness. And there must be some kind of—somebody must—if you look at human functioning and nature— there must be some purpose, somebody behind something . . . it is not just a coincidence.

Jarl, who lives in Stockholm, is a member of the Swedish navy. He is 41 years old and serves as a submarine officer. Although he never goes to church and thinks that there is "nothing" after death, he does have his personal beliefs:

I believe in a higher power than myself. I'm not sure if it's God yet, but I do believe in something—that there's a higher power. That there is something which I can leave things to, let go of those things—this higher power takes care of. I'm more of a spiritual person than religious, I would say . . . I have chosen to believe in this higher power. I think that it's connected to some sort of God, and I think you just have to believe that is there, the fact of something I believe in . . . that's my faith. And I think it's very difficult to rationally explain what this faith is. I mean, that's the whole point of it. I mean this is something that is kind of unexplainable in a way, you can't really put it down in a mathematical theory or you can't prove it, but I believe that it is there because I think certain things happen in life which I can't explain, but they do. It could be happy things or sad things, whatever . . . I'm sort of defining my own God and higher power. I wouldn't say I'm all there yet. I'm still exploring.

I also interviewed Annelise, a 47-year-old native of Aarhus who works as a manager at a telecommunications company. When I asked her if her parents were religious, she said that she didn't actually know because they "never, ever discussed religion." Annelise never goes to church, not even at Christmas. She thinks the stories of the Bible are old legends made up by humans, not to be taken literally. So she is quite irreligious—but not completely. For when I asked her about God, this was her reply:

I believe in something bigger than me, but I don't know what it is. . . . Because—there's something. I don't believe in the old man with the big beard, but I believe there's something. I don't think humans are so perfect that we can handle anything and everything. So something must help us. And this something has to be some God or whatever.

There was also Frank, who was my neighbor for the latter half of our stay in Denmark. He is a musician and a member of one of Denmark's most well-known rock bands. He is 46 years old, married to a social worker, and has two children. Religion is definitely not a major part of Frank's life. He almost never goes to church and he only had his kids baptized to please his wife's dying grandmother. However, Frank is not entirely secular. As a young man he experimented with meditation and dabbled in Eastern spirituality, and he still is somewhat spiritual in his outlook today:

It would be fair to say that if I found out that there is no God—there is no guiding principle—I would say I'm not surprised because it could very well be so. But if you ask what I really believe, I think I believe there is a principle . . . God, a force, some say love, some say . . . I think there is a very—"it will eventually go this way". . . . Yeah, I think there is, and I believe there is a way we should behave to not be in conflict with that principle. I prefer to see it as there is something that has set it all in motion and is watching very patiently and maybe guiding us a little bit if we are still enough to listen to or feel the guidance.

•   •   •

Below are extended excerpts from three interviews with three different people I would consider deeply religious or distinctly spiritual: Dorthe, Laura, and Johanne.

I'll begin with two people who were among the most religious that I met while living in Scandinavia: Dorthe and Laura. Dorthe is a strongly

believing Christian who is actually very similar in her religious orientation to a typical American Christian fundamentalist. Laura is a committed
follower of the revived Nordic polytheistic religion *Asatru*. What makes
Dorthe and Laura atypically religious is that they are both quite actively
engaged within their religious communities—they meet regularly with
their co-religionists for prayer or ritual, study or worship—and they also
both proclaim very strong and literal beliefs in supernatural gods, beliefs
which are at the center of their lives and identities. The last person in this
chapter is Johanne. She is not nearly as actively or strongly religious as
Dorthe or Laura. And yet, in her own way, she is still quite spiritual.

Dorthe

Dorthe is 40 years old. She grew up in Odense, Denmark's third largest
city. Although unemployed at the time of the interview, she has a master's
degree in law and usually works as a legal consultant. She is not married
and has no children, but she has a steady boyfriend who lives in Copenhagen. Politically, she supports the right-of-center Conservative party. She
is also a strong supporter of Israel, where she lived for a year in the early
1990s.

Dorthe was raised by believing Christian parents, and although she is
Christian herself, she wears a Jewish Star of David around her neck and
told me that "if you can be a Zionist without being Jewish, I am." I got in
touch with Dorthe through a mutual acquaintance, Jytte, who works as an
administrator at the university. Both Dorthe and Jytte are members of a
small but very committed group of strongly believing Christians that meet
weekly to pray and study the Bible. I interviewed them both—as well as
others from their congregation—but it is Dorthe's interview that I will
quote from here.

Do you consider yourself a religious person?

*Um-m-m . . . yes, I think I would. As a matter of fact, I don't think that
Christianity is a religion in the usual way you consider something a religion.
But if I have to say yes or no, I would say yes.*

And if Christianity is not a religion, what do you consider a religion?

*I consider where people try to reach something . . . reach God, reach a higher
level in life or something like that. I consider it a religion. But in Christianity,
it doesn't—it's not about the human being trying to reach God, it's about God
reaching down to the human being. And that's the difference.*

Okay, I see. And do you believe in God?

Yes, I do.

And could you explain what is the God you believe in?

To me, it's the God I read about in the Bible. The one who created Adam and Eve and who is ruling in history all the way from Adam and Eve and is still ruling.

Okay, and so when you read in the Bible passages where—let's say children are killed by God; for example, there are many stories where—God kills the Egyptian children just because pharaoh, what do you . . . ?

But they were killed because that was the way God was ruling.

So it is a very literal God you believe in?

Yes, I do because I think if I don't believe that he is literal, then I have a problem on other matters. Because then it will be my opinion that is deciding what God is, and I don't think that.

Would you call yourself a Christian fundamentalist or not? How do you feel about that term?

I think a fundamentalist seems very negative, but—because, you see, what people normally define as fundamentalist, it's usually somebody who's very . . . ehh . . . right wing, very . . . extreme in many ways. Also, very often combining religion and politics, and if that's a fundamentalist, then I'm definitely not a fundamentalist. But if it comes to the point where I say that I believe in the God that I can read about in the Bible and I take it literally, well then I am a fundamentalist.

What is your view of Jesus?

He is the Son of God and He is God also.

And do you believe there is a devil?

Yes, I do.

Can you tell me about this devil?

He's the opposite of God.

Does he live somewhere?

You mean down in a black hole or something? [laughter] You know, that's a very tough question to answer actually, because I think he comes in many shapes. You cannot say that he is the troll living out in the mountain or something like that, but he is . . . um-m-m . . . he is something evil in the world— which is—and he's something opposite to God. He's something that's trying to destroy everything that's good.

Now, if God is all powerful, why would he let this devil run around? Why not just be rid of him?

Sweep him away? No—I think he's absolutely powerful enough to sweep him away and sometimes I can wonder in my head and say why does God allow this and that to happen? You see so many evil things happening all around the world . . . people killing each other or natural catastrophes like in New Orleans right now. And you can say, but that's not fair. What did these people do? They didn't do anything . . . why does it happen? And I think—first God is definitely strong enough to sweep the devil away, but he has chosen to do it in another way than we usually think would be natural . . . and as long as we live in this world, we see good and we see bad all the time. But down to the basics, God has already eliminated him because what was the important thing was to destroy what he was standing for, and he was standing for everything that has to do with death. And he did that when Jesus died on the cross and rose from the grave—when he conquered death. And when he conquered death, he also said, "Okay, we'll still—I still want to let this world or this earth where all these people are living, I want it to go on because it was basically . . . it was I created it and it was created good, and I want it to go on so that as many people as possible can get to know me." But he also knows that some day in history, he'll say, okay my life will put a stop to it. And I say, okay, this is it, this is the end. And when I read the Bible, it has some passages about the devil in the New Testament. I think it's—told in pictures, you know what I mean? But it tells about the devil will be thrown in the lake with fire and so on, and I think that's a picture of how God will—at the end he'll say, okay no more and then destroy or take away all that evil, because it has been conquered but it's not taken away yet.

So you believe in heaven and hell?

Um-m-m . . . yes, or maybe I should put it another way, because I believe in this earth and the universe. I believe in a hell, yes, but I cannot say that hell is this or hell is there. I can say that hell is where God is not. And where God is not, it must be evil.

In your belief system, do people who are not—who don't accept Jesus as their personal savior—Jews or Hindus or Buddhists or atheists or agnostics or Jains or whatever, or even Christians that don't accept—will they be in that place where God is not for eternity after they die?

Yes.

I see. And tell me about prayer in your life. You must pray. Can you tell me when you pray, how you pray, and what you pray for?

I pray very often . . . um-m-m . . . I pray very often in the morning when I wake up and just a few sentences . . . "thank you for sleeping very good this night" or "thank you for waking up and it's a beautiful day and I can see the blue sky" or whatever. And I also ask God to be with me on this day. And then sometimes when I—during the day, I pray sometimes if something happens, or

I see somebody in the street and say "oh, poor soul" and I pray . . . or I hear an ambulance and say "oh, please God let this man or woman in the ambulance get well," or . . . but I also have usually every day or almost every day, I have a time where I either sit down or walk in the woods or whatever and I pray for myself, my situation, my family, my friends, my country, what's happening in the world, ask God to be with me, I ask him to let me live according to what he wants from me, ask him to look after me.

Have you ever had an experience that you would call miraculous or holy or something actually happen to you that you might call a religious experience?

A few years ago, I was in a kind of depression with my life. I was—it came out as a kind of scare—I was scared all the time. I couldn't define what it was, but I was scared all the time. And . . . at a point I was so deep down, that I said God please let me die, I don't want to live any more because I think it's just so . . . well, everything is so black around me, and I don't know what to do and, you know, just depressed. And I prayed to God several times to let me die, but I didn't want to take my own life. I don't think I dared to do it, actually, but be- cause I had some urge to live also. But, then one night I was asleep in bed and I had a dream . . . and in that dream I dreamt that I was dying, and it came out very strangely because I didn't, you know, just walk out in front of a bus or something, but I dreamt that I could see Jesus coming down to get me and to take me. And it was not . . . well, it was the shape of a man, but very bright . . . there was light all over. And I felt this happiness . . . and said, yes, yes, I'm going to die, I'm going to be with Jesus . . . yes, that's great. And then I woke up and I was extremely disappointed.

To be awake?

Awake and to see that this was only a dream, it was not the reality. And I was so disappointed and then it came to me almost immediately—"I want you to live," you know, as if God was talking to me—"I want you to live." And for some reason, I was still disappointed but I said, yeah, I think there's a reason to live. I started to feel better in some way, and I also accepted it in some way. And a few years later, I had another experience that told me this is for real, I want you to live. Because there is a lot of snow here, and . . . you know it was very icy on the streets and I was standing over here in the traffic light to catch the bus to go up to Randers, you know the town—where I was working at the time—and then the bus didn't come because of the snow and the ice and so on. And I was standing there with a colleague and we were talking and we were standing in the middle of the street where the buses could run and could stop and pick us up. Then we were standing there, I don't know, almost an hour or so and then nothing happened and then we agreed, okay let's just walk. Then we started walking and we had only been walking a few steps, 50 meters or something like that, then there was a big Coca-Cola truck coming around the corner, then it slipped on the road and all the . . . you know, the boxes with the Coca-Cola bottles fell down where we had been standing. Exactly where we had been standing. You know we got it all in our head . . . if it we hadn't moved, and then again it came to my head . . . okay, Dorthe, God wants you to live. You know what I mean?

Yeah, thank you for sharing. Wow. Amazing. You know, the statistics say that most Danes don't believe in a literal God—they don't believe in heaven or hell or sin or Jesus. So, do you feel like you are in a minority?

Yeah, sure.

Tell me about that—I mean—in other words, most of the people you know are not believing, right?

That's right.

So what's that like being a minority in such a secular country?

In some ways it's sad. I remember once when—I have a degree in journalism, also—I was at the Danish School of Journalism and we had just finished our education and were having a big party and so on, and I was sitting talking to some of my school mates then. And we were talking about religious matters also, and they were asking me a few questions and so on, and then one of them suddenly said to me, "Dorthe, if you really believe that if we don't believe in Jesus then we'll go to hell or be separated from God, that must be very sad for you." And that was exactly my feeling, because it is sad in a way. Because to me this is something good. It has given me so much, and I feel sad inside when I experience that people say, "Yeah, that's fine for you, but I don't believe that." But it's also their choice and I can't force them in any way. I don't want to force them in any way, because they—if they should believe in the same way as I do, I mean I think it's very important that it comes as some kind of revelation to them, not something they choose . . . just, "Okay, I want to believe that." Because it goes so deep down that you cannot just choose it. You have to be convinced in your soul that this is right . . . It more makes me sad, as I said, but . . . in some way . . . it also makes me . . . how can I say it . . . a little proud.

Okay.

I have—it's like, you know—swimming against the flood in some way, and maybe it's because I am who I am.

Do people ever get—do you ever feel that people tease you or don't like you because of your beliefs? Or are people generally tolerant and kind?

Um-m-m . . . usually tolerant. Sometimes, I won't say they tease me or some-thing like that, but still they think, "Oh, she's crazy." [laughter]

Let's switch to this other topic if that is OK. Denmark was the first country to let homosexuals marry—to get legal status as a married couple and certain rights and privileges. Um . . . how do you feel about that and is that something you are glad or proud of, or something you're ashamed and troubled by?

I'm ashamed about it. Because I think it's—still I believe that—when God created man and woman, that was his way he wanted it to be. I mean, two men or two women cannot have children. But a man and a woman can have chil-dren. And . . . uh-h . . . I don't think God ever intended men to live together or women to live together as a married couple. And I also think it's a big shame be-cause when you go to this registered partnership, as we call it—you go through the church to get the blessing from the church also, I think you tell the homosex-ual what you're doing here is just so vile. And you say—when you give them the blessing or the minister is giving them the blessing of the church, he's also saying I bless you because God wants you two to be together. And I think that's a big lie to put into these people's heads. And I think that's actually very shameful, but it's also wrong. Because you tell them something that's wrong. Because the church stands as some authority, and the church says this is fine, this is okay, and this is very good . . . as long as you love each other it's good. But that's not the way it works, as I read the Bible. And therefore I think it's a big—it's a very big shame, and I think it's embarrassing to be known all over the world: "Ah, Denmark the small country with the homosexual marriages." But that doesn't mean that I—I think we should treat homosexuals bad or anything like that, because they are equal when it comes to the way they're treated in society. As citizens—yes. And you cannot say to a man, "Oh, you can't get this job because you're a homo-sexual" or whatever. No, of course not. One of my neighbors is a homosexual or a lesbian, and I like her very much and she's a good neighbor and a good friend. One of my friends in my congregation was married to a man who came out that he was a homosexual and they got a divorce, but he's still a friend of mine. I don't understand the way he is living, I don't understand the way my neighbor is living, because it's so far from my way of thinking. But—and when it comes to my religious beliefs, I think it's wrong, but when it comes to society, you have to treat them as equals. . . . Because I think it's . . . it's so difficult to understand somebody who's homosexual when you're not homosexual yourself. And I know that they would say to me, "Yes, but as much as you love Peter (my boyfriend), I love this man standing next to me or this woman standing next to me." And I cannot get it into my head because it's so far from my way of thinking. Um-

m-m . . . and in some way, I find it . . . disgusting. But that's still an emotional question. And it's difficult because I—still you have to—as well as you have to love your atheist friend, you also love your homosexual friend, and I think Jesus would do the same.

Laura

Although very religious in a way similar to Dorthe, Laura is not a Christian. She is a believer in *Asatru*, the modern revival of the ancient Nordic pagan religion. I got in touch with Laura simply by doing a little research into the various *Asatru* movements in Denmark. I found the website of one particular group, and then sent out an e-mail asking them if any of their members would be interested in doing an interview with me. Laura responded, so we met in my office at the university for the interview. There aren't many active *Asatru* believers in Scandinavia—certainly less than 1 percent of the population—but Laura's religion does have a certain degree of legitimacy in Danish society; her group was recognized by the Danish government as an "official" or "legitimate" religion in 2003.

Laura is 29 years old. She was raised in a small village in Jutland, but now lives in Aarhus, where she works in the sales department of a large company. She lives with her boyfriend, has one child, is university-educated, and in terms of politics, supports the farthest left party in Denmark, *Enhedslisten*. I asked her about her involvement in *Asatru*:

I've only been involved for a couple of years, actually—in this group. I also belonged to something like this for five, six years, something like that before. And I've always been religious. I've been—interpreted that differently throughout my life.

What does that mean to you when you say you've always been religious?

Actually, it means that—I think that people have a center in their brain for religion and that particular sense has always been activated with me—or in me—and I think some people have that sense at some point in their life and some people never really feel it. But I've always felt that in religion I had a contact with something, and I grew up actually as a Christian. My grandmother was very religious in something—charismatic Christianity . . . so I followed her, just coming to church with her and praying. I've always liked this praying and visions and music and celebrating—stuff like that. And then when I was 12, 13, 14, I started to find out that there were too many prohibitions, and also I realized I wasn't monotheistic.

So when you were little did you believe in God and Jesus?

Yes, yes, because it was the only terms I knew. So I thought that religion was Christianity, so—but I also thought that the Danish national church was boring. But the charismatic church was not so boring, because there was music and all these strange things. I always thought—like healing by putting hands on people. Actually, stuff that is kind of lively. So I thought that was the place for me because I was religious, but most of the time I was just religious with myself. I have a connection now with Thor, particularly, but also with some of the other gods. And I have actually the same connections that I used to have with Jesus or God. It was just the names that I knew at the time. And then there were too many things I wasn't allowed to do when I grew up and I couldn't listen to the music I wanted to listen to and I couldn't dress like I wanted to and it was just not me any more. But I kind of believed still. But then I started reading a lot of courses and started in high school and university, all through about 10 years and more—I just became wiser and I learned a lot about religions and the world, and then I was interested in magic and the occult. But nothing that I wanted to follow—just interested and I knew that . . . I had some kind of magic in me . . . I feel that, in a way that I can understand magic. Some people are more magic than other people—or living it out or something like that. I think there is more between the heaven and the earth, as we say in Denmark. Being Scandinavian and being Nordic, quite some years ago now, I found out that maybe that would be a good way—that would be the way for me, and I felt Thor especially, was the god for me and I started practicing the rituals very free, so I go out in my garden and pour some whisky on the ground and that's what I need to do that day. Then three years or so ago I started with fellow Asa believers.

With others?

We're 500 now—and we have a group here in Aarhus with 50 people.

Okay, wow.

So that's quite a few.

Let's talk a little bit about Thor. I mean, now for you is Thor—forgive me if I word this wrong—I'm trying to understand—is Thor to you the same way as Jesus or God is to a believing Christian? For example, Christians will believe that God is really there and he has power and you can pray to him . . . is that how you see Thor, as well? Or is it more just sort of a name you give to something that you can't describe?

The real way is the first way. Of course, we don't pray in the same way. I pray because I've learned that. I don't direct my prayers at Thor, I direct them at all the gods in the whole region—it's all the powers. So I direct some kind of prayers, it's just unsaid thoughts that when I need to gain something I just talk things through it myself—not Thor, but all. Actually, our thoughts don't interfere too much and we don't go to them when we have this celebration at the two solstices and equinox . . . we have this four times a year and some few more, but we have these big celebrations. Then I feel at that point that I get some powers. Actually, for me it changes at every equinox or solstice—I think to myself, do I want to be more in touch with Thor or the sun? I feel like I need power, just power and to work through, and I need to be a little more gentle and take care of myself. But I think Thor is—is when I need to do something in the world or to the world, and the sun or the changing of the seasons is when I need to work with myself. So—but actually, the gods, they're real to me—but I don't ask them for things . . . when I really want something or to thank all the entities, then I have a ceremony.

So they are there?

Yes, but not in a Christian way, because I think the Christian way is so na- ïve. You don't have any responsibility yourself, you don't have to be good. I think you have to be true to yourself, and I think you have to be decent and honest and all these things, but I don't think you have to live by a codex of what you can do and what you can't do. So the gods don't interfere . . . sometimes they do . . . there's a special goddess that when you get married you promise some- thing in her name—the Spring Goddess. I'm not used to talking about her in English. You've been married—I haven't been married—but when you do you promise her something and I think that she would interfere, you would feel it if you didn't live up to that promise. Of course, you promise to stay with this spouse until you don't want anymore, so if you decide together that you don't want any more, it's fine. It's not like in the Christian religion where you have to stay together. It's up to the human . . . to the individual. But I think the other gods wouldn't interfere in the same way, but sometimes I can feel that I need to do something, I need to be strong, and I have Thor just behind me and I have a vision of him, like from out of the corner of my eye. I just feel that he's there . . . also Freja.

I love Freja.

Yeah, I love Freja, too. But I also think that she is also subjected to—very square impressions, you know, they think of "oh, this is so nice"—she is beauti- ful, but there is much more to her—and also the other goddesses. A lot of the other goddesses are not well known and people don't think of them in a special way . . . and to have a group of other Asatru women, we talk about the god- desses and try to talk about their characteristics and what are they and what can they do.

And how do you find out your information? Is it books or just meditating or like—how does one know about the goddesses and who they are and what they do?

There are, of course, the eddas that you probably know, which have some detailed information about . . . but then there's also another way of finding out and that's—it's kind of "shaman traveling." It's practiced by women. I don't do it myself, but I'm very interested and I think maybe I will be able to do it. It's something like transcendental getting contact, so a lot of women—no, not a lot—some few women do this in Denmark now that I know. They just sit out one night by the fire or something and then somehow get some information. Also I know something . . . I don't sit by the fire and feel that I go out of my mind and into another world, but I have my picture. Also dreams that we share have some meaning. We don't have . . . in this group we also don't have a priest, but we have some persons that perform the rituals more than others. I've also performed rituals, so in a way I'm also a priestess, but I've not done it so much, but there are some people who have done it so much. There's this one man . . . and he's a little bit old now, and eccentric but he's also very wise and when he's not drunk, [laughs] he can tell some very interesting stories that he has from his dreams.

Okay, interesting. And when you get together for the solstice—can you describe some of the typical things that happen when you get together? What are some of the things—do you dance, do you sing, do you do rituals?

Actually, it's the same every time. It's not the same—but it's the same—we do it, of course, differently and we eat different foods, but we meet at a cabin so that we can sleep over and have fires and—a scout cabin or something, so we have some nature. We just meet up in the afternoon on a Saturday because people have to be off work and stuff, and then we meet and then at sundown we go—in winter solstice it's 3:00 in the afternoon and the summer solstice we do it around 9:00. Then we go and—the essential thing is that everybody stands in a circle. Sometimes there's a fire in the middle, sometimes we have statues of the gods and also we have jewelry and other stuff that we want to—what's the word, you know we have to ritually . . . ?

Consecrate?

Yes, consecrate . . . I think that would be the word actually, and we put it in the middle also. We start—and we hold each other's hands, maybe we let go and maybe we just keep holding. It's up to the priest or priestess . . . we just call them that—performers—special words for these two people that perform. They have designed this ritual so before we leave the cabin and go, we stand in a circle and say we're going to do like this. Then we stand there and sometimes there's music and singing and sometimes there's something else . . . a special offering or something. At the spring equinox it's often—and then we have a horn—a drinking horn with mead or beer or water . . . especially also in the spring it's a time for water. Then we have this horn and it goes around in a circle from person to person, either one time or twice or three times depending on what the performers have designed. Then we say—we hail to the gods and we can make some wishes and we pray to our ancestors. It's different every time, but also kind of the same. Either you can just hold the horn and do what you want to do in silence . . . if you want to just think . . . or you can swear something out loud or you can just say, "Hail to my ancestors, hail Thor," and just pass it on.

And how about your parents? What do they think of . . . ?

I just have my mother—actually, I've never known my father. I come from a rather strange family. My father was, you know, a gypsy. Not a gypsy like this race, but he was walking with this baby carriage and many knives—and I never knew him because he died when I was 12 or 13, something like that. But my mother, she doesn't like it too much, because—like my grandmother was in this church and my mother never really was, but also she has these Christian sympathies, so when we celebrate Christmas, for instance, I celebrate Christmas with my family. It's nice, but she wants to sing hymns and I don't want to. But also my mother is cool—she's very cool with stuff like leftist politics, so she doesn't like it too much, but she doesn't really have a problem with it. So there's really been no conflict, but we don't talk that much about it. Then one of my sisters, she actually doesn't know that I belong—well, I think she knows, but we don't talk about it because she's very conservative and . . . I like her very much, but we talk about other stuff. Then my other sister, I think she's going to become Asatru like me because she has that in her.

Johanne

Johanne is a novelist and painter who grew up on a quiet island in northwest Jutland. She currently lives in a small village outside of Aarhus. She is 38 years old and married to a Lutheran minister. They have four children. In addition to her painting and creative writing, she is pursuing a Ph.D. in religious studies. We met at the university, became friends, and our families spent a lot of time together throughout the year. By the time we sat down for an interview, Johanne was quite familiar with the research I was doing. She had heard a talk that I had given at the university on my early findings, and we often discussed our ongoing research with one another over lunch. Johanne was somewhat critical of my work; she felt that Danes were actually more religious or spiritual than I was portraying them. I delved into that topic at the beginning of the interview, asking her if she really thought that there was more religion or spirituality among Scandinavians than what I was finding in my interviews.

Yes. I think . . . like you've got a very traditional concept of what religion is—like "this is about Christianity, this is about believing in God, this is about Jesus, this is about . . . " you know, all the traditional terms, and I think in terms of that—you're right. We have been secularized and you won't find many people fitting into that concept of religion anymore.

Okay.

What I'm suggesting is that—well, everything, of course, depends on how you define religion—but if you define religion in new terms, then you may find that our society is extremely religious. Only in new ways you would not have mentioned before . . . only it takes new shapes today.

Could you give me some examples?

Um-m-m . . . linguistic . . . linguistic stuff—when people talk in their everyday life. For instance, it's very common to—when you talk to anyone, even in this place—or like, "This book was kind of looking for me". . . . "It was meant for me to find this book". . . . "There was a meaning that this took place" . . . "I really feel that this happened because I had to learn this." A lot of expressions like that—all the time. "This happened to me because I needed it to happen in this situation." You know, just small expressions all the time, but it's a very delicate matter. And I'm not sure what to look for really. I'm sure there is something there, and it's pretty much—based on my intuition, I think.

If I were to ask you, "Do you believe in God?"—and I'm not going to say what that means, just that question—how would you respond?

It's none of your business. [laughter] *No, I would be polite, but I would kind of want to talk about something else. I would probably try to turn the conversation . . . into the other person's belief.*

And that is because?

Because I don't know what I believe. Because I'm like most Danes . . . shy and I think whatever I say it doesn't cover it, and it's just—and I feel if God needs these discussions because—I don't know what I believe—I don't know. I'm . . . um-m-m . . . it's all around, I can say like anything. One day I would explain myself in terms of this and this, and other days in terms of this and this. And it would be just like conversation. It would be like . . . it's something I cannot express because I haven't even expressed it to myself.

When you hear the word "God," what comes to mind? What does it mean? What meanings do you attach to God?

[long pause] Um-m-m . . . I think just something . . . something higher than me. I mean in a very—just something that happens up there. I think that's about it. Um-m-m . . . something yellow, I think.

Yellow?

Yeah . . . it does have a color, I think. But it's just . . . um-m-m . . . I . . . [long pause] . . . I used to be more . . . [long pause] . . . I don't remember if we ever talked about this, but when I went to the Academy of Art—I'd been there I think. . . .

I know that you went to the Academy of Art here—at the university, right?

Yes, yes, for five years. It was my education, really. And then after one year— every year we had these examinations, like—you had to present whatever you had painted for a year on a big stage and all the students would be there, and the professors and, you would—yeah. So I painted these very religious pictures, in the sense that they were like angels and—I'm using symbols from the Bible. This was before I met Mikkel. And then someone asked me when I was on the stage and I showed all these pictures and they were all about these religious themes, and then she said, "Are you a Christian?" And I was standing in front of all these students and—I didn't answer just right away, and then someone else, I think the professor said, "Do you believe in God?" [laughter] On stage at the Academy of Art when we are talking about this and then I said, "Yes, I believe in God." And it was just something I said—I don't know whether I did believe in God . . . but it was just something like . . . I'd been walking around to several old churches trying, you know . . . I was brought up in a home where you never go to church, never spoke about God, religion, totally . . . and so, I—I tried—I longed for something like everybody else, and so I started going to all these churches trying to find out is there a God, something like that, and then I got quite convinced there is a God and I believe in God. So this was the first time I actually expressed it.

Okay.

And there was just a silence in the room. And I just watched all these faces and . . . I think, at least, I could see that they despised what I said. They thought, "Wow, this is really—how low you can go? I mean this is an Academy of Art . . . what is she doing here? She should be a pastor or something like that. She believes in God." It was like the worst thing you could ever have said.

And—the next two years, I regretted it so much because I think that everybody had this picture of, "Oh she believes in God." And . . . and I felt it to be like a lie. It was—I liked what I said, but I still thought that I had been lying. It's very difficult to explain . . . um-m-m . . . because just expressing that I believe in God, not even telling what I think God is, but just expressing that was too much for me.

And were there—when you said afterward for the next two years there was this, "Oh well, that's Johanne, she believes in God," I mean—would you use the word stigma?

Yes, yes.

I mean, was it a stigma—like it was a negative—or was it like "Oh, it's Johanne, she believes in God, isn't she amazing" . . . ?

No, the first one.

It was a negative?

Yeah . . .

Did students ever come up to you, one on one, and want to pursue it with you and be like—I mean, did you have them come up to you and say—or they just sort of left it alone?

Well, I remember one student that just—she was a very bright student. Her name was Marianne, she was from Norway, and we were actually good friends. And she was like—long, black hair—and I just remember she came to me one day. I had just painted this big painting and everybody said "Wow"—I was good at painting, but they thought that my way—what I painted in this religion dimension was absolutely stupid. But she came and I just remember, she looked at that picture and I had been painting all night and I hadn't had any sleep, and then she said, "When you go to the bathroom, do you ever really, really shit, you know, and get red in your face and just—I want to hear you tell me about being at the bathroom. I want to be able to imagine you just shitting this big shit in the bathroom—or don't you even do that?" It was just like— she didn't mean to be rude or anything, but she was—this religious dimension was so . . . so far from what took place at the Academy of Art, so she just longed for me to be just like . . .

A human?

Yeah. [laughs]

That's quite a story . . .

But I also remember—this is where I'm really superstitious . . . I decided that it wasn't for me to attend the Academy of Arts and I wanted to start studying here and—because everybody told me that you cannot live on painting. So when I started my studies here, I went to a party. We were sitting in a group, all of these new students, and we had to say why we wanted to study religion. And so I originally wanted to study theology and I was actually—I almost started, because I had—when I was 18—no I must have been 20—I had a disease and I was sure it was just like—it was nothing, but I thought I was going to die for a couple of days, and then I took a walk and then I promised whatever was higher than me that IF I survived, I would give my life to God . . . I never told anyone about this. So I survived, so I wanted to study theology. But I changed my mind because I didn't want to read Latin and all that stuff, so I started studying religion instead. So this first night we were supposed to tell each other why we were going to study this. And then I actually said . . . I said it again . . . I said I believe in God. It was like two years after I had said it at the Art Academy. I said it again, but this was another setting. And I felt good about it, because . . . okay, nobody—and then Mikkel came in the room [her current husband]. *And we met each other. It was exactly that night. So you know afterward, in my superstitious thinking, I've been linking the two, and—okay, so once I promised something that I would give my life to God and then the night I expressed it in the right setting I met this man who devoted, in a way, his life to God, although not in a way that I imagined. Yeah, so that is like a magical dimension of expressing things, to me.*

Do you do anything in your life that makes you feel, whatever it is—a sense of the sacred—if you want to feel the "yellow," is there anything you do?

It's there all the time.

All the time?

Yeah, just as a vague presence, I think, yeah. I don't do anything like meditate or go to the church or any—no, no.

Do you ever use the word "sin" in your life? What is the Danish word for sin? Is it meaningless?

No, it's not—um-m-m—well, I—well in a way it is and in a way it's not. In an intellectual sense, it's absolutely meaningless. As an emotion, it's not— you can say it's an emotion. You know—like four years ago, Mikkel and I had been to a party, and had to drive all the way back home . . . and on the way back home Mikkel had to prepare himself for a TV program. There would be a broadcast of a service he was to hold and he had to give a sermon. And he could not write the sermon. It puzzled him what was he going to say, and so we decided to discuss it in the car on our way back home. And he had to give this sermon on a very special text on the Bible—what's the name in English—you know, the persons always in the Bible who the others don't like—they wanted to get taxes from people—so there's this small text and the person, he says, "Oh, praise the Lord, I'm much better than the other people," and the sinner—he's a sinner, this tax collector, he's really the sinner, he says, "Oh Lord, I'm doing everything bad, I'm just so low, so lousy, can do nothing right." And Mikkel had to write something about that. And we were discussing this, and . . . then sitting there in the car just—I got really disillusioned. And then I said to Mikkel, I don't want to discuss this old stupid stuff written 2,000 years ago, this is just like . . . ah-h-h . . . let's do something else. . . . I was just feeling empty. I was feeling that whatever I had like a belief or something, it was nothing. Let's realize that we are civilized persons, this is just an old story, and we hang onto it. And it was just really, really—it felt empty in the car and suddenly I think the kids must have fallen asleep or something like that, and we were just driving on the road and nobody said anything, and Mikkel, I think he felt empty in a very special way, too. "Okay, let's leave it, it's nothing." Whatever we tried to do with this story, it's—and then something very strange happened. Suddenly— I'm sorry, I know this must sound absolutely idiotic to you, but . . .

No, no.

Then suddenly I just started to speak without intending to. And then I got like . . . I think I called it to myself like a revelation. I've never tried anything like that before. But finding that in the car on the main road, I just started to speak and I was seeing stuff. I saw like a corpse passing by and I saw the faculty of theology burning and disappearing into the sky. I saw . . . I mean it's not like I was out of my mind or anything. It was . . .

You had these images?

Yes, something like that, and I kept talking in a very fluent way, very . . . like I was not talking myself. And then I saw Martin Luther and his whole—what you call it, the Reformation and—and then I started talking about this Reformation, that this was not enough. We had to get back to something even more fundamental than just . . . yeah, just making a revolution against the Catholic church and we had to get back into even more fundamental—and then—it's all that we know in the Bible, everything is just bullshit, everything is bullshit. I didn't say bullshit, but I said it in a very poetic language, and then suddenly I just saw all these corpses in the sky and—in a very split second, it was like everything stopped and I just saw just a glimpse of something. And then I said to Mikkel, and all this is just nothing—the real stuff is something completely different. So I think—and I was crying all the time and Mikkel said it was like I was in a trance, and he just kept driving and it was very sad and very, very strange. And then I just stopped and we parked . . . and we stopped near to a castle and we sat down there and Mikkel was like—what was this? I never tried anything like it—and I was like, nor did I. It was very, very, very strange.

Okay . . .

And also, did I ever tell you about what happened . . . well, one more story like that. This is a very strange one. This is one I'm not laughing at. This is not about having a revelation or something divine. This happened when Eva was I think two years old. She went to the preschool and they said to me, "Eva has to bring her jacket tomorrow because we're going to Aarhus by train to see Santa." It was in December. Okay. So I went back home and then I had this feeling, I don't want Eva to go and see Santa tomorrow. I was fearful. I was afraid of something. I didn't understand because I'm not like—I'm usually not afraid of things concerning my kids. I'm not like that. So I said to Mikkel, "It's so strange, I don't want Eva to go to Aarhus." I mean I know they'd take care of her and they've been there several times and it's just like everyday, but I got this strange feeling. He thought I was way out of line. But I kept telling him, and we took a bath at night and I said it's so strange, I think I can see Eva lying on the tracks in front of the train. And Mikkel said, "You are turning into something—I don't know—you're losing it." But I told him what I saw. And so the next day . . . Mikkel said, "Of course she's going to see Santa, stop it." So the next day I drove her to the kindergarten and she brought her jacket and stuff, and then I had to say good-bye to her, and I was like—I really had to stop myself now because I'm so scared—I saw her lying on the track. But I said good-bye and twice when I got—on my way back home from the kindergarten I stopped the car and said I had to go and get her. I did not. So I stayed at home and I was writing and working and all the time I was waiting for the phone to ring and tell me something was wrong. The phone never rang, okay. Once we got to 2:00 o'clock in the afternoon, I was—"Ah, how stupid of you," and this was nothing. And then Mikkel had to go and get the kids, and then when he got back home he said, "There's something I've got to tell you." So, the grown-up said to Mikkel when he got there, "Please come to the office, we have to talk to you about something, something very, very—well, upsetting, happened today. Once we got to Aarhus in the train, we had about 8 or 10 kids and there were three grown-ups and they helped them all to get off the train and then suddenly Eva was missing. And we didn't understand because we did it all the time and then one of us started screaming and then Eva was lying on the track. Very silent, just like that, with her coat. We didn't understand, but the train was not in motion, so we got the train to stop motion and then we got her off." So two of the grown-ups were crying like–God—because they never experienced this before. They were so upset but nothing happened. So Mikkel said to them, "Oh my God, Johanne told me. She told me last night that she sees Eva exactly how you express it now." And then they just—"Please tell us next time if she ever sees anything like that again. Please tell us." And then— well, I was feeling very strange afterward because I don't believe in stuff like that . . . but the point is—and I even told Mikkel this was—I was reassured that I really had had this experience because I told Mikkel.

• • •

What struck me about both Dorthe and Johanne is that their deeply held religious or spiritual beliefs definitely made them feel somewhat like "outsiders" at times. To believe firmly in God, for example, set them apart from their peers. Johanne talked about how when she revealed her belief in God while an art student, this revelation caused her fellow students to think she was rather odd and somewhat strange, almost slightly abnormal or even inhuman—recall the one woman who asked Johanne if she ever had a significant bowel movement! Dorthe similarly spoke about her discussions at parties with people who do not share her strong religious beliefs and that—although they may not tease her—they do regard her as perhaps a little bizarre. She characterized her religious identity in Denmark as something that sets her apart from the mainstream; she sometimes feels as if she were—in her own words— "swimming against the flood." In 1968, sociologist Peter Berger predicted that as the modern world became more secular, religious believers would find themselves more and more alienated; he said that by the twenty-first century, "religious believers are likely to be found only in small sects, huddled together to resist a worldwide secular culture."[3] This "worldwide secular culture" that Berger predicted 40 years ago has certainly not materialized, of course. If anything, the opposite of Berger's prediction is extant today: in most countries religious people dominate, and it is the nonbelievers, the secularists, the atheists, and the agnostics who are most likely to be found in small groups, huddled together, trying to resist a ubiquitous religious fervor from which they feel alienated and slightly threatened by. But in modern Scandinavia, Berger's characterization of the fate of religious believers isn't too far off the mark. Individuals like Dorthe are indeed a distinct minority, almost akin to a distinct counter-culture, and she and her comrades in faith do gather weekly in their small groups to pray to God, study the Bible, and also experience a sense of solidarity that is more and more necessary as the wider culture around them grows increasingly indifferent to their religious belief and practice.

A second observation concerns Johanne's personal spirituality. It was quite idiosyncratic. On the one hand, she seldom goes to church—maybe three or four times a year, she told me—even though she is married to the village pastor. She does believe in God, but is at quite a loss to explain much about that God; she has few words to describe God (one of them being "yellow"). In other words, her "belief" is certainly there. It is sincere and deep. But what is it, exactly? That is very difficult for her to express. She has also had some dramatic spiritual or nonrational experiences, such as the "trance" she got into while driving with her husband—full of visions and religious insights—and the powerful premonition she had of the danger her daughter would face one day at the train station. In short, Johanne's religious or spiritual identity is quite present and important, but more than anything else, it is personal and amorphous. Her religious identity would not fit neatly into a box. It is hard to label. The point here is that it is essential for us to recognize that for many people, their personal religion is just that, something not easily defined, not readily explicable, not standard or typical, but there, just the same.

Finally, a word about Laura, the neo-pagan. While her group is very small, it is present and growing. They meet, they celebrate, and they worship the gods and goddesses of old. Who could have foreseen this revitalization of *Asatru*? Would anyone living back in the 1800s have predicted that, in the early twenty-first century, pagan religion would be recognized as legitimate by the government of Denmark? The point here is simply to assert that one can never predict or foresee what lies ahead when it comes to humans and religion. The trajectory is always a mystery, if not a downright surprise.

Religion and spirituality, though weak, are certainly still alive in Denmark and Sweden.[4] There's no doubt about it. The individuals profiled in this chapter are of course atypical, but their existence is evidence that one would be mistaken to characterize modern Scandinavia as a totally or wholly secular culture.

8

Cultural Religion

> A traditional religion is not necessarily one fraught with deep theological conviction for its followers, nor one followed with devout piety. It is rather the religion which in the final analysis lies at the deepest level of consciousness and cultural identity.
>
> —Hans Raun Iversen[1]

WHAT DOES IT mean to be Christian? Many people might suggest that a Christian is someone who believes that Jesus is the Son of God and also simultaneously God, and that about 2,000 years ago he was crucified for the sins of humanity but was subsequently resurrected. They might go on to suggest that if we believe in him we will spend eternity with God in heaven after we die, as is all more or less explained in the book that came from God, the Bible. This account of Christian identity is all well and good. But during my year in Scandinavia, I came face to face with a very different version of what it means to be a Christian. Most Danes and Swedes will say that yes, they are Christian. But few will say that they believe in the traditional tenets of the Christian faith as stated above. After all, only about 30 percent of Danes and Swedes believe that Jesus was simultaneously both man and God, only about 30 percent of Danes and Swedes believe in life after death, and less than 10 percent of Danes and Swedes believe that the Bible is the actual word of God.[2] And yet at the same time, the vast majority—around 80 percent of Danes and Swedes—are dues- or tax-paying members of their national church. Whereas Grace Davie has described many contemporary Europeans as being *implicitly* religious in that they may be believers without actively belonging to a church or congregation,[3] the situation is just the opposite in Scandinavia where, in the words of Ole Riis, the majority of men and women actually "belong without believing."[4]

For contemporary Danes and Swedes, to be Christian is simply not limited or confined to the acceptance of a narrow set of supernatural beliefs. Being Christian is linked to their culture, it is part of their collective heritage, and it is manifested in their childhood experiences and family traditions. Being Christian is a conduit for significant rites of passage: birth, confirmation, marriage, and death. It has to do with holidays, songs, stories, and food. It is perhaps akin to what Daniele Hervieu-Leger refers to as a "chain of memory."[5] As for the redeeming blood of Jesus, or the Virgin Birth, or heaven and hell, or "justification by faith," or the Book of Revelation—these things are marginal if not downright absent from their subjective experience of what it means to be Christian.

Talking to Danes and Swedes about their beliefs, worldviews, and identities actually reminded me a lot of Jews. I grew up in a Jewish family and was raised among Jews—none of whom actually believed in the literal teachings of the Jewish religion. All my relatives were Jewish, nearly all of my parents' friends were Jewish, many of my friends at school were Jewish, I attended years of Jewish summer camp, as well as years of Hebrew school—and yet I rarely (if ever?) came to know a single Jew throughout all of these experiences who sincerely believed that Moses actually received the Ten Commandments from God on Mount Sinai. In Hebrew school we learned about the story of Abraham nearly killing his son as a sacrifice to God. But no one—not even the teachers—actually believed it ever happened. At Passover every year, my extended family—aunts, uncles, nieces, nephews, cousins, grand-parents, friends—gathers around the Seder table to celebrate the story of how God delivered the Jewish people from bondage in Egypt. We recite the biblical story and say the prayers that go along with it, and yet no one actually believes the darn thing. This Passover ritual is essentially about getting together with family, eating good food, and participating in a Jewish cultural tradition. But it isn't about worshipping God—not at all. I should also mention that while in graduate school I spent two years doing qualitative research among a Jewish community in Oregon;[6] of the many Jews that I observed and interviewed during that time, only a handful were religious believers. The majority were nonbelievers. Active in their Jewish community and in their synagogue? Sure. But nonbelievers all the same. And as for the year that I lived in Israel, most of the people that I met there, particularly the kibbutzniks, were as decidedly secular as the Jews of Los Angeles and Oregon. Granted, a small minority of Jews in the world are deeply devout and sincere believers in God and the literal words of the Torah (the first five books of what Christians call the "Old Testament"). But they are a distinct minority, comprising only about 6 percent of American Jews and 14 percent of Israeli Jews.[7]

While living among Scandinavians, I was struck by the fact that Danes and Swedes were also, like many Jews, taught about the biblical stories as children, they learned religious songs and hymns, celebrated various religious holidays with their families, and they nearly all had Christian socialization experiences, most commonly in the form of confirmation classes. And yet, while the vast majority of Danes and Swedes that I interviewed had generally fond feelings about these ostensibly religious experiences, like the Jews I grew up with, hardly any of them believed in the basic theological content.

Scandinavians and Jews

A strong case could thus be made that Christians in Scandinavia are actually a lot like contemporary Jews, at least when it comes to contemporary religious identity. In fact, they are about as similar as any two religious communities can be. Consider the following:

- Concerning monthly church attendance rates, 12 percent of Danes and 9 percent of Swedes attend church at least once a month.[8] This is strikingly similar to Jews; 13 percent of Israeli Jews and 11 percent of American Jews attend synagogue at least once a month.[9]
- Compared to other Christian nations in the world, Denmark and Sweden have among the lowest rates of belief in God.[10] Similarly, when compared to other religious groups in the United States, Jews have among the lowest rates of belief in God.[11]
- As the data throughout this book have illustrated, Danes and Swedes score among the lowest in all international surveys of religiosity; a similar phenomenon is seen when it comes to Jews, for as Benjamin Beit-Hallahmi asserts, "modern Jews are highly secularized, scoring low on every measure of religious belief and religious participation in every known study."[12]
- Scandinavians are among the most approving/accepting peoples in the world when it comes to premarital sex.[13] Similarly, Jews are the most approving/accepting of premarital sex of any religious group in the United States.[14]
- Danes and Swedes are world leaders in supporting abortion rights.[15] Similarly, Jews are the most supportive of abortion rights of any religious group in the United States.[16]

- Danes and Swedes are world leaders when it comes to accepting/approving homosexuality.[17] And yet again, of all religious groups in the United States, Jews are far and away the most accepting/approving of homosexuality.[18]
- When it comes to politics, Danes and Swedes are among the most economically left-leaning peoples in the democratic world, favoring strong welfare policies, supporting heavily progressive taxation, supporting unions, etc. Similarly, of all religious groups in the United States, Jews are consistently the most left-leaning; Jews comprise the religious group in the United States that is most strongly supportive of the Democratic party.[19]
- If there is one common ethos that typifies Scandinavian culture, it is a commitment to social equality.[20] And in a recent poll of American Jews, when asked what was the most important aspect of their Jewish identity, the number one answer—with 54 percent of Jews expressing this sentiment—was "a commitment to social equality." As for "religious observance," only 15 percent of Jews polled cited this as the central aspect of their Jewish identity.[21]

But on top of these interesting similarities, the most essential and important similarity between Scandinavian Christians and contemporary Jews is this: *both maintain a definite sense of belonging to a given historical religious tradition, and both engage in various practices and celebratory rituals of their given religion, and yet among both peoples, actual belief in the literal teachings of their given religion is extremely low.* Danes and Swedes see themselves as Christian, and Jews see themselves as Jewish, yet in neither case is God or deep religious faith a central or even necessary component of these identities. The fact is, when we look at religion in the lives of most Danes, Swedes, and Jews, what we are really looking at is what could be more accurately or appropriately called *cultural religion*, a concept first clearly put forth (and only a few years ago!) by the American sociologist of religion, N. J. Demerath.[22]

Cultural Religion

First we must define "religion," which is a notoriously difficult task.[23] Countless definitions of religion have been proposed by social scientists over the years (I will spare you a listing), but suffice it to say that the definitional vat is so sticky, that some recent sociologists of religion have chosen to opt out altogether, declining to offer one![24] Be that as it may, here is my attempt at a definition: Religion refers to concepts, rituals, experiences, and institutions that humans construct based upon their belief in the supernatural, otherworldly, or spiritual. For me, it is the *supernatural* element that is key. I agree with Stark and Bainbridge that "a religion lacking supernatural assumptions is no religion at all."[25] The key difference between people who worship Jesus and those who worship Jimi Hendrix, or between people who regularly gather in groups to fervently sing songs praising their favorite soccer team and those who regularly gather in groups to fervently sing songs praising God, or between people who earnestly celebrate Thanksgiving and those who earnestly celebrate Easter— ultimately boils down to belief in a supernatural, otherworldly, or spiritual element. After all, when music fans refer to Jimi Hendrix as "God," they certainly don't mean it in the same way that Southern Baptist missionaries refer to Jesus as "Lord." The former is a metaphoric cliché, the latter is a sincere expression of truthful belief in a supernatural being. While hardcore soccer fans may think that their favorite players are the greatest beings on the planet, they don't sincerely believe that they fell to the earth from heaven or that their mothers were virgins. OK, you get the point. For something to be "religious," there must be an element of supernatural, otherworldly, or spiritual belief.

Now let's get back to Scandinavians and Jews. Given our definition of religion developed above, what then do we make of, say, a typical Danish wedding? How is it to be characterized or understood? On the face of it, we see that the bride and groom are united under the auspices of a pastor, within the hallowed walls of an old church, amidst invocations of God and Jesus. And yet even some minimal investigating will reveal that hardly anyone actually believes in a literal God or that Jesus is up in heaven blessing their union—not the bride nor the groom, not the majority of those in attendance, and maybe not even the pastor herself (in Denmark, it is possible to be both and a pastor and an atheist).[26] Or what do we make of a Jewish teenager's bar mitzvah in California? It takes place in the presumably sacred walls of a fine synagogue, ancient prayers are recited in which God is invoked and thanked, traditional Jewish head coverings are donned, the Bible is read, and yet hardly anyone in attendance—including the Jewish teenager and his parents, and probably even the rabbi—sincerely believes in the literal content of what is being said, recited, and sung; in fact, only 10 percent of American Jews believe that the Bible is the actual word of God.[27]

So what is going on, then? What is going on in these two examples—and countless more that can be readily invoked—is something that is actually quite common the world over: people participating in something ostensibly religious, without actually believing its supernatural elements.

Millions of people eat or refuse to eat certain foods, they sing songs or recite prayers, fast or feast, baptize or circumcise their children, wear amulets or head coverings, make markings or imprints on their bodies, celebrate holidays, dance or assemble, and engage in a plethora of ceremonies, rites, rituals, and traditions—not because of any deep belief in the otherworldly, or to please or placate God, or to ensure their immortality—but because it feels special, or because it gives their lives a sense of rhythm and poignancy, or because it brings families together, or because it makes them feel like they are part of something grand and auspicious, or because it is fun, or because it somehow intangibly connects them with previous and future generations, or because they like the music, or because it symbolically declares allegiance to a group or nation, or because it enriches communal bonds, or simply because of cultural inertia, in other words, "that's just what we do."

In short, there are countless reasons why people are part of a religious tradition other than—and sometimes even *in spite of*—the supernatural elements there within. Again, we're talking cultural religion. Not "civil religion,"[28] which is something qualitatively different, but cultural religion. And it is certainly ubiquitous; N. J. Demerath suggests that "in many societies around the world—and perhaps especially in Europe—cultural religion may represent the single largest category of religious orientation."[29]

Definition and Core Components

My definition of cultural religion—which is admittedly steeped in my experiences among Jews and my research among Scandinavians—is as follows: *cultural religion is the phenomenon of people identifying with historically religious traditions, and engaging in ostensibly religious practices, without truly believing in the supernatural content thereof.* Cultural religion can thus be said to contain two main elements or components: the first is a matter of people's self or group identification, and the second is in the realm of nominally religious activities people engage in, such as various practices, rituals, or ceremonies.

Let's briefly look at the first, *identification.*

In the months following the terrorist attacks of September 11, 2001, I was curious how the Muslims in my community of Claremont, California, were faring. Were they the victims of any verbal attacks? Were they experiencing a hostile work environment? How were their neighbors treating them? To get answers to these questions, I decided to do some interviews. I didn't have any close Muslim acquaintances, so I started asking around. It turned out that, unbeknownst to me, one of the administrators at my college was Muslim (she was originally from Malaysia). I then found a student to interview (he was on exchange from Saudi Arabia), and I also interviewed a couple that my father knew, and who happened to live fairly close to me (they were from Turkey). Finally, I called up an imam at a nearby mosque and interviewed him (he was from Pakistan). So my sample size was five. Not a grand sample, I admit, nor was it randomly generated. Nonetheless, the interviews were quite fascinating. The good news was that not one of the five had experienced much in the way of hostility from their fellow Americans. But what was really interesting to me was this: out of the five Muslims that I interviewed, four of them (all but the imam) were nonbelievers. That is, *they identified as Muslims, but rejected the supernatural beliefs of Islam.* The administrator who grew up in Malaysia, Beth, described her identity this way:

I was raised as a Muslim, but even so, all throughout my childhood there was a strong realization that I'm not, you know, like all the other Muslims that I grew up with, like my relatives, and so on. We celebrated the Muslim holidays, we did some of the things that one would do as a Muslim, but only in the most external ways. We fasted during the fasting month, we did Ramadan, we did what we call Hari Raya, which is celebrating the Eid, with my relatives. And we prepared the food during the month and all that during Ramadan—we'd get up in the middle of the night to eat so that we could fast during the day. Did all that. I grew up doing all that stuff, but not with any sense of the religious implications of any of these things—didn't at all get a sense of—you know— "virtuousness." Just joining in with what the family is doing and what our relatives are doing. Not feeling close to God or anything like that. A social, cultural experience.

The three other Muslims expressed their identity in a remarkably similar fashion: they were Muslim because of where they came from, the identities of their parents and grandparents, the traditions that they grew up with, the culture they knew best, and so on. And yet, despite identifying as Muslims, they did not accept any of the spiritual or otherworldly claims of the Islamic faith. As for Scandinavians, as I mentioned in the Introduction to this book, nearly all of the people that I interviewed in Denmark and Sweden answered "yes" when I asked them if they were a Christian. And yet, when I then asked them what that meant to them, the answers were almost never theologically based.

Here are some typical responses to the question "What does being Christian mean to you?":

From Annelise, a 47-year-old manager at a telecommunications company:

Being an okay person, being nice to people, not hurting anyone, helping when help is needed, that sort of thing. But nothing spectacular, you know. Just being nice.

It doesn't mean to you that "I believe in Jesus as my—"

No, it doesn't.

From Dag, a 36-year-old career coach:

It means that you have the values to believe in people.

Do you think a person can be a Christian and not believe in God?

Yeah. I think you can be Christian without believing in God. You believe in the values and the ideals, but you don't necessarily believe there is a God.

From Anika, a 36-year-old stay-at-home mom:

Being Christian means to look out for the poor and the challenged in our society . . . to feel compassion, to be able to think of other people than yourself . . . to look out for the weak, the poor . . . to not discriminate . . . but to think that everybody has the same value.

From Jakob, a 35-year-old preschool teacher:

Do you believe in God?

No, I never think I believe in God, no.

Would you call yourself an atheist?

I think perhaps I'm an atheist, but I haven't really given that a lot of thought. But I don't believe in God.

Would you call yourself a Christian?

Yeah, I think so.

And what does that mean?

I think it's because people in Denmark are Christians. And it's a term you use when you speak with people from other countries. So people often ask you—are you religious or what's your religion?—then it's easy to say I'm Christian.

From Ellen, a 29-year-old elementary school teacher:

I think of myself as a Christian. I think it means that I respect the church and if I ever get married I want to definitely get married in the church.

From Tyge, a 62-year-old retired shop steward:

I like the traditions. I don't believe in God, but I like the traditions. I would say I'm a Christian. It means I like the traditions. I just like that we have a church.

Do you go to church at Christmas time?

Sometimes. Very seldom.

What do you do at Christmas?

Like old things—dancing around the Christmas tree . . . a good, healthy meal. [laughter]

From Maren, a 43-year-old manager at a computer company:

It means to me that you have some basic attitudes about the way you see other people—the way I raise my children. How should I put it? Eh-h-h . . . I think that if you see—I look at Christian people as loving people. Love is one of the things in the Christian faith or—that I see strongly and that's important to me. Also, how I treat other people and especially in these days when you hear a lot about immigrants and so on. I think that my Christianity comes out a bit and says that's wrong to treat other people like that. So if you understand it, it's like the basic attitude in me is Christian.

From Hedda, a 66-year-old retired laboratory technician:

I'm a Christian, yes, in some way. I believe in doing good things to other people and being a kind person.

Do you believe in God?

No.

From Mona, a 30-year-old physical therapist:

I am Christian because I grew up in a Christian society. Our way of thinking is Christian, so I think—how you act to people. It's the way.

From Hans, a 50-year-old elementary school teacher:

Mostly I would say I'm a cultural Christian, more than deeply religious. But I think the values from Christianity—I think it's very good. For me also, to practice being a normal human being toward others. So in that sense, yes I'm a Christian . . . if I look at someone who is deeply religious—every week he goes to church, every day he is praying to God and so on—I'm not that. But Christianity has brought us—in our society, in our culture—I think it's very good because it gives me . . . something to refer to—how to behave as a good person, perhaps. You have something to refer to . . . an "ethical frame"—is that it? Yeah. So that's mostly what I mean about cultural Christian.

From my interview with Helle, a 44-year-old secretary:

Would you call yourself a Christian?

Uh-huh. Yes.

What does that mean to you?

Well, there's a very good word that's been described by our Ministry of Church Affairs—he says a lot of the Danish people are cultural Christians. I don't know if you've heard.

Do you agree with him?

Yes.

Would you say you are more of a cultural Christian?

Yes, very much . . . it means to acknowledge that our culture is based on Christian values and to acknowledge my upbringing, and to acknowledge the role of the church in society, I think.

Those are just some selected answers from ten Scandinavians. Multiply them by a factor of 10 and you'll get a good idea of the volume of responses that I got along these very same lines. Sure, there were a handful of people who cited the Bible, God, and Jesus as central to what it means to be a Christian. And there were a handful of others who said that they weren't Christian and didn't accept that designation, because they had quit the church and considered themselves atheists or humanists. But the vast majority of Danes and Swedes definitely identified as Christian—yet it was an identification that was generally devoid of the key religious beliefs of the Christian faith.

At a minimum, then, cultural religion manifests itself at a basic level of personal or group identification with a given religion—without belief in its paranormal ingredients. Millions of people, from Christians in Scandinavia to Jews in California to Muslims raised in Malaysia, associate themselves with—and label themselves as being a member of—a traditional religious group, but their identification is largely secular or cultural in nature, having to do with a variety of reasons, experiences, concepts, or values that aren't steeped in a personal commitment (or even familiarity!) with supernatural claims.

A second major component of cultural religion, and perhaps the most salient and significant, entails the variety of activities that people actually engage in, such as rituals, holidays, ceremonies, and life-cycle rites of passage—without faith or belief. Examples of this facet of cultural religion are abundant in Scandinavia. For instance, a recent poll in Denmark asked men and woman what was the most important thing for them when it came to the holiday of Easter; 58 percent said spending time with family, 41 percent said getting time off work, 31 percent said the arrival of spring and end of winter, while only 11 percent said the death and resurrection of Jesus.[30]

Consider baptism.

The vast majority of Danes and Swedes baptize their babies. Ostensibly, this is a very religious or holy ceremony. It takes place within the sacred walls of the church, the presiding pastor reads biblical passages, Christian prayers are said, and God and Jesus are invoked. And the historical or traditional reason for baptizing babies—at least according to Martin Luther's Small Catechism of 1529—is as follows: "Baptism effects forgiveness of sins, delivers from death and the devil, and grants eternal salvation to all who believe, as the Word and promise of God declare."[31] OK, well, so that is what Martin Luther asserted back in the sixteenth century. But what about the Nordic Lutherans of today? There is no question that the baptizing of babies is one of the most important, lovely, and special ceremonies that Danes and Swedes engage in. There is no question that it is emotionally significant, and that it is rife with meaning for the parents, grandparents, and relatives of the baptized baby. But it is meaning that is familial, or cultural, or traditional in nature. Not supernatural. As Palm and Trost explain concerning baptism in Sweden, "For most parents . . . the religious aspect is of minor importance, and the church ceremony is just part of the ritual. They use the christening ceremony as an excuse to have a party to introduce their baby to their relatives and friends."[32] The undeniable fact is, almost everyone who witnesses, enjoys, and engages in the baptizing of babies in Denmark and Sweden doesn't actually believe in the literal existence of sin or the devil, the deliverance from death, or eternal salvation as promised by God. I doubt if even most Danish or Swedish pastors truly believe it.

Consider Laurits, a 50-year-old division head of the Danish Dairy Board, who had this to share concerning his daughter's baptism:

At the time I was not so convinced that there was a God. We had a lot of discussion with a priest at the time, a very good priest. And he said, well, I'll put it this way: "Maybe you shouldn't take the concept of God so literally, so seriously." He said you should think of it this way: that there's good things and there's bad things, and the ceremony of baptism is one that you want to give this kid to get the good things. I think that's a good way of putting it. Yes, and it's important sometimes to make a certain stop in life and say that this is a milestone and you are celebrating this and that. I think afterwards I had a lot of discussions with people about exactly that—and I always used that argument. I think it's a very good way of putting it.

From Jakob, the 35-year-old preschool teacher quoted earlier, when I asked him why he baptized his son:

I think cultural reasons. And then, he can make his own choice. It's like, I think: I'm a member of the church. I think it's just a tradition that's his also.

Did it have anything to do with God or Jesus?

No.

From Maja, a 28-year-old stay-at-home mom:

We just had our daughter baptized. That's out of tradition. It doesn't really mean that much to me—having her baptized. It's more my boyfriend's wish . . . it's okay with me, it's fine, but it's not that important . . . I think in his family it's a bigger deal, I guess.

From Lisa, a 39-year-old legislative tax consultant, as to the reason why she baptized her children:

Because I think it's more like a nice tradition . . . and I think it's more like a cultural thing than a religious thing, I think. It's a tradition.

Do you believe in God?

No, I don't believe in God in that way, but I think I believe in some sort of power or something that's—what do you say?—a "destiny" or something. I wouldn't say that I believe in God.

What do you say to your children when they ask about God?

I tell them that's bull. [laughter]

From Nea, a 40-year-old manager at a television station:

Did you have your daughter baptized?

Yes.

Why?

Because that's just the way it should be. [laughter]

Laurits, Jakob, Maja, Lisa, Nea—their words are quite typical of what I found in my year's worth of interviewing so many others. The point is clear: the majority of Danes and Swedes participate in the ostensibly and historically religious ritual of baptism for a variety of reasons—from pleasing in-laws, to enjoying it as a nice tradition. But very rarely do they celebrate it with any beliefs about God swelling in their hearts, or deep otherworldly concerns. Baptism as it is practiced in Denmark and Sweden is an example of cultural religion, par excellence.

And the same can be said for so many additional practices in Scandinavian Lutheran society, including the tradition of getting married in a church, the celebrating of Christmas and Easter, having a church funeral, and going through confirmation in one's early teens. At this point, for me to start quoting all the men and women who explained to me their various reasons for engaging in these rituals, holidays, ceremonies, and life-cycle rites of passage would simply be redundant. And I am sure you already can guess what their answers would be: they engage in these things for a variety of reasons *other than* a deep belief in God, Jesus, heaven, hell, or the future of their souls. In fact, many people that I interviewed engaged in these holidays, rituals, and traditions not in a state of mere indifference to such supernatural beliefs, *but even while in direct disagreement* with them. And again, this is also the case for most contemporary Jews.

Some Additional Elements of Cultural Religion

Although personal or group identification and participation in various rituals, holidays, and life-cycle ceremonies constitute two key elements of cultural religion, there are certainly others that deserve to be briefly mentioned.

First, there is the matter of a culturally religious orientation to religious edifices, namely churches. For the culturally religious in Scandinavia, churches are seen as generally good things. It is nice to see them. It feels nice, when driving along a country road at night, to pass by an old stone church, lit up, kindly glowing on the hillside. For most Danes and Swedes, the church is additionally a symbol of their national identity, or in the words of Franklin Scott, the churches in Scandinavia are "community monuments."[33] I don't know how it is in Sweden, but certainly in Denmark many people view the church as a structural emblem of the country itself: its history, heritage, people, and ethos. That said, the church, of course, is not a place to go to very often—recall that Danes and Swedes have the lowest rate of church attendance in the world. And yet, they do still *like* the church. They like the buildings to be there—at least at a distance. They enjoy the sound of church bells ringing throughout the cities and towns every Sunday morning, even though it doesn't motivate them to actually partake in a church service.

A second aspect of cultural religiosity observable in Scandinavia entails a certain orientation to sacred scriptures—particularly the Bible. What I found was that while almost nobody ever reads or studies the Bible, and while even fewer people considered it to be divine in nature—only 7 percent of Danes and 3 percent of Swedes consider the Bible the actual word of God[34]—nearly everyone has a more or less positive appraisal of it. They consider it a "good" book, an ancient repository of decent morals and values, a venerable collection of important stories full of wisdom and insight, an important work of history, and even in a certain sense a bedrock of their civilization. But again, it is not viewed as something that fell from the sky, or was fashioned by angels, or written according to the will of some Immortal, Eternal, Omniscient, and Omnipotent Deity.

A third aspect of cultural religiosity—particularly in the Scandinavian Christian variety—is a definite reluctance to label oneself an atheist, even if one does not believe in God. I was always curious about this phenomenon, for whenever I looked at surveys of religious belief, I noticed a peculiar thing: the percentage of people who say that they don't believe in God is always significantly higher than the percentage who claim to be atheist.[35] How is this possible? Don't a lack of belief in God and atheism amount to basically the same thing? Perhaps technically—but not in the minds or subjective identities of the culturally religious. Although I did interview many Danes and Swedes who accepted the identification "atheist" (such as Christian and Lene, whom I focused on in earlier chapters), the distinct majority of Danes and Swedes who told me that they didn't believe in God simultaneously also rejected being labeled an atheist. For them, the term "atheist" was too negative, too condemning. It has a hostile ring which they prefer not to associate themselves with. For instance, Frederik, a 70-year-old retired literature professor, quipped that an atheist is "the personal enemy of God." Hedda, a 66-year-old high school teacher, told me that she doesn't believe in God, but also would not call herself an atheist because "I'm not that fanatic—'atheist' is too strong."

For many others who eschew the designation atheist, while they don't believe in God, per se, they do believe in "something." This was actually a very frequent response: "No, I don't believe in God . . . but I do believe in *something.*" Every time I asked people what this something entailed, they were almost always unable to articulate it. This "something" just wasn't anything they could describe, nor was it anything that they placed a great deal of faith in, nor that they were too concerned about. It wasn't central to their being, and it didn't comprise a religious faith. But when asked, there it was: "I believe in something, but I don't know what exactly." I found it to be akin to a sort of gentle agnosticism—a small feeling that there was more to life than a strictly material or empirical reality, but of course what that something else was exactly, no one could know. The most common phrase, which people offered up many times, was "Well, there's more between heaven and earth, you know . . . "

Cultural Religion and Cognitive Dissonance

Why would someone have their child baptized if they didn't believe in God or the blessings of Jesus? Why would someone have their child circumcised, if they were an atheist? Are such people confused? Hypo-critical? It could be said that being culturally religious results in cognitive dissonance, a popular term used to denote a potentially uncomfortable or tension-creating situation in which people engage in behaviors that are in conflict with their beliefs.

Most of the Danes and Swedes that I interviewed weren't troubled all that much about engaging in religious rituals and reciting prayers, despite their lack of personal faith. They just do it—no big deal. I did interview some people, however, who couldn't reconcile their lack of faith with overt religious involvement. One prominent example is that of Mia, a 34-year-old museum curator who grew up in Copenhagen. Mia does not believe in God (but don't call her an atheist!), she doesn't believe that Jesus was divine (but adds that the nature of Jesus just isn't something that she ever thinks about), and she was raised by nonbelieving parents. Mia quit the church in her early thirties, and now gives the money that she formerly paid in church taxes to Amnesty International. This evolved from a situation in which she just could not reconcile her lack of belief in the Lutheran religion with the possibility of being a godparent to her best friend's baby. It was a tough quandary, but in the end, she felt that she had to act in accordance with her secular beliefs. As she explained:

I said no to becoming a godparent. And this was to a child that I am very, very close to. But I could not—I just wouldn't give the oath in the church. It was really a hard decision for me, because it not only involved my own view of religion, but when the parents ask you, of course, it's in a way their—a question of—I cannot do this. So in part they are saying to you, "Would you be the most important person? This is our tradition, with our ritual for doing this." So when I say no to that, I felt that I would say no to all the other things. I discussed that a lot with myself, and it was—no. I would fill out all the forms that he could have my kidney, he could have whatever—I would do a lot of things for him—now in the natural time thing—I would also take care of him if his parents weren't there. All these things . . . I am there for him 100 percent in all matters, but I cannot say yes to that I will raise him in Christian beliefs, and I cannot accept that this ritual is being performed in the church.

And how did your best friend react when you explained this—that you couldn't do it because of that specific issue?

She was sorry, but she knew already when she asked me it would be a tricky thing to ask me, so she respects my decision.

Konrad is a 39-year-old computer technician from Stockholm. Konrad declined to go through with the confirmation ceremony when he was 14 because he thought that to do so would be hypocritical, given his lack of faith:

That was quite unusual. In my class in school there was only me and the class punk rocker who didn't get confirmed. I thought, well I don't believe in that, so why should I? Not many of the other kids believed in it either, but they were promised gifts and stuff from their parents if they did. So they only did it because of the gifts. And I thought: that's stupid. I don't believe in that— anything in that—so why should I?

Mads is a 52-year-old worker at a slaughterhouse. He quit the church many years ago, and considers himself a strong nonbeliever. As he explained to me (via a translator):

When I became older I became annoyed at being a member of this association that I don't believe in. And especially when I started to earn money. I didn't want to—automatically you pay tax to this association. And I didn't want to do that when I didn't believe in it.

While there were a handful of others like Mia, Konrad, and Mads that I interviewed—people who quit the church, or declined to be confirmed, or refused to get married in the church because they simply weren't believers—most Danes and Swedes continue to be a member of a church, and identify as a Christian, and engage in various holidays and rituals, even though they don't believe in the supernatural stuff. Their beliefs and identities/activities may thus not be in strict accord—but it doesn't seem to concern or bother them all that much. The joy they get from participating in the traditions of their religion seems to far outweigh any tension or discomfort they may experience as a result of any amount of cognitive dissonance.

Concluding Thoughts

Cultural religion is perhaps strongest and most easily discernable among Jews, Danes, and Swedes—as this chapter has attempted to illustrate. But what about other religions and other peoples out there? How strong is cultural religion among, say, Thai Buddhists or Orthodox Serbs or Mormons in Utah? I wonder if perhaps even in countries that are supposedly very religious, a significant chunk of the people there may actually be more culturally religious than truly religious. Take the example of Poland, which according to international surveys is considered to be one of the most religious countries in Europe. Professor Demerath reports that while he was recently teaching a course at a university in Warsaw, he asked the students about their own religious beliefs. Here is what he found:

> They all said they were Catholics, but beyond that seemed puzzled, reticent, and not a little embarrassed. I wondered if the distinction between religious Jews and cultural Jews might be applicable? At this suggestion, they visibly brightened and clamored to speak. That was precisely it: they were "cultural Catholics." They weren't really believers . . . still, Catholicism was part of their national and family cultural heritage.[36]

Of course, these students at a university in Warsaw are not representative of wider Polish society, which is surely rife with faithful and devout Catholics. There are undoubtedly millions of true believers not only in Poland, but the world over. Hundreds of millions. If not billions. And Sam Harris is correct to point out that many of the faithful do in fact "believe what they say they believe."[37] But it is important to recognize that there are also millions of *culturally religious* folk out there—probably more than most people think—and they are nearly always overlooked in discussions, surveys, and analyses that claim to address and reflect the state of religion in our world today.

9

Back to the USA

MY FAMILY AND I left Denmark at the end of June 2006. We flew up to Norway, where we spent three weeks inhaling the air, swimming the waters, hiking the trails, and pondering the lichens of the most devastatingly gorgeous country on earth, and then we flew back to the United States after over a year of living in Scandinavia. Our first stop was Colorado, where we spent some time with my in-laws. On our second day there, we were invited to their good friends' house for a hearty dinner. After the meal, the man of the house showed me his "new toy," a small gun. As he showed me all its fine (and lethal) attributes, I couldn't help but think how funny and strange it was that within 48 hours of being back in America, I was in the immediate vicinity of a handgun—and that it belonged to a man who considers himself a born-again Christian, no less. "Well, Phil," I thought to myself, "I think you're not in Denmark anymore."

It was a thought that echoed through my mind many times upon re-entry to the United States. One incident really stands out. In the first or second month that I was back in my hometown of Claremont, I was standing in line at my community bank. While I waited for my turn at the teller's counter, I couldn't help but overhear a conversation that was taking place at the other end of the room. A customer was sitting at the desk of a bank manager, consulting with her on how to handle her overwhelming debt. Here is what the bank manager advised her to do (in a fairly loud voice, no less, so that everyone in the bank could hear): "You need to gather up all your debt statements—your credit card bills, mortgage bills, loan documents, overdue notices—and put them in an envelope. Then you need to take that envelope to my pastor. He is a real man of God, and he has a special power when it comes to removing debt. If you take this envelope to him, he will pray over it and bless it and anoint it. Then you just need to give $50 a month to his ministry, and within a year, God will see to it that your debt is all gone. I promise you. He is powerful. I have given this advice to so many people and it works every time." What was so noteworthy to me about this incident was that not only was it shocking for me to hear a bank employee giving such "advice" to a customer in need of some serious financial help—but that no one else in the bank (and there was quite a line that day) seemed to think that what she was saying was weird or unacceptable. I was the only one standing there with a slack jaw.

This is one religious country.

Many of the Scandinavians that I interviewed said the same thing. Lots of them had spent time in the states, and they always commented on how religious Americans are. Lisa, from Stockholm and the mother of three, told me about an experience that she had when she was visiting some American friends of her husband's in Seattle. It was the first time in her life that she had ever met someone who actually believed in the story of Adam and Eve. In this case, it was the wife of her husband's friend. One day the two mothers took their children to the natural history museum, and while they were there, Lisa overheard her explaining to her children that all the displays relating to evolution weren't true, that it was all just make-believe:

I thought it was a little bit spooky, because she tried to fool her kids about something that the rest of the world believes very much in. I think it would be very interesting to have a real discussion with her—but not in front of her kids.

Jonas, a 25-year-old man from the west coast of Denmark, told me about a time that he visited a girlfriend and her family in a small town in Texas, and what he observed while attending her local church:

Everything in that society seemed to revolve around the church . . . it was scary. But it was interesting as well. I saw people falling over and being healed and I was just—"Jesus Christ, could you stop this? You're fooling yourselves." Of course, I didn't say this out loud. But that's what I was thinking. I just saw—I'd never gone to church and I never believed, so I was on the outside looking in, sort of. And I saw the things they used—to do this—they have a band playing the same noise all the time, and the preacher is, of course, very, very good at articulation, and his voice just takes people somewhere else. It's not what he's saying, pretty much. Of course, some of it is in the beginning. But later on it's just his voice—the droning of his voice—that just hypnotized people. They want to be hypnotized. That's my view of it, anyway.

Lasse, a 25-year-old medical student from Sweden, told me about his experiences visiting some distant cousins and their friends in the Pacific Northwest. One night at his cousin's house, Lasse's lack of religious faith came up. As he explained:

That was actually at a dinner with his best friends. We were like—me and three other couples. And then he was asking, "What is your faith, Lasse?"

And they were all—and I said—"Well, I'm an atheist." And they were like—
HUH?! That was like I was swearing, almost. They were like—"WHAT are
you doing, man?! How can you—?" They didn't know what to say. They were
really surprised. Yeah. And I was really surprised that they were surprised.
Why would they be so caring what I believe? I'm still the same, you know. And
I was so surprised how much it meant to them—what I believe. I mean, they
were still nice to me and it didn't have such a big impact on our further con-
versations. But still, at the time when I said it, they were shocked. And I was
surprised that they were so surprised.

Kjerstin is a 24-year-old university student from Sweden's west coast.
When she was a teenager, she went to Florida and lived with a host family
for a month while on a program to study English.

They were really, really nice . . . but they talked to me about religion and I
noticed that they were wanting me to believe. But they weren't forcing me or
anything. It wasn't—they accepted my opinions. But it was hard because they
asked me about sex before marriage, and they asked me about homosexuals
and where I would draw the line. Would I think it's okay for homosexuals to
marry in the church, or would I think it'd be okay if they got children? I was
16 at the time. I wasn't completely sure of what I believed in, but what shocked
me was that they told me that they thought AIDS was the act of God to punish
homosexuals. And—they were so nice and such a great family—and then all
of a sudden they say something like that. I don't know—I don't get it. I was
shocked. I didn't know what to respond. I just said something like, okay that's
not my opinion and I don't want to discuss it, because I didn't want to create
any hard feelings between us since I was living with them.

Religion: Scandinavia and the USA

Why are Americans so religious? This was a question that was often posed
to me while I was abroad, and it has been a question that I have been continually mulling over, deeply, ever since my return. It is a huge and complex question, and certainly one that cannot be answered simply. But in
this final chapter, I'd like to consider some possibilities, however cursorily.
Based on my experience in and study of Scandinavia, and my experience
in and study of religion in the United States, I would offer the following
potential answers concerning this major puzzle as to why Denmark and
Sweden are the least religious countries in the democratic world, while
America is the most religious country in the democratic world.

First we must consider the role that a strong Christian faith played—or didn't play—in the *historical foundations* of these countries. As discussed in Chapter 6, Danes and Swedes had Christianity imposed upon them by chieftains and kings. That is, Christianity was instituted in a "top-down" dynamic, and there is a very good possibility that true Christian faith barely managed to sink all that deeply into the hearts and minds of the Danes and Swedes over the centuries. But Christianity started quite differently in the early colonies of what would eventually become the United States. The first Europeans to establish lasting settlements in New England were strongly believing Christians. The Pilgrims were a pious lot, and the Puritans were perhaps what we might regard today as fundamentalists. They saw themselves as the true people of God, who came to North America to establish a pure, ascetic, and strong Christian society. The Puritans were intolerant of other religious faiths, and dissenters were banned, whipped, and—in the case of some unfortunate Quakers—even executed. The point is that Christianity was part of America's earliest foundations, and in a "grassroots" or popular way. It was established and promulgated not by rulers or kings, as was the case in Scandinavia, but by the people themselves. In short, unlike the situation in early Denmark and Sweden, religion was very strong and widely embraced at the very genesis of what would become the United States.

Second, there is the matter of *immigration*. Until only about 30 years ago, Denmark and Sweden were among the most homogenous nations in the Western world, and had little or no significant waves of foreign immigration. As for the United States—it *is* a nation of immigrants. With the exception of the Native Americans (who comprise less than 2 percent of the American population), everyone who lives in the United States today is the descendant of immigrants. Between the late 1600s and late 1700s, immigrants from Scotland, Ireland, England, and Germany poured in, along with (enslaved) Africans. Throughout the 1800s, more European immigrants came—including Scandinavians, the Dutch, the French—as well as Chinese immigrants. Between 1880 and 1925, millions of Italians, Poles, Jews, Russians, Greeks, Hungarians, etc., poured in to North America, and since 1965, some 20 million people have immigrated to the United States, from all over Asia, India, Latin America, Pakistan, Iran, etc. How might this be a factor in explaining different rates of religiosity in Scandinavia and the USA? Simply that when immigrants come to a new land, they often turn to religion for a sense of ethnic solidarity and community. Sociologists have long recognized this phenomenon: immigration is consistently correlated with increased religiosity.[1]

A third factor has to do with the *high degree of racial, ethnic, class, and cultural diversity* one finds in the United States, particularly when compared to relatively small—and until very recently—homogenous Denmark and Sweden. My experiences, interviews, and observations led me to conclude that most Danes and Swedes feel a very strong sense of "belonging" to a people simply by virtue of being Danish or Swedish. They feel connected to one another, to a greater or lesser degree. Yet for many people in the United States, that taken-for-granted sense of belonging and connectedness is not automatically tied to simply being an "American." The fact is, Americans are far more divided or "socially distanced" from one another along ethnic, racial, class, and cultural lines to a degree that is simply not found in Scandinavia (of course, with the exception of the recent arrival of new immigrants). I suspect that religion in the United States often serves as a provider of intimate community and that religiosity fosters a sense of belonging and connectedness for many Americans, a sense of belonging and connectedness that they don't necessarily get simply by virtue of their national identity, the way one finds among most Danes and Swedes. For as Jan Lindhardt, a bishop in Denmark, once quipped, "The Danes don't need to go to church on Sundays because they can go to their Danishness every day of the week."[2]

A fourth factor involves *the separation of church and state*. As we have seen in Denmark and Sweden, the Lutheran Church is a *national* church; it was supported by the kings and queens of centuries past, and is still supported by taxes in Denmark and, until about six years ago, in Sweden. The link/relationship between government and religion in Scandinavia has always been strong and cozy. Not so in the United States. There has never been a National Church of America, and thanks to the first clause of the First Amendment to the U.S. Constitution, the government cannot be in the business of establishing religion throughout the land. Although the First Amendment certainly gets interpreted differently by different courts, the overall effect of the law has been consistent: to establish a fairly firm wall, or at least a strong chain-link fence, between religion and government. Whether the framers of the Constitution intended it or not, the First Amendment has actually played a significant role in helping to keep religion alive and well in this country. Basically, it made sure that no state-supported monopoly religion could reign over the land, as has been the case for centuries in Denmark and Sweden. Instead, the United States has been characterized by religious pluralism—an extreme degree of pluralism, unlike anywhere else on the planet—where virtually every single religion, faith, denomination, creed, and spiritual system is represented somewhere, by someone. This means that not only are there many more choices for people seeking religious involvement, but the plurality of religions may also spur greater interest via excessive marketing.

A fifth and unavoidably obvious difference between the United States and Scandinavia is the degree to which *religion is aggressively marketed.* As was discussed previously, because the Lutheranism of Denmark and Sweden is a state-subsidized, monopoly-like religion, there is little need or incentive for pastors or bishops to heavily "sell" their religion to the public. I recall interviewing one pastor in Denmark who very candidly stated that he wasn't really into public speaking and that he found giving sermons rather difficult, but he loved poring over books of philosophy and theology. Thus, being employed by the Danish state as a Lutheran pastor was a great gig: sure, he had to give a sermon a few times a month, but it was usually only to a handful of people—often old ladies—and yet for much of the rest of the time he could hole up in his office and study, read, and write. I had a Danish friend who also described the pastor in her hometown in similar terms: not much of a public go-getter, but more of a thoughtful bookworm. In the United States, such pastors would have a hard time paying their church's electric bills. And they'd have a really tough time keeping the place afloat, for studying ancient texts all day isn't the way to attract parishioners in America. Here in the United States, there is a situation akin to that of an unregulated market economy, where competition reigns supreme. Since no religion, no church, and no clergyman can receive funds from the government, any religious institution that wants to remain open and vital has to seek support from its own members. The result is an unrelenting, unending barrage of marketing techniques used to attract people to given religious establishments. In America, churches will do whatever it takes to attract "customers": dynamic and charismatic pastors, great bands, top-notch digital TV screens, powerpoint presentations, comfortable pews, free doughnuts, free child care, free Internet access, free Starbucks coffee—you name it. And religious denominations and congregations advertise all over the place: on TV, on the radio, on billboards, on the Internet. I regularly receive postcards in the mail—sent directly to my home—inviting me to attend this or that church. And these postcards are often very slick, with high-quality graphics, inviting images, and catchy phrases like "Try a church with an edge!" or "Undreamed of Possibilities Await. . . ." The point is, unlike in Scandinavia, religion is excessively marketed in the United States, and it seems to net results.

Finally—and this is specifically related to the work of Pippa Norris and Ronald Inglehart covered in Chapter 6—comes the drastically different *levels of security* one finds when contrasting Scandinavian society to American society. I don't think it is a mere coincidence that the nations of Scandinavia (the most irreligious) have the lowest poverty rates of all developed democracies and the United States (the most religious) has the highest. After all, research shows that the poor are much more likely to be religious than the rich. Not only are poorer nations more likely to be religious than wealthier nations, but even within the United States the pattern is clear: poor Americans are far more likely to pray daily and consider religion "very important" than wealthy Americans,[3] and poor Americans are more likely to believe in heaven, hell, and the devil than wealthy Americans.[4] Of course, poverty is not the only cause of religiosity. And obviously many wealthy people hold strong religious beliefs. Yet there is an undeniably salient correlation between rates of poverty and rates of religiosity. And in the United States, it isn't just poverty, but numerous sources of insecurity that can propel someone to seek comfort in religion. Millions of Americans—over 45 million, to be exact—don't have health insurance. Millions of people can't find affordable housing. The United States is admittedly one of the wealthiest nations in the world, but that wealth is not widely nor evenly distributed. Far from it; the wealth in America is heavily concentrated in certain hands, so that there exists a huge gulf between the haves and the have-nots, particularly when it comes to decent health care, affordable housing, healthy food, not to mention well-supported schools or competent legal representation. And the possibility of homelessness looms over the heads of millions. As Inglehart and Norris explain:

> The United States is exceptionally high in religiosity in large part . . . because it is also one of the most unequal postindustrial societies . . . Relatively high levels of economic insecurity are experienced by many sectors of U.S. society, despite American affluence. . . . Many American families, even in the professional middle class, face risks of unemployment, the dangers of sudden ill health without adequate private medical insurance. Vulnerability to becoming a victim of crime, and the problems of paying for long-term care of the elderly.[5]

The situation regarding social security in Denmark and Sweden couldn't be any more different than what it is in the United States. Not only do the Scandinavian nations spread their wealth around to a degree unparalleled among developed democracies—so that the gap between rich and poor is remarkably small—but the tangible, day-to-day support people experience in their lives is exceptional. If a person loses a job in Scandinavia, they don't lose their medical care, nor will they lose the roof over their heads. No matter how down-and-out someone is in Scandinavia, they can always find food, shelter, and health care. And everyone knows that they (and their loved ones) will receive good care in their old age. And there is plenty of affordable, excellent child care to go around. And free job training. And free education. Life in Scandinavia may be a lot of things, but precarious simply isn't one of them.

Morten

I'd like to conclude this chapter by presenting the experiences and words of Morten, who represents a particularly fascinating case of religious—and subsequent irreligious—identity. Morten turned out to be a very special informant for me because I first interviewed him while he was living in Denmark, and then was fortuitously able to interview him over a year later, after he had spent nine months living in the United States. His experience in America really changed him, in ways that neither he nor I could possibly have been able to foresee.

I first met Morten because he was the husband of one of my colleagues at the University of Aarhus, and also because his children attended the same preschool as mine. We hung out quite a bit that year, and became good friends. He is 37 years old. He grew up in a very small village on Sjaelland. He is well educated, holding a master's degree in history and science, and works as an upper-level manager in one of Denmark's most successful companies. Although I talked with him all year long about my research, and about Danish society, politics, religion, etc.—when it came time to do a formal interview, I was fairly surprised. Morten, it turned out, was actually a believer.

In the pages that follow, I will present excerpts from both interviews with Morten; the first one was conducted in Denmark in December 2005, and the second one was conducted in California in June 2007. Below are excerpts from that first interview.

Let's start with your parents. Were they religious at all?
No.
When you say "no," what do you mean?

Um . . . they are Christian and they have been through confirmation. And married in church and I'm baptized Christian. And then my brothers are as well. But they're not religious at all.

Do they believe in God?

My mother is dead—but she didn't. And my father doesn't.

What about your grandparents . . . ?

I didn't know them that well, but I would say—my guess would be no.

Okay, let's talk about you. Are you a member of the national church?

Yeah.

Why?

At some point in my life, when I was starting at the university, I made some friends and they all decided to exit the church, because some of them were there by tradition and some of them were not. But the ones in there by tradition, being in a scientific environment, said, "I do not believe in God, so I do not want to pay for the church." Maybe it was money, too, but still—and at that point I had to make a decision and I was like, oh I don't think I will exit the church.

And what made you decide that?

[laughter] I don't know, I don't know. Maybe I thought God could come in handy at a later point in my life, I don't know.

Okay, and did you baptize your children?

Yeah.

Why did you do that?

Um-m-m . . . I would say that I baptized them because I . . . [long pause] . . . I kind of believe in God. [laughter] Okay, it's not—a lot of people say that they believe in "something" and to me that's too—that's too floppy. I think it's an easy answer, you know. It's like "maybe there are spirits in the woods" and like that. When we were married we had to make a decision: is this going to be in a church or not? Some of my friends have said, "I will not be married in the church because I do not believe in God." And some of my friends have said, "I do not believe in God but I don't care, so let's just get married in the church." And some of the women do not believe in God. They just say it's romantic and it's nice. But when we had to decide, I kind of had to think it over, because I didn't want to get married in the church if it was just a ritual—or because it was a nice place to get married. And I had this experience when I was a young—well, I was in the university—that I kind of thought I was in trouble being sick—ill. And I kind of made a pact: I said, "Okay God, this is—now this is your turn, if I'm okay now, then I would believe in you." To that extent, I made a promise, so I had to stick to that.

You mean you got better?

I was not ill, it was just symptoms, you know. It's too much detail, but. . . .

You thought you might be really ill—

Yeah, and then I wasn't.

And you sort of had this conversation with God?

Yeah, it was if you save me now, then I will believe. And I have to stick to that, I think.

You were how old when this happened?

Twenty. And then so I'll say when I need help—I pray to God and ask for help. I kind of think that I can pray to God and ask him for help, but I'm not sure that there is a God that listens, you know. So I'm not sure if I'll get any help . . . but I still ask for it. And I have seen no signs that I get help, so . . . it's just like, well I do it, it's like when—in the church the priests are telling us things like, "If you are in a dark room and you light up a candle, the candle will light up the whole room. The candle is Jesus and God, and He lights up the whole world." And that's—that's not the feeling I have. It's not like when everything is dark I have God to help me. It's like if everything is dark, I can ask God for help, but I have to do other things myself as well.

Okay.

It helps me at least.

It's comforting?

Yeah, yeah. And sometimes it's neurotic, I think, because when I have to take off in an airplane, then I always say "Heavenly Father" and say that he has to keep this plane in the air and land it safely. But maybe that's just a neurotic thing, but . . .

So just to be clear then, I mean, the God that is in the Bible that, you know, makes the world and makes Adam and Eve and talks to Moses and gives the Ten Commandments, I mean, is that the God that you believe in, or is it a little bit different?

It's a hard question to ask because it's—I have this dual—I know it's not like I believe in intelligent design. I believe in big bang and evolution and all that stuff. But when I think of big bang we have this singularity of all the matters in one point, but what was before that? And . . . I could believe if someone told me, well God made the singularity and made the big bang, I would say "Hey, fair enough." But I do not believe that He created the earth in six days, no.

Okay, Morten . . . do you think that we have a soul or a spirit inside or do you think we're just bodies?

Yes, I think we have a soul.

And why do you think that?

The obvious answer is because I can feel that there is one in me, so why not—yeah, I think so. Yeah. But I wouldn't rule out that it's just chemistry and things in my brain making me believe that's so. But still—rationally I can say to myself, well that's just your brain pulling a trick on you, but . . . why not? I think that maybe there's something there.

• • •

About half a year after this interview, Morten's wife got a nine-month visiting professorship at a university in California, some two hours north of Claremont. It was great fun to have them so close—our families got together many times, and it was wonderful for us to hear our kids speaking Danish with their kids, and to talk with them about all their observations of life in America. Toward the end of their stay, Morten told me that his feelings about religion had changed. Nine months in America—rather than strengthen or deepen his Christian faith—had caused him to seriously question it. Here are excerpts from that last interview:

Okay, so Morten, you've been here more than half a year?

Yeah.

And when you first came here you started to go to churches, right?

Yeah, yeah.

Tell me about that.

Um, well, I've been to about five, six, seven different churches . . . the first thing that struck me when I came here is that here people are much more— what do you call it—not official, but they are more "showing" their religion here. At least their Christian religion. At home, in Denmark, people are—if people are religious, it's something private. They kind of keep it at home or within themselves and go to church and have experiences there, but it's not like they need to put bumper stickers on their cars saying that they're religious. And so what struck me was that people—like the people begging for money here say "God bless you," and it's on the bumper sticker "I got Hope" or whatever. And some people actually have bumper stickers saying that they are not religious here, which I've never seen at home. And, to me, that feels a little superficial that they have to tell everybody that they are so and so religious and they believe so and so in Jesus Christ and all this. Are they saying this because they want other people to see that they are? So that struck me. And you have radio shows that are talking about how to act as a good Christian and stuff like that. We don't have that at home. People here are much more religious Christian-wise than in Denmark. To me, you should base your society or your culture on logic and science and things you can prove and things you can disprove, or whatever. But here, people just believe that Jesus is the Son of God and he is God and that he did miracles and all that stuff. And, for me, that doesn't really comply with a scientific and logic-based society. And that puzzled me because I thought the United States would be more like Denmark—believing in, you know, rationality. That was strange to me and that people here were more explicit about their beliefs. I mean, saying with a straight face that "I had cancer, but I prayed to Jesus and he cured me." You can't make that work if you're a rational person. But people here actually believe, or at least say they believe, that Jesus cured them. Like he can pick who to cure and who not to cure. That's not a thing I've seen before and I didn't think you were like that here. But then there's television, too. And a thing I saw—the politicians and a lot of people in TV and media are very explicitly saying that they believe in God. For instance—I know that President Bush is religious, but he's much more religious than I thought, you know, and—if people in Denmark knew that he said that he consulted with God before he invaded Iraq and actually meant that, I think the Danes would be pretty scared of what this guy is capable of doing. Because what if God tells him to do something—and that's not a good idea? I don't think Danes think Iraq is a good idea, but, you know, if you're not basing your things on rational thought but kind of hearing this voice in your head and feeling that God is talking to you, then that could be considered being a little mentally ill. I don't say he is that, but you know that could be maybe the notion of Bush in Denmark if they really knew. That puzzled me, or scared me, actually.

Yeah.

Okay, I saw a faith program on TV where they had taken Barack Obama and John Edwards and Hillary Clinton and talked to them about their faith. What struck me most was that I had the notion that, okay, the Republicans today are very religious, but for rational-thinking people like myself, you can always vote for the Democrats because they are not into this religious movement or whatever. But when I saw Hillary Clinton on the news, she was saying stuff like—she was asked a question like, "How did you handle that your husband was being unfaithful to you?" And she said, "Well, you know, I believe in God and I have this group of people I can pray with and I have this big group network of people who prayed for me to get over this, and I prayed myself." And I was just like, what is Hillary Clinton praying?! I don't know. It's just scary— that even the Democrats are so religious. So if I was to live here I would have a problem voting for a president, because I don't want a religious leader.

And why is that?

I think it's okay to be religious, but if you base your judgments of how to rule your country on religious beliefs, then you can get in a lot of trouble.

Um—it's—to me, the Muslim movements like Al-Queda in Afghanistan are religious fanatics who can just see one side of the story and they have an ideology of religion that has to conquer the world and there's just one way to be. And, to me, when I'm hearing politicians here in the United States talk about religion, I feel they talk about it the same way they do in Afghanistan. It's—to some extent, of course, it's not as extreme—but still . . .

Okay . . . and what about in the six months you've been living here—do you see religion just kind of in daily life?

Yeah, yeah. I've talked to people about it because I was getting curious because it had a big impact on me. It was so weird to be here because I didn't think you were like that in the United States. So I talked to people, and to me, it's, you know, for instance, I asked one of my kid's friend's father. I asked him, "Do you go to church?" And he said, "No, no, but I study the Bible at home; I make home studies." And I had this feeling that he thought he had to say that—that he was embarrassed for not going to church. Maybe because he didn't know that I didn't care, but still he said, "I just believe in reading the Bible at home and studying it and reading it and telling my kids what it's all about." So I think there is like the consensus in Denmark is if you're religious—you don't talk that much about it. And here the consensus is that you believe in God and you have to be strong and really want to take a debate with people if you say you're not. That's exactly the opposite at home.

Did your feelings about religion or God change after living here for six months?

Yeah, it did.

Tell me about that.

Yeah, because when I came here I believed in God and I was Christian—but in a Danish way. So there's a lot of stuff in the Bible that just doesn't make sense, but—you know—sure, I thought God was up there and he helped us, he tried to make a book and we tried to behave according to the book, and you know, humans make errors so maybe the book isn't 100 percent correct, but you can kind of do it. But when I came here and saw all the people being so—explicit—like Jesus died and he was the Son of God and he was born by a virgin. And I added it all up and said, okay if I need to say I'm a Christian, then I need to believe in all this stuff. Because there's so much that you have to buy into in order to be Christian. And I didn't buy into it. I don't believe it. I don't believe in Jesus being God incarnated as a human being on earth, and I don't believe that his mother was a virgin and I don't even think he performed that many miracles, you know, like walking on water, turning water into wine—could have maybe helped some people curing them, but not by making miracles.

Just maybe giving them the sense of faith in God and that could maybe help them to some extent. And then I kind of said to myself I can't really be a Christian anymore because I don't—because if I just believe in 10 percent of the stuff I need to, then I won't consider myself a Christian any more. Because I could see that here people were more devoted to Christianity in the way you should be. Back home, people will just tell you they're Christian, but they don't— they're not—they just don't know it. They think they're Christian because everybody is, but not because they buy into all these concepts of believing in all the miracles. They will say maybe there's more between heaven and earth than you can explain, and I think that's true, but it has nothing to do with God and Jesus and all that stuff. So I'm going home at least an agnostic, maybe an atheist, I don't know. [laughs] But I saw a lot of good things here—and I had a lot of thoughts about why do people here believe in God and what is the purpose for them doing it, and I went to a lot of churches. I can see that back home in Denmark if you go to a church you have a lot of rituals and the sermon is pretty boring. You have organ music and you sing hymns or psalms or whatever, and they're very old and if you're not going to church every Sunday, you don't know them that well and they're horrible to sing. The words don't make sense, so that's the boring part. And the priests are dressed up very formal with black dresses and all that stuff. And it's just a lot of rituals, and it's very, very boring—so nobody goes to church. But here it's much more—the priests are talking about stuff you really need to talk about. And they play music that is great to listen to and you like it. I loved singing with them—good lyrics—and they have powerpoints showing the lyrics instead of having a little book. And they have concepts like let's all rise and greet our fellow men standing next to you and say "I'm glad you're here, I love you, it's great being together." I liked that. That's a good concept. And they had this—let's pray and everybody that has something you want to pray for raise your hand. They said, "Well, my son is in Iraq and I'm very worried that he will be killed, can we pray for him being safe back home?" I can understand that. Or my mother-in-law has cancer, can we pray for that? Saying all these things and people in union prayed for helping people, and I liked that. Um—but the thing I liked about it was that you are joined in a community of people, you're talking about your problems, you're saying to everybody else, "I'm sad that my son is not here; I'm afraid he will die," and people say "Okay, we're here for you and we will all wish or pray,"—I would say wish—for him to come home safely. And that's a very, very strong concept. I just don't think it has anything to do with God. Maybe I would go to a church if I lived here in order to get that. And they greet you. When you come to church they say: "Oh, we're so glad you come here to our church, oh it's so great, oh you come from Denmark, that's a wonderful country. My nephew went there and he loved it," and all this stuff. And they have for kids—they take kids aside and they take care of them, so it's very—it feels like the churches here are in a more free-market position. They have to fight and make it good . . . But I still don't want to have Jesus Christ belief in it.

And you think this change really came about from living in the United States?

Yes, exactly it did.

Fascinating.

One can say that back home I said I believed in God, but it wasn't—it didn't fill up that much of my day. It's just something I said if people asked me—I would say yeah I think I believe, at least, in something. But being here made me evaluate my beliefs and say, well, do you actually believe in that? And . . . no, I don't. I don't think so, no. Jesus—he's not the Son of God. I know he is not. Maybe he's a prophet or something, I don't know, but he's not the Son of God and I know that now. I kind of ignored the fact at home because nobody really challenged me on that, nobody said that it's true that he's the Son of God. They just think, well, whatever.

So when you go back to Denmark, if someone were to ask you, what would say to them about the religion here? How would you summarize—I mean how would you explain it to other Danes?

I think I would say to them, maybe you don't believe me, but the American society is—all politics and media discussions—is based on that everybody is very devoted Christians. Meaning that you cannot hold an office, you cannot be a president, you cannot be whatever, if you don't publicly say that you believe in God and all of your sentences end with God bless America or whatever. That we, as Danes, have to be very, very careful with joining the United States when they want us to go to war or they want us to join them in whatever endeavors they want us to join with them, because the religious fanatics in the United States have a very, very high influence on what's going to happen in the United States, and I don't think Danes know that. I think that if Danes knew that, they would be very—I don't think they would be afraid—but I think they would say, "No, no, we don't want to be a part of that." And I don't think they know. But I'm going to tell them.

• • •

Morten's experience illustrates the degree to which both religious identity and secular identity are closely linked to one's social surroundings and social interactions. Yes, religious faith is a deeply personal matter, but it is also affected by, and inexorably enmeshed within, one's cultural environment. Back home in Denmark, where religion is such a *non-topic*, most people can live their lives without regularly thinking about belief in God or the divinity of Jesus or the immortality of the soul. And their lack of strong religious faith is not necessarily some personally chosen orientation, arrived at through a lengthy process of intense individual soul-searching or extended existential debates. Rather, it is usually an unreflexive, taken-for-granted secularity; people living their lives largely indifferent— or sometimes utterly oblivious—to basic religious questions or theological concerns, because that's "just the way it is" in Scandinavia. And when religion is such a non-topic in a given culture, it also means that someone like Morten—who considered himself Christian and believed in God back home—could maintain a fairly religious orientation without having to regularly confront just what such an orientation might truly imply, at least on a deeper theological level. But when Morten came to the United States, where religion is so strong and people wear their religious beliefs on their sleeves (and bumper stickers), he suddenly found himself scrutinizing just what it is that he claimed to believe, and just what it truly means to say one believes in God or is a Christian. And despite enjoying the American church services he attended—the good music, the decent sermons, the sense of community and vocal concern for each other's personal hardships—he came to realize that he just didn't buy the essentially supernatural components of the Christian faith. He returned to Denmark a nonbeliever—"an agnostic, maybe an atheist," in his own words.

• • •

I wonder what the Denmark that Morten returned to is like these days. It has been well over a year since I was there. And I wonder what the future of religion and secularity will look like in Scandinavia in the decades ahead. As religion glows ever hotter the world over, will the relatively secular nations of Denmark and Sweden hold fast to their irreligious ways, maintaining faith not in resurrections but in reason, basing their society not on the worship of God, but on the welfare of their fellow citizens, and finding meaning not from the otherworldly, but from one another, in the here and now? Or will the deep religious faith of the wider world seep into Scandinavia in the years ahead, causing greater numbers to pack the churches on Sunday mornings, infusing the Danes and Swedes with a rekindled or newly embraced love of the Lord? It is impossible to say. As a mere social scientist, I cannot make any grand predictions concerning the future trajectory of the human experience here on this earth. But what I can at least do is attempt to paint a portrait of a society that currently exists, right now, at the beginning of the twenty-first century, just below the Artic Circle, between Torshavn and Liepaja, wherein most people don't believe much in God, don't accept the supernatural claims of religion as literally true, seldom go to church at all, and live their lives in a largely secular culture wherein death is calmly if not stoically accepted as simply a natural phenomenon and the ultimate meaning of life is nothing more or less than what you make of it. The existence of this relatively irreligious society suggests that religious faith—while admittedly widespread—is not natural or innate to the human condition. Nor is religion a necessary ingredient for a healthy, peaceful, prosperous, and (have I already said it?) deeply good society.

Appendix

Sample Characteristics and Methodology

ALTHOUGH I HAD countless conversations with literally hundreds of Scandinavians over the course of my stay there, I conducted 149 formal interviews. By formal, I mean that these individuals knew that they were being interviewed for my book and consented to the interview, a designated time was set aside to conduct the actual interview, and a structured set of questions was referred to throughout the interview. Although I regularly referred to this set of prewritten questions, the interviews generally proceeded as open-ended conversations, and I allowed each conversation to meander where it would, rather than forcing a standard format or order of questions and responses. I also rewrote and restructured my questions many times over the course of the year, as my interviewing experience grew more varied and extensive.

Of these 149 formal interviews, 121 were conducted face-to-face, and 28 were conducted over the phone. One hundred fourteen of the interviews were one-on-one, while 35 people were interviewed in pairs (usually husband and wife couples) or in groups of 3 or 4 (usually sets of friends or colleagues). One hundred thirty-one of the interviews were tape-recorded with the consent of the informants (telephone interviews were recorded via speaker phone), and 18 of the interviews were conducted without a tape recorder, but extensive notes were taken which were typed up immediately following the interview. Of the 131 interviews that were tape-recorded, 122 were transcribed/typed up for analysis, but 9 were damaged or lost in the mail en route from Denmark to the United States. Most interviews lasted about one hour. Some interviews lasted longer (over two hours), and a few interviews were shorter, around a half an hour.

Of those who were formally interviewed, 75 were men and 74 were women. One hundred three were Danish, 39 were Swedish, and 7 were immigrants to Denmark from Chile, Iran, or Turkey. In terms of the education levels of my informants, it was somewhat difficult to neatly correlate the Scandinavian and American educational systems, as they are quite distinct. However, that said, approximately 34 percent had completed the equivalent of a university degree, approximately 15 percent had completed some university courses but never achieved a degree or were currently enrolled at a college or university, approximately 11 percent had completed the equivalent of a high school education, approximately 11 percent had completed some sort of specific professional training (such as how to be a social worker, businessman, preschool teacher, etc.), approximately 15 percent had completed some form of specific vocational training (such as how to be a tool maker, photographer, nurse, physical therapist, etc.), and approximately 14 percent had completed somewhere between the sixth and ninth grades.

Out of the 149 informants, approximately 23 percent had been raised in small towns (population less than 5,000), approximately 41 percent had been raised in one of Denmark or Sweden's three largest cities, and approximately 33 percent had been raised in medium-sized towns (larger than 5,000 people, but not one of the three largest cities in Denmark or Sweden).

Concerning age, 3 percent of my informants were between the ages of 15 and 19, 21 percent were between 20 and 29, 25 percent were between 30 and 39, 17 percent were between 40 and 49, 15 percent were between 50 and 59, 9 percent were between 60 and 69, 7 percent were between 70 and 79, and 3 percent were age 80 or older.

The largest shortcoming of my sample is that it was a convenience sample and hence nonrandom. And because my sample was nonrandom, that means that valid generalizability to the wider Danish and Swedish populations is not possible. Informants were found through a number of ways, the first being what is traditionally known as a "snowball" process. I began by interviewing people that I knew through my daily life: the employees that worked at the corner market where I shopped, the teachers at my daughters' schools, the parents of the students in my daughters' classes, the janitor that cleaned my office, the secretaries at the university, my neighbors, etc. Once I interviewed them, I asked to interview their friends, relatives, and colleagues, and thus my sample grew in this fashion. I also found informants through friends and relatives in the United States who had friends, relatives, or colleagues in Denmark or Sweden; I would call or e-mail these people and introduce myself as a friend or relative of so-and-so, and ask if it would be possible to do an interview. And again, I subsequently asked these people for further contacts and potential informants. However, many informants were obtained not through social ties, but simply by my seeking out a certain "type" of profession or person and then interviewing "whoever I got." For example, when I wanted to interview some police officers, I simply called the police station in Aarhus and said that I was an American sociologist doing research on Scandinavian culture, and asked if there was anyone that I could interview, and I then interviewed whoever they assigned to me. I did the same thing with the inhabitants of several old age homes, employees of a mental institution, students at local high schools, etc. I also ended up interviewing many people that I met in unplanned situations, for example, I would find myself on a train sitting next to people, and then interview them. Or I would meet people on a park bench while watching my kids playing, or I would meet people at some party or public event and then ask to interview them. Finally, I interviewed a few people because they contacted me directly, having seen an article on me and my research in a local newspaper. In sum, I interviewed whoever I could find, based on whatever contacts I had or could pursue.

Notes

Introduction

1. Peter L. Berger, "Reflections on the Sociology of Religion Today," *Sociology of Religion* 62, 4 (2001): 443–54.

2. I have also spent time in Sweden. I lived for two short spells with friends in Stockholm in the 1990s, and I have also visited the city of Gothenburg, as well as spent time in the countryside of Småland.

3. For an in-depth discussion of my research methods, including my sampling methods, the demographic characteristics of my sample, etc., pleased see the Appendix.

4. For 31 days in September and October 2006, I counted the number of police that I saw while living in Claremont. The total: 36.

5. As in the words of Keith Ward: "Our whole understanding of morality really does depend upon the existence of God, upon seeing human conduct in the context of a wider spiritual realm, if it is to make sense." See Keith Ward, *In Defence of the Soul* (Oxford: Oneworld Publications, 1992), 31.

6. This is from an op-ed piece in the *Calgary Sun* on September 9, 1997, and was quoted in Michael Shermer, *The Science of Good and Evil* (New York: Henry Holt, 2004), 152.

7. Byron Nordstrom, *Scandinavia Since 1500* (Minneapolis: University of Minnesota Press, 2000).

8. Ole Riis, "Patterns of Secularization in Scandinavia," in *Scandinavian Values: Religion and Morality in the Nordic Countries*, edited by Thorleif Pettersson and Ole Riis (Uppsala: ACTA Universitatis Upsaliensis, 1994).

9. Andrew Buckser, *After the Rescue: Jewish Identity and Community in Contemporary Denmark* (New York: Palgrave Macmillan, 2003), 59.

10. Eva Hamberg, "Christendom in Decline: the Swedish Case," in *The Decline of Christendom in Western Europe, 1750-2000*, ed. Hugh McLeod and Werner Ustorf (New York: Cambridge University Press, 2003), 48.

11. Survey results on the God question vary. Andrew Greeley (2003) found that 57 percent of Danes and 54 percent of Swedes claim to believe in God, but simultaneously that only 34 percent of Danes and 26 percent of Swedes could be considered "theists." Botvar (1998) found that only 20 percent of

Danes and 18 percent of Swedes claim to believe in a "personal God." Bond-eson (2003) found that 51 percent of Danes and 26 percent of Swedes believe in a "personal God." And yet Lambert (2003) reports that 24 percent of Danes and 16 percent of Swedes believe in a "personal God." See Andrew Greeley, *Religion in Europe at the End of the Second Millennium* (New Brunswick, N.J.: Transaction Publishers, 2003); Pal Ketil Botvar, "Kristen tro I Norden. Priva-tisering og Svekkelse av religiose dogmer," in *Folkkyrkor och Religios Pluralism –Den Nordiska Religosa Modellen*, ed. Goran Gustafsson and Thorleif Petters-son (Stockholm: Verbum, 2000); Ulla Bondeson, *Nordic Moral Climates: Value Continuities and Discontinuities in Denmark, Finland, Norway, and Sweden* (New Brunswick, N.J.: Transaction Publishers, 2003); Yves Lambert, "New Christi-anity, Indifference, and Diffused Spirituality," in *The Decline of Christendom in Western Europe, 1750–2000*, ed. Hugh McLeod and Ustorf Werner (New York: Cambridge University Press, 2003).

12. "Something's Happy in the State of Denmark," *Los Angeles Times*, June 10, 2006.

13. Such as Annetta Nunn, the police chief of Birmingham, Alabama, did in August 2006.

14. As Governor Mike Huckabee of Arkansas did in January 2006.

15. Although I have used the term "pastor" here, the Danes and Swedes that I interviewed did not use that term. They almost always referred to their pastors or ministers as "priests" (the word is *præst* in Danish). They also sometimes referred to them as "vicars," and two of the three pastors that I interviewed used that spe-cific term to describe themselves. I have chosen to use "pastor" because for most Americans it denotes a Protestant affiliation, whereas "priest" usually refers to Catholics. As for "vicar," most Americans rarely, if ever, use that term.

16. Claus Vincents, "Danskern tror (også) på Darwin," *Kristeligt Dagblad*, Au-gust 12, 2006, p. 1.

17. Dean Hoge, Bention Johnson, and Donald Luidens, *Vanishing Boundaries: The Religion of Mainline Protestant Baby Boomers* (Louisville, Ky.: Westminster/ John Knox Press, 1994).

18. Ronald Inglehart, Miguel Basanez, Jaime Diez-Medrano, Loek Halman, and Ruud Luijkx, *Human Beliefs and Values: A Cross-Cultural Sourcebook Based on the 1999-2002 Value Surveys* (Buenos Aires: Siglo Veintiuon Editores, 2004).

19. Ibid.

20. Ibid.

21. These words are taken from a speech given by Anders Fogh Rasmussen and translated in Lars Decik, "The Paradox of Secularism in Denmark: From Emancipation to Ethnocentrism?" in *Secularism and Secularity: Contemporary International Perspectives*, ed. Barry Kosmin and Ariela Keysar (Hartford, Conn.: Institute for the Study of Secularism in Society and Culture, 2007), 129.

22. Such as the Creation Museum in Kentucky.

Chapter 1

1. Ayaan Hirsi Ali, *Infidel* (New York: Free Press, 2007), 239–40.

2. Michael E. McCullough and Timothy B. Smith, "Religion and Health," in *Handbook of the Sociology of Religion*, ed. Michele Dillon (New York: Cambridge University Press, 2003).

3. Phil Zuckerman, "Is Faith Good for Us?" *Free Inquiry* 26, 5 (2006): 35–38; Gregory S. Paul, "Cross-National Correlations of Quantifiable Societal Health with Popular Religiosity and Secularism in the Prosperous Democracies," *Journal of Religion and Society* 7, 1 (2005): 1–17.

4. These quotes from Pat Roberston come directly from the film *With God on Our Side: George W. Bush and the Rise of the Religious Right*, by Calvin Skaggs, David Van Taylor, and Ali Pomeroy, Lumiere Productions, 2004.

5. Pat Robertson, *The New Millennium* (Dallas: Word Publishing, 1990), 181.

6. Ann Coulter, *Godless: The Church of Liberalism* (New York: Three Rivers Press, 2006), 3.

7. Ibid., 280.

8. Bill O'Reilly, *Culture Warrior* (New York: Broadway, 2006), 19.

9. Ibid., 72.

10. Ibid., 176.

11. Rush Limbaugh, *See, I Told You So* (New York: Pocket Star Books, 1993), 95.

12. William Bennett, John Dilulio, Jr., and John Walters, *Body Count: Moral Poverty and How to Win America's War Against Crime and Drugs* (New York: Simon and Schuster, 1996), 208.

13. William Bennett, *The De-Valuing of America* (New York: Summit Books, 1992), 215.

14. Paul Weyrich, quoted in the film *With God on Our Side: George W. Bush and the Rise of the Religious Right*, by Calvin Skaggs, David Van Taylor, and Ali Pomeroy, Lumiere Productions, 2004.

15. Keith Ward, *In Defence of the Soul* (Oxford: Oneworld, 1998).

16. Ibid., 8, 10.

17. John D. Caputo, *On Religion* (New York: Routledge, 2001).

18. Inglehart et al., *Human Beliefs and Values.*   19.   Paul Froese, "After Atheism: An Analysis of Religious Monopolies in the Post-Communist World," *Sociology of Religion* 65, 1 (2004): 57–75. See also Rodney Stark, *Exploring the Religious Life* (Baltimore: Johns Hopkins University Press, 2004), 151.

20. Ibid.

21. D. L. Overmeyer, editor, *Religion in China Today* (Cambridge: Cambridge University Press, 2003).

22. Fenggang Yang, "Between Secularist Ideology and Desecularizing Reality: The Birth and Growth of Religious Research in Communist China," *Sociology of Religion* 65, 2 (2004): 101–19.

23. Robert Putnam, *Bowling Alone* (New York: Touchstone, 2000), 23.

24. Goran Gustafsson, "Religious Change in the Five Scandinavian Countries, 1930–1980," in *Scandinavian Values: Religion and Morality in the Nordic Countries*, ed. Thorleif Pettersson and Ole Rise (Uppsala: ACTA Universitatis Upsaliensis, 1994); Gyfli Gislason, "In Defense of Small Nations," in *Norden—the Passion for Equality*, ed. Stephen Graubard (Oslo: Norwegian University Press, 1986).

25. See Bondeson, *Nordic Moral Climates: Value Continuities and Discontinuities in Denmark, Finland, Norway, and Sweden* (New Brunswick, N.J.: Transaction Publishers, 2003). However, Inglehart et al., *Human Beliefs and Values*, reports higher rates of belief in God, with 69 percent of Danes and 53 percent of Swedes believing in God. Andrew Greeley found that 57 percent of Danes and 54 percent of Swedes believe in God (*Religion in Europe at the End of the Second Millennium*, New Brunswick, N.J.: Transaction Publishers, 2003). However, regardless of which survey is the most accurate, the fact remains that belief in God in Denmark and Sweden is dramatically lower that in nearly all other nations in the world.

26. Yves Lambert, "New Christianity, Indifference, and Diffused Spirituality," in *The Decline of Christendom in Western Europe, 1750–2000*, ed. Hugh McLeod and Ustorf Werner (New York: Cambridge University Press, 2003).

27. Inglehart et al., *Human Beliefs and Values*.

28. Ibid.

29. Ibid.

30. Ibid.

31. Ibid.

32. Pal Ketil Botvar, "Kristen tro I Norden. Privatisering og Svekkelse av religiose dogmer," in *Folkkyrkor och Religios Pluralism –Den Nordiska Religosa Modellen*, ed. Goran Gustafsson and Thorleif Pettersson (Stockholm: Verbum, 2000).

33. George Gallup, Jr., and D. Michael Lindsay, *Surveying the Religious Landscape* (Harrisburg, Pa.: Morehouse Publishing, 1999).

34. Inglehart et al., *Human Beliefs and Values*.

35. Pippa Norris and Ronald Inglehart, *Sacred and Secular: Religion and Politics Worldwide* (New York: Cambridge University Press, 2004).

36. Greeley, *Religion in Europe*.

37. Ibid.

38. Yves Lambert, "A Turning Point in Religious Evolution in Europe," *Journal of Contemporary Religion* 19, 1 (2004): 29–45.

39. Peter Gundelach, *Det er dansk* (Copenhagen: Hans Reitzels Forlag, 2002).

40. Ronald Inglehart and Pippa Norris, *Rising Tide: Gender Equality and Cultural Change around the World* (New York: Cambridge University Press, 2003); Phil Zuckerman, "Atheism: Contemporary Numbers and Patterns," in *The Cambridge Companion to Atheism*, ed. Michael Martin (Cambridge: Cambridge University Press, 2007).

41. *Human Development Report* of the United Nations (New York: Palgrave Macmillan, 2006).

42. *Human Development Report* of the United Nations (New York: United Nations Development Programme, 2005).

43. UNICEF REPORT, 2007, "The State of the World's Children"; go to www.unicef.org/sowc07/.

44. *Human Development Report* of the United Nations (New York: Palgrave Macmillan, 2006).

45. *Global Competitiveness Report 2006–2007*, World Economic Forum; go to www.weforum.org/en/initiatives/gcp/Global percent20Competitiveness percent20Report/index.htm.

46. *Human Development Report*, 2005.

47. Ibid.

48. Karen Christopher, Paula England, Timothy Smeeding, and Katherin Ross Philips, "The Gender Gap in Poverty in Modern Nations: Single Motherhood, the Market, and the State," *Sociological Perspectives* 45, 3 (2002): 219–42.

49. *Human Development Report*, 2005.

50. *Human Development Report*, 2006.

51. Thomas Kurian, *Illustrated Book of World Rankings* (Armonk, N.Y.: M. E. Sharpe, 2001).

52. Transparency International 2006, "Corruption Perceptions Index"; go to www.infoplease.com/ipa/A0781359.html.

53. Paul, "Cross–National Correlations of Quantifiable Societal Health," 1–17.

54. Byron Nordstrom, *Scandinavia Since 1500* (Minneapolis: University of Minnesota Press, 2000), 347.

55. Of course, I am not the first or only person to point this out. In a provocative article published in 2005 (cited above), Gregory S. Paul reported that nations with high rates of belief in God also had higher rates of homicide, juvenile and early adult mortality, STD infections, teen pregnancy, and abortion than nations in which belief in God is relatively low.

56. Stephen Graubard, editor, *Norden—the Passion for Equality* (Oslo: Norwegian University Press), 1986.

57. Christian Smith, "Why Christianity Works: An Emotions-Focused Phenomenological Account," *Sociology of Religion* 68, 2 (2007): 165–78.

58. Martin Luther King, Jr., *Strength to Love* (Philadelphia: Fortress Press, 1963).

59. Go to: www.cbctrust.com.

60. Inglehart et al., *Human Beliefs and Values*.

Chapter 2

1. Dean Hamer, *The God Gene: How Faith Is Hardwired into Our Genetics* (New York: Doubleday, 2004), 6.

2. Rodney Stark and Roger Finke, *Acts of Faith* (Berkeley: University of California Press, 2000); Rodney Stark and William Sims Bainbridge, *The Future of*

Religion (Berkeley: University of California Press, 1985); Rodney Stark and William Sims Bainbridge, *A Theory of Religion* (New York: Peter Lang, 1987).

3. Andrew Greeley, *Unsecular Man: The Persistence of Religion* (New York: Dell, 1972), 1.

4. Ibid., 16.

5. Justin Barrett, *Why Would Anyone Believe in God?* (Walnut Creek, Calif.: Alta Mira Press, 2004), 108.

6. Christian Smith, *Moral, Believing Animals: Human Personhood and Culture* (New York: Oxford University Press, 2003), 104.

Chapter 3

1. Belief in life after death, according to a recent survey published by Ulla Bondeson, may be as low as 30 percent in Denmark and 33 percent in Sweden. Other surveys find that the percentages are somewhat higher, for example, Andrew Greeley reports that 41 percent of Danes and 51 percent of Swedes believe in life after death. If the "true" percentage is somewhere in between these two surveys, that still means that a clear majority of Danes and Swedes do *not* believe in life after death, and that rates of belief in life after death in Scandinavia are among the lowest in the world. See Bondeson, *Nordic Moral Climates*; Andrew Greeley, *Religion in Europe at the End of the Second Millennium* (New Brunswick, N.J.: Transaction Publishers, 2003).

2. See also K. A. Opuku, "Death and Immortality in the African Religious Traditions," in *Death and Immortality in the Religions of the World*, ed. Paul Badham and Linda Badham (New York: New Era Books, 1987); Ralph Hood and Ronald Morris, "Toward a Theory of Death Transcendence," *Journal for the Scientific Study of Religion* 22, 4 (1983): 353–65; R. Kastenbaum and P. T. Costa, "Psychological Perspectives on Death," *Annual Review of Psychology* 28 (1977): 225–49.

3. See Bryan S. Turner, *Religion and Social Theory* (Thousand Oaks, Calif.: Sage Publications), 1991, chap. 10.

4. William Sims Bainbridge, "A Prophet's Reward: Dynamics of Religious Exchange," in *Sacred Markets and Sacred Canopies*, ed. Ted G. Jelen (Lanham, Md.: Rowman and Littlefield, 2002), 84.

5. Ronald Inglehart, Miguel Basanez, and Alejandro Moreno, *Human Values and Beliefs: A Cross-Cultural Sourcebook* (Ann Arbor: University of Michigan Press, 1998).

6. Bronislaw Malinowski, *Magic, Science, and Religion* (New York: Anchor, 1954), 47.

7. Sigmund Freud, *The Future of an Illusion* (New York: W. W. Norton, 1961 [1927]), 19.

8. Robert Hinde, *Why Gods Persist: A Scientific Approach to Religion* (London: Routledge, 1999).

9. Charlotte Perkins Gilman, *His Religion and Hers* (New York: Century, 1923), 18.

10. Hamer, *The God Gene*, 143.

11. Peter Berger, *The Sacred Canopy* (New York: Anchor Books, 1967), 51.

12. Stark and Bainbridge, *The Future of Religion*, 7.

13. Greeley, *Unsecular Man*, 55.

14. Berger, *The Sacred Canopy*, 56 and 58.

15. Kenneth Pargament, *The Psychology of Religion and Coping* (New York: Guilford Press, 1997), 95.

16. Barrett, *Why Would Anyone Believe in God?* 51.

17. Max Weber, "The Social Psychology of the World Religions," in *From Max Weber: Essays in Sociology*, ed. Hans Gerth and C. Wright Mills (New York: Oxford University Press, 1946).

18. To quote Andrew Greeley: "The fallacy of equating what goes on in the intellectual community—and only a segment of that—with the whole of society is one that has been so long enshrined among academics" (*Unsecular Man*, p. 3).

19. Zygmunt Bauman, *Postmodernity and Its Discontents* (Oxford: Polity Press, 1997), 170–71.

20. According to recent survey results presented by Norris and Inglehart (*Sacred and Secular*, 75), a minority of Danes and Swedes (37 percent) claim to think about the meaning of life "often." Although this is an increase—up from 29 percent for Danes and 20 percent for Swedes in 1981—it still illustrates that a distinct majority of Danes and Swedes do not think about the meaning of life all that much. And also, it is important to remember that thinking about the meaning of life need not necessarily be considered a "religious" endeavor, as some have claimed. Secular people can ponder the meaning of life often, though that does not mean they are engaging in a spiritual or religious quest.

21. Peter Gundelach, Hans Raun Iversen, and Margit Warburg, *At the Heart of Denmark: Institutional Forms and Mental Patterns* (forthcoming).

Chapter 4

1. As in Chapter 2, the interviews presented here are edited excerpts and do not comprise each interview in its entirety.

2. David Hay, *Religious Experience Today: Studying the Facts* (London: Mowbray, 1990), 9.

3. Robert Bellah, *Beyond Belief* (New York: Harper and Row, 1970, 206), 223.

4. Bauman, *Postmodernity and Its Discontents*, 170.

Chapter 5

1. Benjamin Beit-Hallahmi, "Atheists: A Psychological Profile," in *The Cambridge Companion to Atheism*, ed. Michael Martin (Cambridge: Cambridge University Press, 2007), 30.

2. Talal Asad, *Formations of the Secular: Christianity, Islam, and Modernity* (Palo Alto: Stanford University Press, 2003), 17.

3. A few notable exceptions—that is, books that deal with what it means to be secular—include: Bruce Hunsbereger and Bob Altemeyer, *Atheists: A Groundbreaking Study of America's Nonbelievers* (Amherst: Prometheus Books, 2006); Barry Kosmin and Ariela Keysar, editors, *Secularism and Secularity: Contemporary International Perspectives* (Hartford, Conn.: Institute for the Study of Secularism in Society and Culture, 2007); Colin Campbell, *Toward a Sociology of Irreligion* (New York: Herder and Herder, 1972).

4. Zuckerman, "Atheism: Contemporary Numbers and Patterns."

5. For some major works on secularization, see Karel Dobbelaere, *Secularization: An Analysis at Three Levels* (Bruxelles: P.I.E.-Peter Lang, 2002); William Swatos and Daniel Olson, *The Secularization Debate* (Lanham, Md.: Rowman and Littlefield, 2000); Steve Bruce, *God Is Dead: Secularization in the West* (Oxford: Blackwell, 2002); Peter Berger, editor, *The Desecularization of the World: Resurgent Religion and World Politics* (Grand Rapids, Mich.: William B. Eerdmans, 1999); David Martin, *A General Theory of Secularization* (New York: Harper and Row, 1978); Peter Glasner, *The Sociology of Secularization: A Critique of a Concept* (London: Routledge Kegan Paul, 1977); Berger, *The Sacred Canopy*1967. My position on secularization is as follows: it is not inevitable, as several early social theorists predicted. But neither is it impossible, as Rodney Stark and others have recently argued. Instead, a loss of religion in a given society is merely *possible*. And that does not mean it is irreversible either, for religiosity can wax and wane over generations, dying out and then suddenly reemerging. There is no question that religion in Europe—in terms of both belief and participation—has declined over the past 100 years, but that does not mean we know exactly why, nor that the decline will necessarily continue, for a religious revival is always possible.

6. Sam Harris, *The End of Faith: Religion, Terror, and the Future of Reason* (New York: W. W. Norton, 2004); Richard Dawkins, *The God Delusion* (Boston: Houghton Mifflin, 2006); Christopher Hitchens, *God Is Not Great: How Religion Poisons Everything* (New York: Twelve, 2007).

7. The pioneering work of Frank Pasquale delves into the various shades and contours of irreligion among Americans who are secular.

8. Per Salomonsen, *Religion i dag: Et sociologisk metodestudium* (Copenhagen: G.E.C. Gads Forlag, 1971).

9. Ibid., 361.

10. Callum Brown, *The Death of Christian Britain* (New York: Routledge, 2001), 182.

Chapter 6

1. Berger, ed., *The Desecularization of the World*, 11.

2. Hugh McLeod and Werner Ustorf, *The Decline of Christendom in Western Europe, 1750–2000* (New York: Cambridge University Press, 2003); Phil

Zuckerman, "Secularization: Europe —Yes; United States—No," *Skeptical Inquirer* 28, 2 (2004): 49–52.

3. See, for example, Andrew Higgins, "In Europe, God Is (Not) Dead," *Wall Street Journal*, July 14, 2007, A1.

4. Jeffrey Fleishman, "Bell Tolls for Germany's Churches," *Los Angeles Times*, April 22, 2007, 1, section A.

5. Jack Shand, "The Decline of Traditional Religious Beliefs in Germany," *Sociology of Religion* 59, 2 (1998): 179–84.

6. Manfred Te Grotenhuis and Peer Scheepers, "Churches in Dutch: Causes of Religious Disaffiliation in the Netherlands, 1937–1995," *Journal for the Scientific Study of Religion* 40, 4 (2001): 591–606.

7. Frank Lechner, "Secularization in the Netherlands?" *Journal for the Scientific Study of Religion* 35, 3 (1996): 252–64.

8. McLeod and Ustorf, *The Decline of Christendom in Western Europe*, 3.

9. Bruce, *God Is Dead*; Steve Bruce, "Christianity in Britain, R.I.P." *Sociology of Religion* 62, 2 (2001): 191–203; Brown, *The Death of Christian Britain*; Robin Gil, C. Kirck Hadaway, and Penny Long Marler, "Is Religious Belief Declining in Britain?" *Journal for the Scientific Study of Religion* 37, 3 (1998): 507–16.

10. Eva Hamberg, "Stability and Change in Religious Beliefs, Practice, and Attitudes: A Swedish Panel Study," *Journal for the Scientific Study of Religion* 30, 1 (1991): 63–80.

11. Irving Palm and Jan Trost, "Family and Religion in Sweden," in *Family, Religion, and Social Change in Diverse Societies*, ed. Sharon Houseknecht and Jerry Pankurst (New York: Oxford University Press, 2000), 108.

12. Andrew Buckser, *After the Rescue: Jewish Identity and Community in Contemporary Denmark* (New York: Palgrave Macmillan, 2003), 59.

13. Norris and Inglehart, *Sacred and Secular*, 2004, 90.

14. Steve Bruce, *Choice and Religion: A Critique of Rational Choice* (Oxford: Oxford University Press, 1999), 220.

15. Rodney Stark and Roger Finke, "Beyond Church and Sect: Dynamics and Stability in Religious Economies," in *Sacred Markets, Sacred Canopies*, ed. Ted G. Jelen (Lanham, Md.: Rowman and Littlefield, 2002); Stark and Finke, *Acts of Faith*; Riger Finke and Rodney Stark, "The Dynamics of Religious Economies," in *Handbook of the Sociology of Religion*, ed. Michele Dillon (New York: Cambridge University Press, 2003); Rodney Stark and Laurence Iannaccone, "A Supply-Side Reinterpretation of the Secularization of Europe," *Journal for the Scientific Study of Religion* 33 (1994): 230–52; Laurence Iannaccone, "Religious Markets and the Economics of Religion," *Social Compass* 39 (1992): 123–211.

16. "Seeker churches" in America do just that—they go into communities and try to find out what it is that people want in a church and what would make people who don't go to church go, and they thus create congregations based on the premise that interest in religion can be increased with the proper marketing

techniques; see Kimon Howland Sargeant, *Seeker Churches: Promoting Traditional Religion in a Nontraditional Way* (New Brunswick, N.J.: Rutgers University Press, 2000).

17. Eva Hamberg, "Christendom in Decline: the Swedish Case," in *The Decline of Christendom in Western Europe, 1750–2000*, ed. Hugh McLeod and Werner Ustorf (New York: Cambridge University Press, 2003).

18. Ibid.; also see www.km.dk.

19. Go to www.da.wikipedia.org/wiki.frikirke.

20. Hamberg, "Christendom in Decline: the Swedish Case."

21. Lambert, "New Christianity, Indifference, and Diffused Spirituality."

22. For critiques of Rodney Stark's work, particularly when applied to Scandinavia, see Steve Bruce, "The Poverty of Economism or the Social Limits on Maximizing," in *Sacred Markets and Sacred Canopies*, ed. Ted G. Jelen (Lanham, Md.: Rowman and Littlefield, 2002); Steve Bruce, "The Supply-Side Model of Religion: The Nordic and Baltic States," *Journal for the Scientific Study of Religion* 39, 1 (2000): 32–46; Bruce, *Choice and Religion*; Joseph Bryant, "Cost-Benefit Accounting and the Piety Business: Is Homo Religiosus, at Bottom, Homo Economicus?" *Method and Theory in the Study of Religion* 12, 4 (2000): 520–48.

23. The conclusion of Norris and Inglehart's extensive study into the matter is that "there is no significant relationship between participation and pluralism across the broader distribution of societies worldwide." See Norris and Inglehart, *Sacred and Secular,* 101. See also Mark Chaves and Philip Gorski, "Religious Pluralism and Religious Participation," *Annual Review of Sociology* 27 (2001): 261–81; Daniel Olson and Kirk Hadaway, "Religious Pluralism and Affiliation Among Canadian Counties and Cities," *Journal for the Scientific Study of Religion* 38, 4 (1999): 490–508.

24. Norris and Inglehart, *Sacred and Secular.*

25. Ibid., 5.

26. From Karl Marx's 1844 *Contribution to the Critique of Hegel's Philosophy of Right,* quoted in Robert Tucker, *The Marx-Engels Reader,* 2d ed. (New York: W. W. Norton, 1978), 54.

27. Neil Kent, *The Soul of the North* (London: Reaktion Books, 2000), 120.

28. Donald Connery, *The Scandinavians* (New York: Simon and Schuster, 1966), 5.

29. Eric Einhorn and John Logue, *Modern Welfare States: Scandinavian Politics and Policy in the Global Age* (Westport, Vt.: Praeger), 2003.

30. *Human Development Report* of the United Nations, 2005; *Human Development Report* of the United Nations, 2006.

31. Go to www.visionofhumanity.com.

32. Brown, *The Death of Christian Britain.*

33. Ibid., 1.

34. Ibid., 10.

35. Ibid., 192.

36. Tony Walter and Grace Davie, "The Religiosity of Women in the Modern West," *British Journal of Sociology* 49, 4 (1998): 640–60.

37. Alan Miller and Rodney Stark, "Gender and Religiousness," *American Journal of Sociology* 107 (2002): 1399–1423; Miller and Stark, "Risk and Religion: An Explanation of Gender Differences in Religiosity," *Journal for the Scientific Study of Religion* 34 (1995): 63–75.

38. Inger Furseth, "Women's Role in Historic Religious and Political Movements" *Sociology of Religion* 62, 1 (2001): 105–29; Susan Sundback, "Nation and Gender Reflected in Scandinavian Religiousness," in *Scandinavian Values: Religion and Morality in the Nordic Countries*, ed. Thorleif Pettersson and Ole Riis (Uppsala: ACTA Universitatis Upsaliensis, 1994); Berndt Gustafsson, *The Christian Faith in Sweden* (Stockholm: Verbum, 1968).

39. Ole Riis, "Patterns of Secularization in Scandinavia," in *Scandinavian Values: Religion and Morality in the Nordic Countries*, ed. Thorleif Pettersson and Ole Riis (Uppsala: ACTA Universitatis Upsaliensis, 1994), 122.

40. Bent Rold Andersen, "Rationality and Irrationality of the Nordic Welfare State," in *Norden—The Passion for Equality*, ed. Stephen Graubard (Oslo: Norwegian University Press, 1986).

41. Gundelach, Iversen, and Warburg, *At the Heart of Denmark*

42. Go to www.oecd.org/dev/institutions/GIDdatabse.

43. Go to www.denmark.dk.

44. "The Workplace: A Woman's Domain," The Copenhagen Post, June 7, 2007; go to www.denmark.dk/en/servicemenu/News/GeneralNews/TheWorkplaceAWomansDomain.htm.

45. Bradley Hertel, "Gender, Religious Identity, and Work Force Participation," *Journal for the Scientific Study of Religion* 27, 4 (1998): 574–92.

46. Bruce, *God Is Dead*; Steve Bruce, *Religion in the Modern World: From Cathedrals to Cults* (New York: Oxford University Press, 1996).

47. Martin, *A General Theory of Secularization*.

48. Sheridan Gilley, "Catholicism in Ireland," in *The Decline of Christendom in Western Europe, 1750–2000*, ed. Hugh McLeod and Werner Ustorf (New York: Cambridge University Press, 2003).

49. Phil Zuckerman, ed., *Du Bois on Religion* (Walnut Creek, Calif.: Alta Mira Press, 2000); Andrew Billingsley, *Mighty Like a River: The Black Church and Social Reform* (New York: Oxford University Press, 1999).

50. Andrew Greeley and Michael Hout, *The Truth about Christian Conservatives: What They Think and What They Believe* (Chicago: University of Chicago Press, 2006).

51. Personal correspondence via e-mail, May 10, 2007.

52. Knud Jespersen, *A History of Denmark* (New York: Palgrave Macmillan, 2004), 93–94.

53. The Harris Poll #11, February 26, 2003; go to www.harrisinteractive.com.

54. Georg Gallup, Jr., and D. Michael Lindsay, *Surveying the Religious Landscape* (Harrisburg, Pa.: Morehouse Publishing, 1999), 35.

55. www.http://edition.cnn.com/2002/EDUCATION/11/26/education.rankings.reut/index.html.

56. Go to www.siteselection.com/ssinsider/snapshot/sf011210.htm.

57. *Human Development Report* of the United Nations, 2006.

58. S. S. Acquaviva, *The Decline of the Sacred in Industrial Society* (New York: Harper and Row, 1979); Rodney Stark, "Secularization R.I.P.," *Sociology of Religion* 60 (1999): 249–73.

59. Hilda Elis Davidson, *The Lost Beliefs of Northern Europe* (New York: Routledge, 1993); Hilda Elis Davidson, *Gods and Myths of Northern Europe* (New York: Penguin Books, 1964).

60. Richard Fletcher, *The Barbarian Conversion: From Paganism to Christianity* (New York: Henry Holt, 1997), 374.

61. Ibid., 372–73.

62. Carole Cusack, *The Rise of Christianity in Northern Europe 300–1000* (London: Cassell, 1998), 145; P. H. Sawyer, *Kings and Vikings: Scandinavia and Europe AD 700–1100* (London: Methuen, 1982), 102.

63. Prudence Jones and Nigel Pennick, *A History of Pagan Europe* (New York: Routledge, 1995).

64. George Proctor, *Ancient Scandinavia* (New York: John Day, 1965), 112.

65. Gustafsson, *The Christian Faith in Sweden.*

66. Davidson, *Gods and Myths of Northern Europe*, 23.

67. Palle Lauring, *A History of Denmark* (Copenhagen: Host and Son, 1960), 124.

68. John Flint, "The Secularization of Norwegian Society," *Comparative Studies in Society and History* 6, 3 (1964): 325–44.

69. Sawyer, *Kings and Vikings*, 139.

70. Kent, *The Soul of the North.*

71. Lauring, *A History of Denmark.*

72. Kent, *The Soul of the North.*

73. T. K. Derry, *A History of Scandinavia* (Minneapolis: University of Minnesota Press, 1979), 94.

74. B. J. Hovde, *The Scandinavian Countries, 1720–1865* (Ithaca, N.Y.: Cornell University Press, 1948), 308.

75. Arnold H. Barton, *Scandinavia in the Revolutionary Era, 1760–1815* (Minneapolis: University of Minnesota Press, 1986), 46.

76. Hans Raun Iversen, "Leaving the Distant Church: The Danish Experience," *Religion and the Social Order* 7 (1997): 139–58.

77. Andrew Buckser, *Communities of Faith: Sectarianism, Identity, and Social Change on a Danish Island* (Oxford: Berghahn Books, 1996), 105.

78. Hans Raun Iversen, "Leaving the Distant Church

79. Gerald Strauss, "Lutheranism and Literacy: A Reassessment," in *Religion and Society in Early Modern Europe 1500–1800*, ed. Kaspar von Greyerz (Boston: George Allen and Unwin, 1984).

80. Hamberg, "Christendom in Decline: the Swedish Case."

81. Timothy Tangherlini, "Who Ya Gonna Call?: Ministers and the Mediation of Ghostly Threat in Danish Legal Tradition," *Western Folklore* 57, 2/3 (1998): 153–78; Timothy Tangherlini, "How Do You Know She's a Witch?: Witches, Cunning Folk, and Competition in Denmark," *Western Folklore* 59, 3/4 (2000): 279–303; Gustav Henningsen, "Witchcraft in Denmark," *Folklore* 93, 2 (1982): 131–37; Anders Frojmark, "Demons in the miracula," in *Medieval Spirituality in Scandinavia and Europe*, ed. Lars Bisgaard et al. (Odense: Odense University Press, 2001); Jens Christian Johansen, "Faith, Superstition and Witchcraft in Reformation Scandinavia," in *The Scandinavian Reformation*, ed. Ole Peter Grell (New York: Cambridge University Press, 1995).

82. Bryan Wilson, "Unbelief as an Object of Research," in *The Culture of Unbelief*, ed. Rocco Caporale and Antonio Grumelli (Berkeley: University of California Press, 1971), 247.

Chapter 7

1. For a fuller account of the difference between "religious" and "spiritual," see Robert Fuller, *Spiritual but Not Religious* (New York: Oxford University Press, 2001); Penny Long Marler and Kirk Hadaway, "'Being Religious' or 'Being Spiritual' in America: A Zero-Sum Proposition?" *Journal for the Scientific Study of Religion* 41, 2 (2002): 289–300; Wade Clark Roof, *Spiritual Marketplace: Baby Boomers and the Remaking of American Religion* (Princeton, N.J.: Princeton University Press, 1999).

2. David Harrington Watt, *Bible-Carrying Christians* (New York: Oxford University Press, 2002); Charles Strozier, *Apocalypse: On the Psychology of Fundamentalism in America* (Boston: Beacon Press, 1994); Susan Rose, *Keeping Them Out of the Hands of Satan: Evangelical Schooling in America* (New York: Routledge, 1988); Nancy Ammerman, *Bible Believers* (New Brunswick, N.J.: Rutgers University Press, 1987).

3. Peter Berger quoted in Stark and Finke, *Acts of Faith*, 58.

4. Simon Coleman, *The Globalisation of Charismatic Christianity* (Cambridge: Cambridge University Press, 2000); Buckser, *Communities of Faith*.

Chapter 8

1. Iversen, "Leaving the Distant Church: The Danish Experience," 146.

2. Bondeson, *Nordic Moral Climates*; Botvar, "Kristen tro I Norden. Privatisering og Svekkelse av religiose dogmer."

3. Grace Davie, *Religion in Britain since 1945: Believing without Belonging* (Oxford: Blackwell, 1994).

4. Riis, "Patterns of Secularization in Scandinavia," 99.

5. Daniele Hervieu-Leger, *Religion as a Chain of Memory* (New Brunswick, N.J.: Rutgers University Press, 2000).

6. Phil Zuckerman, *Strife in the Sanctuary: Religious Schism in a Jewish Community* (Walnut Creek, Calif.: Alta Mira Press, 1999).

7. Arnold Dashefsky, Bernard Lazerwitz, and Ephraim Tabory, "A Journey of the 'Straight Way' or the 'Roundabout Path': Jewish Identity in the United States and Israel," in *Handbook of the Sociology of Religion*, ed. Michele Dillon (New York: Cambridge University Press, 2003).

8. Inglehart et al., *Human Beliefs and Values*.

9. Dashefsky, Lazerwitz, and Tabory, "A Journey of the 'Straight Way' or the 'Roundabout Path.'"

10. Inglehart et al., *Human Beliefs and Values*.

11. Kosmin and Keysar, editors, *Secularism and Secularity*.

12. Beit-Hallahmi, "Atheists: A Psychological Profile."

13. Martin Weinberg, Ilsa Lottes, and Frances Shaver, "Sociocultural Correlates of Permissive Sexual Attitudes: A Test of Reiss's Hypothesis About Sweden and the United States," *Journal of Sex Research* 37, 1 (2000): 44–52.

14. John Hoffman and Alan Miller, "Social and Political Attitudes Among Religious Groups: Convergence and Divergence over Time," *Journal for the Scientific Study of Religion* 36, 1 (1997): 52–70.

15. Inglehart et al., *Human Beliefs and Values*.

16. Hoffman and Miller, "Social and Political Attitudes Among Religious Groups," 52–70.

17. Loek Halman, "Scandinavian Values: How Special Are They," in *Scandinavian Values: Religion and Morality in the Nordic Countries*, ed. Thorleif Pettersson and Ole Rise (Uppsala: ACTA Universitatis Upsaliensis, 1994).

18. John Cochran and Leonard Beeghley, "The Influence of Religion on Attitudes Toward Nonmarital Sexuality: A Preliminary Assessment of Reference Group Theory," *Journal for the Scientific Study of Religion* 30, 1 (1991): 45–62.

19. Kosmin and Keysar, editors, *Secularism and Secularity*; Barry Kosmin and Seymour Lachman, *One Nation Under God: Religion in Contemporary American Society* (New York: Crown, 1993).

20. Graubard, editor, *Norden—the Passion for Equality*.

21. Roberta Rosenberg Farber and Chaim Waxman, editors, *Jews in America: A Contemporary Reader* (Waltham, Mass.: Brandeis University Press, 1999).

22. N. J. Demerath, "The Rise of 'Cultural Religion' in European Christianity: Learning from Poland, Northern Ireland, and Sweden," *Social Compass* 47, 1 (2000): 127–39; N. J. Demerath, *Crossing the Gods: World Religions and Worldly Politics* (New Brunswick, N.J.: Rutgers University Press, 2001).

23. Kevin Christiano, William Swatos, and Peter Kivisto, *Sociology of Religion: Contemporary Developments* (Walnut Creek, Calif.: Alta Mira Press, 2002).

24. Inger Furseth and Paal Repstad, *An Introduction to the Sociology of Religion* (Burlington, Vt.: Ashgate, 2006).

25. Stark and Bainbridge, *The Future of Religion*, 3.

26. Consider, for example, the recent case of Danish priest Thorkild Grosboll; his congregation stood by him and supported his tenure despite the fact that he denied a belief in God.

27. Rodney Stark, *One True God: Historical Consequences of Monotheism* (Princeton, N.J.: Princeton University Press, 2001), 213.

28. Bellah, *Beyond Belief*.

29. Demerath, "The Rise of 'Cultural Religion' in European Christianity," 136.

30. Survey results from "Paskemaling," a survey done by Epinion, commissioned by *Kristelig Daglblad*, March 26, 2006.

31. Go to www.wayoflife.org/fbns/fbns/fbns209.html.

32. Palm and Trost, "Family and Religion in Sweden," 111.

33. Franklin Scott, *Scandinavia* (Cambridge, Mass.: Harvard University Press, 1975), 42.

34. Botvar, "Kristen tro I Norden. Privatisering og Svekkelse av religiose dogmer."

35. See, for example, Greeley, *Religion in Europe at the End of the Second Millennium*.

36. Demerath, "The Rise of 'Cultural Religion' in European Christianity," 129–30.

37. Harris, *The End of Faith*, 29.

Chapter 9

1. Richard H. Niebuhr, *The Social Sources of Denominationalism* (Cleveland: Meridian Books, 1929)); Will Herberg, *Protestant Catholic Jew* (New York: Anchor, 1955); Stephen R. Warner and Judith Wittner, editors, *Gatherings in Diaspora: Religious Communities and the New Immigration* (Philadelphia: Temple University Press, 1998); Helen Rose Ebaugh and Janet Saltzman Chafetz, *Religion and the New Immigrants: Continuities and Adaptations in Immigrant Congregations* (Walnut Creek, Calif.: Alta Mira Press, 2000).

2. Jan Lindhardt was quoted in Gundelach, Iversen, and Warburg, *At the Heart of Denmark*.

3. Norris and Inglehart, *Sacred and Secular*, 108–10.

4. *Gallup Poll Monthly*, no. 352, January 1995.

5. Ibid.

Bibliography

Acquaviva, S. S. 1979. *The Decline of the Sacred in Industrial Society*. New York: Harper and Row.

Ali, Ayaan Hirsi. 2007. *Infidel*. New York: Free Press.

Altoun, Richard. 2001. *Understanding Fundamentalism*. Walnut Creek, Calif.: Alta Mira Press.

Ammerman, Nancy. 1987. *Bible Believers*. New Brunswick, N.J.: Rutgers University Press.

Andersen, Bent Rold. 1986. "Rationality and Irrationality of the Nordic Welfare State." In *Norden—The Passion for Equality*, edited by Stephen Graubard. Oslo: Norwegian University Press.

Asad, Talal. 2003. *Formations of the Secular: Christianity, Islam, and Modernity*. Palo Alto: Stanford University Press.

Bainbridge, William Sims. 2002. "A Prophet's Reward: Dynamics of Religious Exchange." In *Sacred Markets and Sacred Canopies*, edited by Ted G. Jelen. Lanham, Md.: Rowman and Littlefield.

Barrett, Justin. 2004. *Why Would Anyone Believe in God?* Walnut Creek, Calif.: Alta Mira Press.

Barton, H. Arnold. 1986. *Scandinavia in the Revolutionary Era, 1760–1815*. Minneapolis: University of Minnesota Press.

Bauman, Zygmunt. 1997. *Postmodernity and Its Discontents*. Oxford: Polity Press.

Becker, Ernest. 1998. *Denial of Death*. New York: Free Press.

Beit-Hallahmi, Benjamin. 2007. "Atheists: A Psychological Profile." In *The Cambridge Companion to Atheism*, edited by Michael Martin. Cambridge: Cambridge University Press.

Bellah, Robert. 1970. *Beyond Belief*. New York: Harper and Row.

Bennett, William. 1992. *The De-Valuing of America*. New York: Summit Books.

Bennett, William, John Dilulio, Jr., and John Walters. 1996. *Body Count: Moral Poverty and How to Win America's War against Crime and Drugs*. New York: Simon and Schuster.

Berger, Peter. 2001. "Reflections on the Sociology of Religion Today." *Sociology of Religion* 62(4): 443—54.

———, ed. 1999. *The Desecularization of the World: Resurgent Religion and World Politics*. Grand Rapids, Mich.: William B. Eerdmans.

———. 1968. "A Bleak Outlook Is Seen for Religion." *New York Times*, April 25, p. 3.

———. 1967. *The Sacred Canopy*. New York: Anchor Books.

Bibby, Reginald. 2002. *Restless Gods: The Renaissance of Religion in Canada*. Toronto: Stoddart.

Billingsley, Andrew. 1999. *Mighty Like a River: The Black Church and Social Reform*. New York: Oxford University Press.

Bondeson, Ulla. 2003. *Nordic Moral Climates: Value Continuities and Discontinuities in Denmark, Finland, Norway, and Sweden*. New Brunswick, N.J.: Transaction Publishers.

Botvar, Pål Ketil. 2000. "Kristen tro I Norden. Privatisering og Svekkelse av religiøse dogmer." In *Folkkyrkor och Religiös Pluralism –Den Nordiska Religosa Modellen*, edited by Göran Gustafsson and Thorleif Pettersson. Stockholm: Verbum.

Brown, Callum. 2001. *The Death of Christian Britain*. New York: Routledge.

Bruce, Steve. 2002a. *God Is Dead: Secularization in the West*. Oxford: Blackwell.

———. 2002b. "The Poverty of Economism or the Social Limits on Maximizing." In *Sacred Markets and Sacred Canopies*, edited by Ted G. Jelen. Lanham, Md.: Rowman and Littlefield.

———. 2001. "Christianity in Britain, R.I.P." *Sociology of Religion* 62(2): 191–203.

———. 2000. "The Supply-Side Model of Religion: The Nordic and Baltic States." *Journal for the Scientific Study of Religion* 39(1): 32–46.

———. 1999. *Choice and Religion: A Critique of Rational Choice*. Oxford: Oxford University Press.

———. 1996. *Religion in the Modern World: From Cathedrals to Cults*. New York: Oxford University Press.

Bryant, Joseph. 2000. "Cost-Benefit Accounting and the Piety Business: Is Homo Religiosus, at Bottom, Homo Economicus?" *Method and Theory in the Study of Religion* 12(4): 520–48.

Buckser, Andrew. 2003. *After the Rescue: Jewish Identity and Community in Contemporary Denmark*. New York: Palgrave Macmillan.

———. 1996. *Communities of Faith: Sectarianism, Identity, and Social Change on a Danish Island*. Oxford: Berghahn Books.

Campbell, Colin. 1972. *Toward a Sociology of Irreligion*. New York: Herder and Herder.

Chaves, Mark, and Philip Gorski. 2001. "Religious Pluralism and Religious Participation." *Annual Review of Sociology* 27: 261–81.

Christiano, Kevin, William Swatos, and Peter Kivisto. 2002. *Sociology of Religion: Contemporary Developments*. Walnut Creek, Calif.: Alta Mira Press.

Christopher, Karen, Paula England, Timothy Smeeding, and Katherin Ross Philips. 2002. "The Gender Gap in Poverty in Modern Nations: Single Motherhood, the Market, and the State." *Sociological Perspectives* 45(3): 219–42.

Cochran, John, and Leonard Beeghley. 1991. "The Influence of Religion on Attitudes Toward Nonmarital Sexuality: A Preliminary Assessment of Reference Group Theory." *Journal for the Scientific Study of Religion* 30(1):45–62.

Coleman, Simon. 2000. *The Globalisation of Charismatic Christianity*. Cambridge: Cambridge University Press.

Connery, Donald. 1966. *The Scandinavians*. New York: Simon and Schuster.

Cusack, Carole. 1998. *The Rise of Christianity in Northern Europe 300–1000*. London: Cassell.

Dashefsky, Arnold, Bernard Lazerwitz, and Ephraim Tabory. 2003. "A Journey of the 'Straight Way' or the 'Roundabout Path'": Jewish Identity in the United States and Israel." In *Handbook of the Sociology of Religion*, edited by Michele Dillon. New York: Cambridge University Press.

Dawkins, Richard. 2006. *The God Delusion*. Boston: Houghton Mifflin.

Davidson, Hilda Ellis. 1993. *The Lost Beliefs of Northern Europe*. New York: Routledge.

———. 1964. *Gods and Myths of Northern Europe*. New York: Penguin Books.

Davie, Grace. 1994. *Religion in Britain since 1945: Believing without Belonging*. Oxford: Blackwell.

Decik, Lars. 2007. "The Paradox of Secularism in Denmark: From Emancipation to Ethnocentrism?" In *Secularism and Secularity: Contemporary International Perspectives*, edited by Barry Kosmin and Ariela Keysar. Hartford, Conn.: Institute for the Study of Secularism in Society and Culture.

Demerath, N. J. 2001. *Crossing the Gods: World Religions and Worldly Politics*. New Brunswick, N.J.: Rutgers University Press.

———. 2000. "The Rise of 'Cultural Religion' in European Christianity: Learning from Poland, Northern Ireland, and Sweden." *Social Compass* 47(1): 127–39.

Derry, T. K. 1979. *A History of Scandinavia*. Minneapolis: University of Minnesota Press.

Dobbelaere, Karel. 2002. *Secularization: An Analysis at Three Levels*. Bruxelles: P.I.E.-Peter Lang.

Ebaugh, Helen Rose, and Janet Saltzman Chafetz. 2000. *Religion and the New Immigrants: Continuities and Adaptations in Immigrant Congregations*. Walnut Creek, Calif.: Alta Mira Press.

Einhorn, Eric, and John Logue. 2003. *Modern Welfare States: Scandinavian Politics and Policy in the Global Age*. Westport, Vt.: Praeger.

Farber, Roberta Rosenberg, and Chaim Waxman, editors. 1999. *Jews in America: A Contemporary Reader*. Waltham, Mass.: Brandeis University Press.

Finke, Roger, and Rodney Stark. 2003. "The Dynamics of Religious Economies." In *Handbook of the Sociology of Religion*, edited by Michele Dillon. New York: Cambridge University Press.

Fleishman, Jeffrey. 2007. "Bell Tolls for Germany's Churches." *Los Angeles Times*, April 22, 2007, page 1, section A.

Fletcher, Richard. 1997. *The Barbarian Conversion: From Paganism to Christianity*. New York: Henry Holt.

Flint, John. 1964. "The Secularization of Norwegian Society." *Comparative Studies in Society and History* 6(3): 325–44.

Freud, Sigmund. 1961 [1927]. *The Future of an Illusion*. New York: W. W. Norton.

Froese, Paul. 2004. "After Atheism: An Analysis of Religious Monopolies in the Post-Communist World." *Sociology of Religion* 65(1): 57–75. See also Stark (2004), p. 151.

Frojmark, Anders. 2001. "Demons in the miracula." In *Medieval Spirituality in Scandinavia and Europe*, edited by Lars Bisgaard, Carsten Selch Jensen, Kurt Villads Jensen, and John Lind. Odense: Odense University Press.

Fuller, Robert. 2001. *Spiritual but Not Religious*. New York: Oxford University Press.

Furseth, Inger. 2006. *From Quest for Truth to Being Oneself: Religious Change in Life Stories*. Frankfurt Am Main: Peter Lang.

———. 2001. "Women's Role in Historic Religious and Political Movements." *Sociology of Religion* 62(1): 105–29.

Furseth, Inger, and Paal Repstad. 2006. *An Introduction to the Sociology of Religion*. Burlington, Vt.: Ashgate.

Gallup, George, Jr., and D. Michael Lindsay. 1999. *Surveying the Religious Landscape*. Harrisburg, Pa.: Morehouse.

Geertz, Clifford. 1973. *The Interpretation of Cultures: Selected Essay*. New York: Basic Books.

Gil, Robin, C. Kirck Hadaway, and Penny Long Marler. 1998. "Is Religious Belief Declining in Britain?" *Journal for the Scientific Study of Religion* 37(3): 507–16.

Gilley, Sheridan. 2003. "Catholicism in Ireland." In *The Decline of Christendom in Western Europe, 1750–2000*, edited by Hugh McLeod and Werner Ustorf. New York: Cambridge University Press.

Gilman, Charlotte Perkins. 1923. *His Religion and Hers*. New York: Century.

Gislason, Gyfli. 1986. "In Defense of Small Nations." In *Norden—the Passion for Equality*, edited by Stephen Graubard. Oslo: Norwegian University Press.

Glasner, Peter. 1977. *The Sociology of Secularization: A Critique of a Concept*. London: Routledge of Kegan Paul.

Graubard, Stephen, editor. 1986. *Norden—the Passion for Equality*. Oslo: Norwegian University Press.

Greeley, Andrew. 2003. *Religion in Europe at the End of the Second Millennium*. New Brunswick, N.J.: Transaction Publishers.

———. 1972. *Unsecular Man: The Persistence of Religion*. New York: Dell.

Greeley, Andrew, and Michael Hout. 2006. *The Truth About Christian Conservatives: What They Think and What They Believe*. Chicago: University of Chicago Press.

Grieve, Gregory Price. 2006. *Retheorizing Religion in Nepal*. New York: Palgrave Macmillan.

Grossbongardt, Annette. 2006. "Less Europe, More Islam." *Spiegel Online*, Nov. 2, 2006. www.spiegel.de.

Grotenhuis, Manfred Te, and Peer Scheepers. 2001. "Churches in Dutch: Causes of Religious Disaffiliation in the Netherlands, 1937–1995." *Journal for the Scientific Study of Religion* 40(4): 591–606.

Gundelach, Peter. 2002. *Det er dansk*. Copenhagen: Hans Reitzels Forlag.

Gundelach, Peter, Hans Raun Iversen, and Margit Warburg. Forthcoming. *At the Heart of Denmark: Institutional Forms and Mental Patterns*.

Gustafsson, Berndt. 1968. *The Christian Faith in Sweden*. Stockholm: Verbum.

Gustafsson, Goran. 1994. "Religious Change in the Five Scandinavian Countries, 1930–1980." In *Scandinavian Values: Religion and Morality in the Nordic Countries*, edited by Thorleif Pettersson and Ole Rise. Uppsala: ACTA Universitatis Upsaliensis.

Halman, Loek. 1994. "Scandinavian Values: How Special Are They?" In *Scandinavian Values: Religion and Morality in the Nordic Countries*, edited by Thorleif Pettersson and Ole Rise. Uppsala: ACTA Universitatis Upsaliensis.

Hamberg, Eva. 2003. "Christendom in Decline: The Swedish Case." In *The Decline of Christendom in Western Europe, 1750–2000*, edited by Hugh McLeod and Werner Ustorf. New York: Cambridge University Press.

———. 1991. "Stability and Change in Religious Beliefs, Practice, and Attitudes: A Swedish Panel Study." *Journal for the Scientific Study of Religion* 30(1): 63–80.

Hamberg, Eva, and Thorleif Pettersson. 2002. "Religious Markets: Supply, Demand, and Rational Choices." In *Sacred Markets, Sacred Canopies*, edited by Ted G. Jelen. Lanham, Md.: Rowman and Littlefield.

Hamer, Dean. 2004. *The God Gene: How Faith Is Hardwired into Our Genetics*. New York: Doubleday.

Harris, Sam. 2004. *The End of Faith: Religion, Terror, and the Future of Reason*. New York: W. W. Norton.

Hay, David. 1990. *Religious Experience Today: Studying the Facts*. London: Mowbray.

Henningsen, Gustav. 1982. "Witchcraft in Denmark." *Folklore* 93 (2): 131–37.

Herberg, Will. 1955. *Protestant Catholic Jew*. New York: Anchor.

Hertel, Bradley. 1988. "Gender, Religious Identity, and Work Force Participation." *Journal for the Scientific Study of Religion* 27(4): 574–92.

Hervieu-Leger, Daniele. 2000. *Religion as a Chain of Memory*. New Brunswick, N.J.: Rutgers University Press.

Higgins, Andrew. 2007. "In Europe, God Is (Not) Dead." *Wall Street Journal*, July 14, page A1.

Hinde, Robert. 1999. *Why Gods Persist: A Scientific Approach to Religion*. London: Routledge.

Hitchens, Christopher. 2007. *God Is Not Great: How Religion Poisons Everything.* New York: Twelve.

Hoffman, John, and Alan Miller. 1997. "Social and Political Attitudes Among Religious Groups: Convergence and Divergence over Time." *Journal for the Scientific Study of Religion* 36 (1): 52–70.

Hoge, Dean, Bention Johnson, and Donald Luidens. 1994. *Vanishing Boundaries: The Religion of Mainline Protestant Baby Boomers.* Louisville, Ky.: Westminster/John Knox Press.

Hood, Ralph, and Ronald Morris. 1983. "Toward a Theory of Death Transcendence." *Journal for the Scientific Study of Religion* 22(4): 353–65.

Hovde, B. J. 1948. *The Scandinavian Countries, 1720–1865.* Ithaca, N.Y.: Cornell University Press.

Hunsberger, Bruce, and Bob Altemeyer. 2006. *Atheists: A Groundbreaking Study of America's Nonbelievers.* Amherst: Prometheus Books.

Iannaccone, Laurence. 1992. "Religious Markets and the Economics of Religion." *Social Compass* 39: 123–211.

Inglehart, Ronald, Miguel Basanez, Jaime Diez-Medrano, Loek Halman, and Ruud Luijkx. 2004. *Human Beliefs and Values: A Cross-Cultural Sourcebook Based on the 1999–2002 Value Surveys.* Buenos Aires: Siglo Veintiuon Editores.

Inglehart, Ronald, Miguel Basanez, and Alejandro Moreno. 1998. *Human Values and Beliefs: A Cross-Cultural Sourcebook.* Ann Arbor: University of Michigan Press.

Inglehart, Ronald, and Pippa Norris. 2003. *Rising Tide: Gender Equality and Cultural Change Around the World.* New York: Cambridge University Press.

Iversen, Hans Raun. 2006. "Secular Religion and Religious Secularism: A Profile of the Religious Development in Denmark Since 1968." *Nordic Journal of Religion and Society* 2: 75–93.

———. 1997. "Leaving the Distant Church: The Danish Experience." *Religion and the Social Order* 7: 139–58.

Jespersen, Knud. 2004. *A History of Denmark.* New York: Palgrave Macmillan.

Johansen, Jens Christian. 1995. "Faith, Superstition and Witchcraft in Reformation Scandinavia." In *The Scandinavian Reformation,* edited by Ole Peter Grell. New York: Cambridge University Press.

Jones, Prudence, and Nigel Pennick. 1995. *A History of Pagan Europe.* New York: Routledge.

Kastenbaum, R., and P. T. Costa. 1977. "Psychological Perspectives on Death." *Annual Review of Psychology* 28: 225–49.

Kent, Neil. 2000. *The Soul of the North.* London: Reaktion Books.

King, Jr., Martin Luther. 1963. *Strength to Love.* Philadelphia: Fortress Press.

Kosmin, Barry, and Ariela Keysar, editors. 2007. *Secularism and Secularity: Contemporary International Perspectives.* Hartford, Conn.: Institute for the Study of Secularism in Society and Culture.

Kosmin, Barry, and Ariela Keysar. 2006. *Religion in a Free Market*. Ithaca, N.Y.: Paramount Market Publishing.

Kosmin, Barry, and Seymour Lachman. 1993. *One Nation Under God: Religion in Contemporary American Society*. New York: Crown.

Lambert, Yves. 2004. "A Turning Point in Religious Evolution in Europe." *Journal of Contemporary Religion* 19(1): 29–45.

———. 2003. "New Christianity, Indifference, and Diffused Spirituality." In *The Decline of Christendom in Western Europe, 1750–2000*, edited by Hugh McLeod and Ustorf Werner. New York: Cambridge University Press.

Lauring, Palle. 1960. *A History of Denmark*. Copenhagen: Host and Son.

Lechner, Frank. 1996. "Secularization in the Netherlands?" *Journal for the Scientific Study of Religion* 35(3): 252–64.

Limbaugh, Rush. 1993. *See, I Told You So*. New York: Pocket Star Books.

Malinowski, Bronislaw. 1954. *Magic, Science, and Religion*. New York: Anchor.

Marler, Penny Long, and Kirk Hadaway. 2002. "'Being Religious' or 'Being Spiritual' in America: A Zero-Sum Proposition?" *Journal for the Scientific Study of Religion* 41(2): 289–300.

Martin, David. 1978. *A General Theory of Secularization*. New York: Harper and Row.

Martin, Michael. 2007. *Cambridge Companion to Atheism*. New York: Cambridge University Press.

McCullough, Michael, and Timothy Smith. 2003. "Religion and Health." In *Handbook of the Sociology of Religion*, edited by Michele Dillon. New York: Cambridge University Press.

McLeod, Hugh, and Werner Ustorf. 2003. *The Decline of Christendom in Western Europe, 1750–2000*. New York: Cambridge University Press.

Miller, Alan, and Rodney Stark. 2002. "Gender and Religiousness." *American Journal of Sociology* 107: 1399–1423.

Miller, Alan S., and John P. Hoffman. 1995. "Risk and Religion: An Explanation of Gender Differences in Religiosity." *Journal for the Scientific Study of Religion* 34: 63–75.

Niebuhr, H. Richard. 1929. *The Social Sources of Denominationalism*. Cleveland: Meridian Books.

Nordstrom, Byron. 2000. *Scandinavia Since 1500*. Minneapolis: University of Minnesota Press.

Norris, Pippa, and Ronald Inglehart. 2004. *Sacred and Secular: Religion and Politics Worldwide*. New York: Cambridge University Press.

Olson, Daniel, and Kirk Hadaway. 1999. "Religious Pluralism and Affiliation Among Canadian Counties and Cities." *Journal for the Scientific Study of Religion* 38(4): 490–508.

Opuku, K. A. 1987. "Death and Immortality in the African Religious Traditions." In *Death and Immortality in the Religions of the World*, edited by Paul Badham and Linda Badham. New York: New Era Books.

Overmeyer, D. L. editor. 2003. *Religion in China Today*. Cambridge: Cambridge University Press.

Palm, Irving, and Jan Trost. 2000. "Family and Religion in Sweden." In *Family, Religion, and Social Change in Diverse Societies*, edited by Sharon Houseknecht and Jerry Pankurst. New York: Oxford University Press.

Pargament, Kenneth. 1997. *The Psychology of Religion and Coping*. New York: Guilford Press.

Pasquale, Frank. 2006. "Varieties of Irreligious Experience in the American Northwest." Paper presented at the annual meeting for the Society for the Scientific Study of Religion, October 21.

Paul, Gregory. 2005. "Cross-National Correlations of Quantifiable Societal Health with Popular Religiosity and Secularism in the Prosperous Democracies." *Journal of Religion and Society* 7(1): 1–17.

Pettersson, Thorleif, and Ole Riis. 1994. *Scandinavian Values: Religion and Morality in the Nordic Countries*. Uppsala: ACTA Universitatis Upsaliensis.

Proctor, George. 1965. *Ancient Scandinavia*. New York: John Day.

Putnam, Robert. 2000. *Bowling Alone*. New York: Touchstone.

Riis, Ole. 1994. "Patterns of Secularization in Scandinavia." In *Scandinavian Values: Religion and Morality in the Nordic Countries*, edited by Thorleif Pettersson and Ole Riis. Uppsala: ACTA Universitatis Upsaliensis.

Roof, Wade Clark. 1999. *Spiritual Marketplace: Baby Boomers and the Remaking of American Religion*. Princeton, N.J.: Princeton University Press.

Rose, Susan. 1988. *Keeping Them Out of the Hands of Satan: Evangelical Schooling in America*. New York: Routledge.

Salomonsen, Per. 1971. *Religion i dag: Et sociologisk metodestudium*. Copenhagen: G.E.C. Gads Forlag.

Sargeant, Kimon Howland. 2000. *Seeker Churches: Promoting Traditional Religion in a Nontraditional Way*. New Brunswick, N.J.: Rutgers University Press.

Sawyer, P. H. 1982. *Kings and Vikings: Scandinavia and Europe AD 700–1100*. London: Methuen.

Scott, Franklin. 1975. *Scandinavia*. Cambridge, Mass.: Harvard University Press.

Shand, Jack. 1998. "The Decline of Traditional Religious Beliefs in Germany." *Sociology of Religion* 59(2): 179–84.

Shermer, Michael. 2004. *The Science of Good and Evil*. New York: Henry Holt.

Smith, Christian. 2007. "Why Christianity Works: An Emotions- Focused Phenomenological Account." *Sociology of Religion* 68(2): 165–78.

———. 2003. *Moral, Believing Animals: Human Personhood and Culture*. New York: Oxford University Press.

Snarey, John. 1996. "The Natural Environment's Impact Upon Religious Ethics: A Cross-Cultural Study." *Journal for the Scientific Study of Religion* 35(2): 85–96.

Stark, Rodney. 2004. *Exploring the Religious Life*. Baltimore, Md.: Johns Hopkins University Press.

———. 2001. *One True God: Historical Consequences of Monotheism.* Princeton, N.J.: Princeton University Press.

———. 1999. Secularization R.I.P. *Sociology of Religion* 60: 249–73.

Stark, Rodney, and William Sims Bainbridge. 1987. *A Theory of Religion.* New York: Peter Lang.

———. 1985. *The Future of Religion.* Berkeley: University of California Press.

Stark, Rodney, and Roger Finke. 2002. "Beyond Church and Sect: Dynamics and Stability in Religious Economies." In *Sacred Markets, Sacred Canopies*, edited by Ted G. Jelen. Lanham, Md.: Rowman and Littlefield.

———. 2000. *Acts of Faith: Explaining the Human Side of Religion.* Berkeley: University of California Press.

Stark, Rodney, Eva Hamberg, and Alan S. Miller. 2004. "Spirituality and Unchurched Religions in America, Sweden, and Japan." In *Exploring the Religious Life*, by Rodney Stark. Baltimore, Md.: Johns Hopkins University Press.

Stark, Rodney, and Laurence Iannaccone. 1994. "A Supply-Side Reinterpretation of the Secularization of Europe." *Journal for the Scientific Study of Religion* 33: 230–52.

Strauss, Gerald. 1984. "Lutheranism and Literacy: A Reassessment." In *Religion and Society in Early Modern Europe 1500–1800*, edited by Kaspar von Greyerz. Boston: George Allen and Unwin.

Strozier, Charles. 1994. *Apocalypse: On the Psychology of Fundamentalism in America.* Boston: Beacon Press.

Sundback, Susan. 1994. "Nation and Gender Reflected in Scandinavian Religiousness." In *Scandinavian Values: Religion and Morality in the Nordic Countries*, edited by Thorleif Pettersson and Ole Riis. Uppsala: ACTA Universitatis Upsaliensis.

Swatos, William, and Daniel Olson. 2000. *The Secularization Debate.* Lanham, Md.: Rowman and Littlefield.

Tangherlini, Timothy. 2000. "How Do You Know She's a Witch?: Witches, Cunning Folk, and Competition in Denmark." *Western Folklore* 59 (3/4): 279–303.

———. 1998. "Who Ya Gonna Call? Ministers and the Mediation of Ghostly Threat in Danish Legal Tradition." *Western Folklore* 57(2/3): 153–78.

Tucker, Robert. 1978. *The Marx-Engels Reader*, 2d ed. New York: W. W. Norton.

Turner, Bryan. 1991. *Religion and Social Theory.* Thousand Oaks, Calif.: Sage.

Turville-Petre, E.O.G. 1964. *Myth and Religion of the North.* London: Weidenfeld and Nicolson.

Tylor, Edward. 1903 [1871]. *Primitive Culture.* London: Murray.

Walter, Tony. 1996. *The Eclipse of Eternity: A Sociology of the Afterlife.* New York: St. Martin's Press.

Walter, Tony, and Grace Davie. 1998. "The Religiosity of Women in the Modern West." *British Journal of Sociology* 49(4): 640–60.

Ward, Keith. 1992. *In Defence of the Soul*. Oxford: Oneworld Publications.

Warner, R. Stephen, and Judith Wittner, editors. 1998. *Gatherings in Diaspora: Religious Communities and the New Immigration*. Philadelphia: Temple University Press.

Watt, David Harrington. 2002. *Bible-Carrying Christians*. New York: Oxford University Press.

Weinberg, Martin, Ilsa Lottes, and Frances Shaver. 2000. "Sociocultural Correlates of Permissive Sexual Attitudes: A Test of Reiss's Hypothesis About Sweden and the United States." *Journal of Sex Research* 37(1): 44–52.

Wilson, Bryan. 1971. "Unbelief as an Object of Research." In *The Culture of Unbelief*, edited by Rocco Caporale and Antonio Grumelli. Berkeley: University of California Press.

Wolfe, Alan. 2003. *The Transformation of American Religion: How We Actually Live Our Faith*. New York: Free Press.

Yang, Fenggang. 2004. "Between Secularist Ideology and Desecularizing Reality: The Birth and Growth of Religious Research in Communist China." *Sociology of Religion* 65(2): 101–19.

Zuckerman, Phil. 2007. "Atheism: Contemporary Numbers and Patterns." In *The Cambridge Companion to Atheism,* edited by Michael Martin. Cambridge: Cambridge University Press.

———. 2006. "Is Faith Good For Us?" *Free Inquiry* 26(5): 35–38.

———. 2004. "Secularization: Europe—Yes; United States—No." *Skeptical Inquirer* 28(2): 49–52.

———, editor. 2000. *Du Bois on Religion*. Walnut Creek, Calif.: Alta Mira Press.

———. 1999. *Strife in the Sanctuary: Religious Schism in a Jewish Community*. Walnut Creek, Calif.: Alta Mira Press.

Index

About the Author

PHIL ZUCKERMAN is an associate professor of sociology at Pitzer College. He is the author of *Invitation to the Sociology of Religion* and *Strife in the Sanctuary: Religious Schism in a Jewish Community.*